STATE GOVERNMENT:

Politics in Wyoming

TIM R. MILLER

KENDALL/HUNT PUBLISHING COMPANY
Dubuque, Iowa, USA • Toronto, Ontario, Canada

B   402362   01

To Professor John T. Hinckley:
A career dedicated to education,
A lifetime devoted to Wyoming.

CONTENTS

PREFACE

Some 50 years ago, the Wyoming State Legislature determined that in order to graduate from the University of Wyoming, students must study the constitutions of the state and nation (or a history option). In 1975, the Wyoming Attorney General ruled that the law also applied to students attending Wyoming community colleges.

Partially because of the 1975 ruling, and partly because of professional creativity on the part of several University of Wyoming political science professors, there has been a recent increase in concern with teaching Wyoming government. This text is a modest attempt to aid those who have dedicated their careers to teaching Wyoming government.

As much as possible, the book tries to instill student interest. All too often, we who teach government hear how boring and dull the field is. Not so, we cry! Understanding politics is basic to being educated men and women, we believe. But to educate students, we must first scratch the crust of their curiosity. Thus, this text attempts to arouse student interest, while familiarizing students with the basics of our state's political system. If, at times, the text seems overly basic, it's because it is. This book is not written for those who already feel comfortable with the working of government. Rather, it is written for the many students who may be taking their first and last course in Wyoming government. To this end, the text should leave students with a fundamental knowledge of Wyoming government. If in the process, a spark of interest and even concern is ignited, so much the better.

Tim R. Miller

ACKNOWLEDGMENTS

The author owes a great debt to numerous people for their help with this project. In particular, sincere gratitude is extended to the following people for their reviews of portions of the manuscript: George Christopulos (State Engineer), Helen Deniston (Auditor's Office), Doug Gibson and Herb Manning (Wyoming Farm Bureau), John Hinckley and Roy Jordan (Northwest Community College), Rodger McDaniel (state senator), Oliver Walter (University of Wyoming), Bill Williams (Wyoming Taxpayers Association), and to officials of the Industrial Siting Administration. The material was edited by K. T. Roes and Patricia Miller.

A special thanks goes to Justice of the Peace Hunter Patrick for his invaluable assistance with the material on the courts.

Also, the author is indebted to Sherri Gray and Patricia Miller for their help with preparation of the manuscript.

CHAPTER

ONE

The Early Years

The Making of a State

The Mountain Men—The First Whites

In James Michener's novel about the development of northern Colorado and southern Wyoming, entitled *Centennial,* Chief Lame Beaver was the first of his tribe to meet a white man. In 1799, the chief met two trappers named Pasquinel and McKeag. The two trappers had separately left St. Louis, traveling up the Missouri River to the Platte, across the great prairie of present-day Nebraska and west into Colorado. Describing the glorious lives of the two adventurers, the author writes:

One sun-filled morning in May, as they were wandering together north of Rattlesnake Buttes looking for antelope, McKeag had a flash of insight; it occurred to him that he and Pasquinel were the freest men in the world. They were bound by nothing; they owed no one allegiance; they could move as they wished over an empire larger than France or Scotland; they slept where they willed, worked when they wished, and ate well from the land's bounty.

As he looked at the boundless horizon that lovely day, he appreciated what freedom meant; no Highland laird before whom he must grab his forelock. Pasquinel was subservient to no Montreal banker. They were free men, utterly free.

He was so moved by this discovery that he wanted to share it with Pasquinel. 'We are free,' he said. And Pasquinel, looking to the east, replied, 'They will be moving upon us soon.' And McKeag felt a shadow encroaching upon his freedom, and after that day he never felt quite so untrammeled.[1]

B.C. by permission of Johnny Hart and Field Enterprises, Inc.

1

Fiction? One author calls it "faction," or fiction based on fact. While isolated whites may have entered present-day Wyoming after the early 1740's, and a few French traders came through the area in the 1790's, the first in a series of trader/explorers, John Coulter, came in the winter of 1807–1808. After that time, a slow immigration of hardy trappers and traders in search of beaver pelts began. And, as in *Centennial,* the adventurers typically came along a route following the Missouri, Platte, and North Platte Rivers.

But, are the fictitious McKeag's observations above overly romantic? Certainly. While the earliest mountain men were brave souls willing to tolerate physical discomfort while gambling their safety for the unlikely possibility of riches, they were seldom the poetic souls of present-day books and movies. The work was "often laborious and otherwise disagreeable—lugging six or eight five-pound traps, wading in ice-cold water, setting traps at just the right place . . . , skinning the victims in freezing temperature . . ."[2] This, plus the ever-present dangers of Indian attacks and accidents, posed challenges to be met by adventurers, not poets.

All in all, the importance of these mountain men upon the area's development is exaggerated. The period of beaver trapping activity was relatively short, from the early 1820's to 1840. And at the peak, in the 1830's, there were probably no more than 200 of them in the state at a given time. The state's foremost historian, T. A. Larson, summarizes their importance:

They explored the area thoroughly, skinned thousands of beaver, lived virtually as savages, and for the most part vanished from history without leaving an imprint, except for a few place names, on modern Wyoming.[3]

The Trail Period—Passing Through

As the trappers left the state at the end of the 1830's and early 1840's, the first homeseekers or settlers entered, usually traveling by wagon, horse or foot, along the Oregon Trail. These pioneers, however, seldom settled in Wyoming. For the most part, they sought the greener pastures of Oregon, California, and Utah, and in some instances chased the 49ers' "golden rainbow" to the gold fields of California.

As the national emigration took place, the area of present-day Wyoming witnessed a great deal of activity, with stagecoaches joining the flow of settlers in the 1850's, the short-lived Pony Express in 1860, and the first transcontinental telegraph soon thereafter. Still, the emigrants, who generally traveled through the dry and desolate southern region, seldom decided to make their homes here:

The travelers spent less than 30 days in Wyoming and left little besides ruts, names and dates on trailside cliffs, a few place names and some graves . . . Already the area which would soon be given the name Wyoming was quite well known to many people. Scarcely anyone, however, had shown any interest in making Wyoming his home—except the Indians.[4]

Enter the Union Pacific Railroad

Congress authorized construction of the first transcontinental railroad with passage of the Pacific Railway Act of 1862. Two companies—the Union Pacific and Central Pacific—were offered large tracts of land along the new line, government loans, and assurances of future government contracts in exchange for building the railroad.[5] With these subsidies as protection for their investments, the Central Pacific built a line east from Sacramento, California, while the Union Pacific

Union Pacific Railroad poster announcing the opening of the transcontinental railroad. Union Pacific Railroad Museum Collection.

worked west from Council Bluffs, Iowa. They met at Promontory Summit, Utah on May 10, 1869.

Construction of the first transcontinental railroad, linking the East and West, was a dramatic event in American history. The commercial impact was tremendous. For the first time, business dealings—with new markets, easier transportation of goods, national corporate perspectives—could span the nation. Likewise, the political, social, and cultural impacts were great. Now the likelihood of the United States of America stretching from ocean to ocean became a matter of time. And anything which stood in the way of this "manifest destiny," whether Indian tribes, geographic landscape, or buffalo herds, was simply a factor to be "overcome." While this perspective had long been accepted by many, the railroad made it both more feasible and imminent. In fact, some commentators have compared the historical significance of astronaut Neil Armstrong's 1969 walk on the moon with the building of the transcontinental railroad a century earlier. Considered in light of their times, both were tremendous accomplishments.

The impact of the railroad upon what came to be known as Wyoming was also dramatic. The Union Pacific selected a route through the southern portion of the region for a variety of reasons, mostly geographic. The route was found by General Grenville Dodge, who headed an early survey team's search for a route through the Rocky Mountains and was subsequently chief engineer of the Union Pacific. The route offered a relatively gentle crossing through South Pass, a natural break in the Rockies located in southern Wyoming.[6]

In practically every sense, the railroad "opened" Wyoming economically, as it did technologically, politically, and (stretching the point) even culturally. But in a more important sense, the railroad opened the region to people. Before the railroad arrived, there simply were few white people in the area. There were native Indians, whites hurriedly traveling on the trails, and a smattering of traders, explorers, and nomads. But, few whites spent considerable time here. The railroad changed all that.

For one thing, thousands of men were employed in construction crews at a given time. Dr. Larson estimates that "perhaps as many as 6,000 men were employed in building the Union Pacific Railroad" at the peak of construction in 1868.[7] As well, U.S. troops were stationed at forts along or near the lines to protect white construction crews and settlers,

and to guard against abuses upon the Indian population.

As the U.P. crews inched westward, new towns leapfrogged along the tracts. Having been given large tracts of land by the government along the line, the railroad often laid out lots for sale to speculators, adventurers, and settlers who would populate the new towns. The new towns and cities—such as Cheyenne, Laramie City, Benton, Green River City, Bryan, and Bear River City—were gambles themselves. While the early settlers usually spoke of the bright futures of their new communities, all too often the towns died abrupt deaths as the railroad crews pushed westward.

Generally, these frontier communities were populated with two types of people. The more

Bear River City. This settlement was one of the "Hell on Wheels Towns" along the UP and it boasted 200 inhabitants at the time of the picture. It was on White Sulphur Creek 965 miles west of Omaha, Nebraska near the present Utah-Wyoming border. Bear River City vanished within a few months after the track crews moved on. Union Pacific Railroad Museum Collection.

constructive people were settlers seeking homes. These were the daring people who took Horace Greeley's advice (although there are disputes about the authenticity of the "Go west young man" remark) and headed west seeking a home and prosperity. These people sought business opportunities in general, but particularly in the cattle industry which boomed in the post-Civil War period. These settlers stayed after the construction crews headed on. The other type of opportunity seekers responded to the "hell-on-wheels" needs of the new frontier. With thousands of construction workers and soldiers living literally in the "boonies," there was a high demand for liquor, prostitutes, and games of chance. It is quite understandable, it seems, that the new communities were filled with people willing to satisfy these desires. In fact, it was not uncommon for such "entrepreneurs" to pro-

vide their services from portable facilities which could stay with the construction crews as they moved westward. This is not to imply, of course, that these services vanished from the towns which did survive, after the railroad moved on. This was clearly not the case.

In fact, it was a colorful, exciting, bawdy era. Readings of the period are filled with stories of prostitution, gambling, drunkenness, murder, and vigilante "justice" such as lynchings. While there were less rowdy activities available in these towns,[8] the description in Sidebar 1–1 verifies that these were rough times, indeed. All in all, the Union Pacific was clearly a catalyst in the events which led to the populating of the region. Clearly, "settlement and railroad may be said to have arrived at virtually the same time, and there is no doubt about which caused the other to come."[9]

Sidebar 1–1
On Territorial Rowdyism

by T. A. Larson
(Former University of Wyoming Professor of History, Member of Wyoming House of Representatives)

The September 19, 1867, issue of the newspaper (*Cheyenne Leader*) reported that a sergeant who had been trying to subdue an intoxicated soldier had fractured the soldier's skull and had accidentally shot himself, that there had been an exchange of shots in a robbery attempt at a gunshop, that a man had been knocked down and robbed, and that there had been much stealing of revolvers and blankets from tents and wagons. In the next issue of the newspaper (September 24) it was reported that there had been a street fight, that a man who had fired a shot at a policeman had been placed on the chain gang at the fort, and that a hundred men had gathered on the street to bet on a dog-

fight. The September 26 issue said that the city marshal had reported two neighbors fined for abusing each other, a drunk fined, a fight, a man mauled by an inebriated "friend," and another man fined for trying "to run things at a saloon." The September 28 issue reported that a drunk had been fined, a man in a camp above town had been cut in a fight, a man had been fined for drawing a gun on a newsman, and a gang had created a "muss" at a house of ill fame.

Undismayed, the *Leader* editor commented on September 28 that it was gratifying "that Cheyenne remains so free of crime and rowdyism in comparison with towns below."

Part of Dakota Territory

As fascinated easterners looked westward in 1868, they saw both a technological "miracle" being accomplished and the growth of rowdy, "hell-on-wheels" towns and small cities. An army doctor who returned to Cheyenne in October, 1867, noted the growth:

When I left here last July all the land was bare, and the only habitations were tents. Cheyenne has now a population of fifteen hundred, two papers, stores, warehouses, hotels, restaurants, gambling halls, etc.[10]

At the same time, the new residents along the U.P. tracks were busy trying to tame their new-found homeland. Accordingly, the years 1868 and 1869 saw considerable political activity in the region. As early as August, 1867, the new residents of Cheyenne had formed a somewhat primitive city government; by October, county officials had been selected.[11]

Since 1864, the area we know as Wyoming had technically been a part of the huge Dakota Territory.

When the Union Pacific Railroad reached Cheyenne in 1867, the Dakota legislature created Laramie County which included all of the present-day Wyoming east of the Continental Divide.[12]

In the county election, voters selected U.P. engineer, John S. Casement to go to Washington to lobby for separation of the area from Dakota and creation of a new territory.[13] While his efforts were short-termed and relatively unsuccessful, they show the tone of thinking in Wyoming (as the area was beginning to be known).

Increasingly, the people living in Cheyenne and to the west were becoming unhappy about being a part of Dakota Territory. There were several reasons for this. Cheyenne is 800 miles from Yankton (the territory's capitol), making communications with Laramie County residents difficult most of the time and impossible in the winter. Also, the Yankton-Cheyenne

areas were separated by land belonging by treaty to Indians, making communication even more difficult. In addition, Dakota Territory was so large that it was only a matter of time before it would be divided. There were other reasons as well. For instance, the two regions had different interests and backgrounds.

The farmers and small-town folks in eastern Dakota had problems of their own without having to cope with those of an alien world several hundred miles away. They knew little and cared less about the needs of hell-on-wheels communities and South Pass mining camps.

There was a political factor, too. The Yankton residents knew that the western region of the territory had more people than the eastern region. In time, they feared, the wild and woolly westerners might actually control their territory! For these reasons, then, Dakota Territory was willing and even impatient to see their western neighbors cut loose.[14]

Approaching Congress and Choosing a Name

For the reasons discussed above, the Dakota legislature (as its session convened in December, 1867) voted unanimously to petition the United States Congress to organize a separate territory out of the southwestern portion of the Dakota Territory. Shortly thereafter, two Cheyenne men were sent to Washington to join in the lobbying effort. The most capable of the lobbyists was Dr. Hiram Latham, a physician for the U.P. who was selected and sponsored by Cheyenne's business and professional community. Dr. Latham bolstered the lobbying efforts of Dakota Territory's congressional delegate (Walter A. Burleigh), former General (and Union Pacific ally) Grenville H. Dodge (who represented Iowa in the House of Representatives at the time), J. S. Casement and others who were anxious for organization of the new territory. As was common on Wyoming's behalf, Dr.

Latham exaggerated the population of the area. He assured Congress that there were 35,000 residents in the region, with another 25,000 to arrive within a year. But a census taken in July, 1869 showed a population of only 8,000.

The lobbying efforts were successful. The Wyoming Organic Act passed the Senate rather easily on June 3, 1868. While the opposition in the House of Representatives was greater than in the Senate, the act passed on July 22 by a vote of 106 to 50. President Andrew Johnson signed the bill which created Wyoming Territory on July 25.[15]

To pass, the legislation had to overcome several objections. There was significant opposition among Colorado representatives and lobbyists, some of which hoped to have portions of Wyoming annexed by Colorado. The Colorado statehood bill was tied up in Congress at the time. Another complaint was that the proposed territory would be an expensive drain on the federal treasury, particulary since the area would be unable to pay the costs of the government services it would need. Also, Republicans who were leading the impeachment efforts against President Johnson did not like the prospect of his getting to fill the jobs, that would be created by passage of the bill, on the basis of presidential patronage. Latham, Dodge, Casement and other friends of Wyoming overcame these arguments.[16]

Of all the issues surrounding independent territorial status, "naming the new territory caused more discussion than any other phase of the Organic Act."[17] Several names were suggested, including Indian tribes (Cheyenne, Sioux, Pawnee, Arapahoe, and Shoshone), rivers (Platte, Sweetwater, Yellowstone, and Big Horn), and a former President (the recently assassinated Lincoln). Instead, Congress chose "Wyoming"—a Delaware Indian term meaning "land of tall mountains and vast plains."

John A. Campbell, first territorial governor (1869-1875). Wyoming State Archives, Museums and Historical Department, University of Wyoming.

Territorial Government

As authorized by Congress, the President was to appoint people to a variety of government positions in the new territory. Because confusion in the last months of the Andrew Johnson presidency kept appointments from being made, U. S. Grant filled the vacancies. President Grant's appointments included John A. Campbell of Ohio to be governor, Edward M. Lee of Connecticut as secretary (a position similar to lieutenant governor in other states), Joseph M. Carey of Pennsylvania to be U.S. Attorney, and John H. Howe of Illinois for chief justice of the new court.[18] While these executive and judicial positions were appointed, delegates to the territorial legislature and U.S. Congress were elected (the delegate to Congress could debate but could not vote as a representative of a territory). As was typ-

Sidebar 1–2
On Early Wyoming Elections

by T. A. Larson
(Former University of Wyoming Professor of History, Member of Wyoming House of Representatives)

Political activity occupied some of the free time of many Wyoming adults, particularly the men. One argument used for electing territorial delegate and legislators at the same time (finally achieved in 1882) was that it would cut in half the excitement and strife which were part of campaigning and voting. For many people, nevertheless, it seems that regular elections brought cheap entertainment and escape from the workaday world. Meeting leaders from other parts of the territory, reading lively political editorials, and participating in torchlight processions must have helped brighten many a man's life.

Politicians played for keeps, packing primary conventions, stuffing ballot boxes, lying about one another, and buying votes with whiskey and money. While the politicans who avoided such methods had a better chance of success in the 1880's than in the 1870's, many reprehensible practices continued. *Bill Barlow's Budget* (Douglas), for instance, charged in May, 1888, that Lusk and other eastern precincts had voted children, canary birds, and poodle dogs in their futile attempt to win the county seat from Douglas. The *Budget* maintained that in Manville, which ran third, 200 out of 226 votes were fraudulent.

Reprinted from *History of Wyoming*, Second Edition, revised by T. A. Larson by permission of University of Nebraska Press. Copyright © 1965, 1978 by the University of Nebraska Press.

ical of early elections in Wyoming, Democrats defeated all opponents, sweeping the election. About Wyoming's first territorial election, Dr. Larson observes, "There were no serious disturbances, only the usual drinking and rowdyism, on election day (See Sidebar 1–2).

The first territorial legislature had a potentially uneasy political situation—a Democratic legislature working with a Republican governor and other Republican officials who were appointed by the Republican president. Still, while Wyoming had its share of political infighting, both before and after 1869, the first legislature set aside most of its political differences (particularly Secretary Lee who worked well with the Democratic legislature). This political "truce" was short-lived. In the next few months, the infighting surfaced again, resulting in Secretary Lee being fired because of difficulties with the Republican state chairman.

The first session of the legislature convened on October 12, 1869. Using Governor Campbell's recommendations and statutes from Nevada, Colorado and Nebraska to guide them, the legislature passed the first laws (or statutes) for the new territory. Among the more important bills passed were acts regulating mines and mine safety, designating Cheyenne as capitol, placing the territorial prison in Laramie, authorizing certain taxes (e.g. a property tax on land, and a $2 poll tax on voters under sixty), and protecting game by outlawing the sale of mountain sheep, elk, deer and antelope during breeding season. The legislature expressed an anti-Union Pacific sentiment, which was rather common at the time, by passing several acts which the railroad opposed.[19] The U.S. Senate, responding to a strong railroad lobby, reversed all the anti-U.P. acts except the law which prohibited "yellow dog" contracts (in which workers are required to sign away their right to sue the employer for its negligences before being hired). Also, the session passed two laws over Governor Campbell's veto—one legalized gambling, the other outlawed marriages between whites and blacks.[20]

These acts alone do not distinguish Wyoming's first territorial legislature. But passage of one other law does. On Friday, November 12, council (i.e., senate) president William H. Bright introduced a resolution to give women the right to vote. On December 10, 1864, the resolution passed.

Thus, the Territory of Wyoming distinguished itself by paving the way for Wyoming to become the first state to recognize the right of women to vote and hold office, some 20 years later. This measure by the first territorial legislature, a truly progressive act in 1869, would ultimately give rise to Wyoming's motto—the Equality State.

In all, the territorial days fluctuated with the young cattle industry, witnessing both periods of dramatic economic prosperity and decline. Gradually, the trend was toward overall economic growth. By 1890, when statehood became a reality, the population had increased to 62,000. With the conclusion of the Indian wars of 1867–77 came an end to major hostilities between white and red men in Wyoming. The hostilities ended with the peaceful tribes being forced onto reservations and the hostile bands being pushed out of Wyoming into Montana and elsewhere. While the cattle and sheep industries had struggled with nature and among themselves to stay in business, they had proved that the cattle industry would survive, and ultimately thrive and prosper in Wyoming. While life was hard in the new territory—with a high, dry, and frequently cruel climate, water shortages, Indian hostilities, and sometimes unbearable loneliness—the rewards were great for the souls who were able to cope with the challenges. Life here was

clearly a gamble; those with enough courage, skill, and luck to meet the challenge often prospered.

On to Statehood—The Early Moves

As noted before, Wyoming's economy, particularly the cattle industry, was much like a roller coaster in the early years. Sometimes it climbed steep heights, other times it raced downward as if out of control. To many leaders of the time, government policies were partly responsible for the periods of slow growth and decline. Land policies, in particular, were thought to be unresponsive to Wyoming's needs. Too often, it seemed, government actions made it difficult for settlers to get enough land and water to prosper. To early leaders like Francis E. Warren and Joseph M. Carey, statehood was the answer. Admission as a state, they reasoned, would give Wyoming the political clout it lacked as a territory and would open the way for the desired federal aid and land policy changes.[21]

The names Warren and Carey loom large in the emerging statehood period, as they do for the years to follow. More than any other men (or women), they were the outstanding political leaders of the statehood movement. Francis E. Warren was born in Massachusetts in 1844. He came to Wyoming in 1868 after winning the Congressional Medal of Honor for gallantry as a member of the Massachusetts Volunteer Infantry during the Civil War. After his arrival in Wyoming, "he became interested in real estate, livestock, mercantile business, and in promoting the first lighting system in Cheyenne." After serving in the Cheyenne city government as council member and mayor, and in a variety of territorial positions (all between 1873 and 1885), the prominent businessman was appointed territorial governor by President Arthur. He served two terms as territorial governor, from 1885 to

1886 and again between 1889 and 1890. When statehood arrived in 1890 and a new government was elected, the voters chose Warren as the first governor of the new state. After serving only six weeks as governor, he resigned to accept the state legislature's appointment (until ratification of the 17th Amendment to the U.S. Constitution, Senators were appointed by the state legislatures) to the U.S. Senate, a position he held (continuously after 1895) for 37 years and four days until his death in 1929. Warren's leaving the governor's mansion for the U.S. Senate set a precedent which has been followed by numerous Wyoming chief executives (in spite of Art. 4, Sec. 2 of Wyoming's constitution which reads "Qualifications of governor— . . . nor shall he be eligible to any other office during the term for which he was elected.") Throughout the latter part of his career, Warren was the "Godfather" of Wyoming politics.[22]

Joseph M. Carey was born in Delaware in 1845. After studying law at the University of Pennsylvania and practicing in Philadelphia, Carey was appointed U.S. Attorney for Wyoming by President Grant, a position he held from 1869–71. He served as Associate Justice of the Territorial Supreme Court from 1871 to 1876. He was mayor of Cheyenne between 1881 and 1885. In 1885, he was elected to represent the Territory in the U.S. House of Representatives. When Wyoming became a state in 1890, Carey was selected by the state legislature (with Warren) to serve in the U.S. Senate. However, in 1895 he was denied reelection by the legislature. The intriguing events surrounding the 1895 rejection of Carey and selection of Warren (brought about by Carey's support for the gold standard which was unpopular in the West, an anti-Cheyenne vote by legislators who did not want to select two senators from that city, and Warren's support by influential newspaper editors[23]) touched off a feud between the two Republican leaders which lasted more than 20 years. After losing his senate seat, Carey retired from politics to practice law. At the turn of the century he became involved in the populist reform movement. In 1910, the former Republican ran on the Democratic ticket and was elected governor. He held that position from 1911 until 1915. During that time he was active in, and symbolic of, the reform movement.[24]

While these two Republican leaders became political opponents after statehood, they were skilled, articulate spokesmen on behalf of Wyoming. Historian L. L. Gould notes the importance of effective political leadership for the statehood movement:

In Joseph M. Carey and Francis E. Warren, the two most prominent resident politicians, Wyoming could claim two public-spirited citizens of recognized ability and impressive skill. Drawn from the ranks of old territorial settlers, Carey and Warren commanded an allegiance from Wyoming residents that was denied to transitory federal officers. By 1880 the shifting balance of power toward the local leaders, added to Wyoming's gains in economic stability, helped to give the movement for statehood its initial impetus.[25]

These two leaders, essential as they were, were not enough to bring about statehood. Several other things had to happen first. Other states, for one thing, were in the statehood line ahead of Wyoming.

After Colorado was admitted in 1876, no additional states were admitted until 1889. Politically, the conditions were not right for expansion during this period. During the 1880's, political control of the federal government was generally divided between Republicans and Democrats. Democrats used the divided control to oppose statehood for northwestern states. Democratic politicians correctly assumed that these areas would vote Republican. If admitted to the Union, they reasoned, the new states would increase Republican strength in the Congress and in the electoral college during presidential voting. In the 1888 election, however, the Republican party gained control of the White House and both houses of Congress. This Republican domination paved the way for admission of North and South Dakota, Montana and Washington in 1889. The new states had larger populations, more enthusiasm, and had started their statehood drives earlier than had Wyoming. But with their admission, Wyoming's turn became more likely.[26]

In the 1888–1889 period, as Wyoming representatives sought passage of the enabling legislation (congressional permission to take the steps toward statehood, such as drafting a constitution), not all Wyoming residents agreed that the territory should become a state. While Republicans seemed in agreement in support of statehood, Democrats were much less unanimous. Democratic leaders were somewhat suspicious. Statehood would increase taxes, they reasoned. And, Republicans would probably dominate the constitutional convention, something they would probably use to their advantage in the first statewide election.[27] Besides, their enemies, Carey and Warren, were leading the statehood movement. This, too, raised suspicions among Democratic leaders.[28]

Calling the Constitutional Convention

By 1889, Wyoming was getting impatient. The 1888 Territorial legislature had petitioned Congress for statehood, and enabling legislation had been passed by two congressional committees. But, nothing more concrete had happened. Tired of waiting, Governor Warren decided to proceed as if the enabling legislation had been passed, which it had not. After seven (out of ten) counties were "persuaded"[29] to pass resolutions "for the election of delegates to a constitutional convention,"[30] the governor issued a proclamation calling for the drafting of a constitution. In the June 3, 1889 proclamation, Warren said, "the territory of Wyoming has the population, material resources, public intelligence and morality necessary to insure a stable government therein."[31] Accordingly, the officials decided to act as if the procedure set forth in Senate bill No. 2445 (which was hung up in the U.S. Senate) had passed.

As directed in Senate bill 2445, 55 delegates were to be chosen to attend the convention, apportioned on the basis of votes cast in the 1888 congressional election. The Wyoming election was set for the second Monday in July, 1889.[32] To make it look as though Wyoming was unanimously in support of statehood, Republicans "tried to cover the proceedings with a bipartisan veil." Even so, Democrats often tried to sabotage the election by keeping voters away. They believed a low turnout would embarrass the Republican talk in Washington about the large population in Wyoming. The Republican strategy was more successful, leaving them in the majority of a "bipartisan" convention (a convention with both Republican and Democratic delegates).[33]

The Convention Meets

When the convention first met in Cheyenne on September 2, 1889, 45 delegates were present. Throughout the proceedings, only 49 delegates attended. The delegates were all men, and included several lawyers and ranchers, veterans of the Union Army, and people born outside Wyoming (including several born outside the U.S.).[34] Laramie attorney Melville C. Brown was elected chairman. While leading a colorful career at best (and scandalous at worst), Brown has generally been credited with performing his duties impartially.[35]

The convention was pressure-packed, with much to do and little time to do it. As with most political gatherings in this country, the convention divided itself into committees

MEMBERS OF THE CONSTITUTIONAL CONVENTION OF WYOMING, 1889.
(Bottom row) left to right: 1. Louise S. Smith, official stenographer; 2. Melville C.
Brown, President of the Convention; 3. Mrs. B. Recker, Asst. Sec'y; 4. Mrs.
Frances Ollerenshaw, enrolling and engrossing clerk; 5. Frank M. Foote. (Second
row) 6. Frederick H. Harvey; 7. Mark Hopkins; 8. H. G. Nickerson; 9. Louis J.
Palmer; 10. John M. McCandlish; 11. Henry A. Coffeen; 12. Edward J. Morris. (Third
row) 13. John F. Carroll (Editor of the Cheyenne Leader); 14. Asbury B. Conaway;
15. John A. Riner; 16. D. A. Preston; 17. A. L. Sutherland; 18. Henry S. Elliott;
19. Henry G. Hay; 20. Thomas R. Reed. (Fourth row) 21. John McGill; 22. George
W. Fox; 23. W. E. Chaplin; 24. E. S. N. Morgan; 25. J. A. Casebeer; 26. John L.
Russell; 27. Mortimer N. Grant; 28. I. S. Bartlett (Newspaper Reporter). (Fifth row)
29. George W. Baxter; 30. C. P. Organ; 31. James A. Johnston; 32. John W. Hoyt;
33. J. C. Argesheimer (Newspaper Reporter) (Sixth row) 34. Herman Glafcke
(Asst. Sec'y of Convention); 35. Clarence D. Clark; 36. Stephen W. Downey. (Top
row) 37. C. W. Holden; 38. O. P. Yelton (Sergeant at Arms); 39. In the shadow
against the door on the left, Meyer Frank. The boy to the left with his hat on,
Corlett Downey. These two boys were the pages in the Convention. The other
children were those who came in to have their picture taken. Wyoming State
Archives, Museums and Historical Department, University of Wyoming.

which specialized in specific subjects. The five
major committees "dealt with the legislative
department; the judiciary; boundaries and apportionment; taxation, revenue, and public
debt; and railroads and telegraphs."[36]

The delegates decided several major issues,
and innumerable smaller ones. For example,
"some members wanted to make it easy to
organize new counties" in order to make it

easier for people to get their county seats. The
convention made it rather difficult for counties
to divide. In addition, they established a state
supreme court separate from the district
courts. During territorial status, the district
court judges had met together to hear appeals,
functioning as a supreme court.

The delegates also considered whether or
not people should be required to read in order
to vote. Reasoning that voters must be able to

read the constitution in order to vote knowledgeably, the members included this provision in the document.[37]

In spirited debate, the convention considered the method for legislative apportionment (what the basis for representation should be). With relative ease, they decided that representation in the house of representatives should be by population. This way, counties with more people would have more legislators. The trouble came regarding the state senate. The less populated counties argued that the counties should all have the same representation, just as all states are equally represented in the U.S. Senate. Opponents found fault with this "federal plan" comparison, correctly pointing out that a county is "simply a medium by which a state conducts its business." States, on the other hand, are independent political entities with equal standing in the federal balance. The convention did what the U.S. Supreme Court would later say all states must do—base representation in both houses of state legislatures solely on population.[38] The more people a county has, the more the representation in the state senate.

Several other issues were debated. Should there be a separate constitutional tax on mined coal? After heavy lobbying by the minerals industry, the delegates said no, because taxes that are written into the constitution would be too difficult to raise. In other words, it would have taken a constitutional amendment to raise the tax on coal. Should Wyoming have a form of civil service, whereby state employees would be hired solely on the basis of their abilities, without consideration of political party membership? The members said no. Patronage, they reasoned, is one of the rewards of politics. Also, the members debated the location of various state institutions.

Two of the most significant issues at the state constitutional convention dealt with state water laws and women's suffrage (right to vote). Wyoming's novel contribution to water law lies in Art. 8, Sec. 1, which declares that most of the water in the state belongs to, and is to be managed by, the state itself. This provision is the key to Wyoming's defense of its water rights against what state officials see as federal incursions into the area of state control over resources (See Chapter 7). Art. 8, Sec. 1 of the Wyoming Constitution reads, "the water of all natural streams, springs, lakes or other collections of still water, within the boundaries of the State, are hereby declared to be the property of the State."

On the issue of women's suffrage, the convention debated separating this portion from the constitution and letting the voters decide whether women should keep their right to vote if and when the territory won statehood. At the time, no state recognized women as voters, with isolated exceptions for school elections. Following impassioned speeches, the delegates voted to keep the provision in the constitution without giving the male population a separate chance to defeat the measure.

On September 30, 1889, the twenty-fifth working day of the session, the convention completed its work. On a roll-call vote the constitution was approved, 37–0. The document was then given to the voters for approval (i.e., ratification). On November 5, 1889, the voters approved the constitution, 6,272 to 1,923. Only Sheridan County opposed it.[39]

A few months later, in personal letters to Carey and soon-to-be Chief Justice of the Wyoming Supreme Court Willis Van Devanter, Warren wrote that he:

. . . believed that the lawmakers had shown too much regard for the rights of miners, settlers, and the less fortunate. In addition, he argued, the legislative apportionment drawn by the convention discriminated against Laramie County in favor of the northern counties. . . . Because the political leaders, Warren and Carey, remained aloof from the convention's proceedings, the gathering could exercise considerable independence; this led Warren in later years to characterize the body as the 'fool Constitutional Convention.'[40]

Most observers, both at the time and since, disagree with Warren's characterization.

Congress Grants Statehood

Because the U.S. Constitution says little about how new states are to be admitted, the process has generally been based upon the precedent established at the outset of the country in the Ordinance of 1787. That precedent says the issue of statehood is to be based upon "such matters as population (with 60,000 supposedly the minimum), agricultural and commercial development, demonstrated capacity for self-government and other factors. . . ."[41] Yet, as history shows, the major issues were usually political ones.

This was the case with Wyoming. Fortunately for Wyoming and its chief lobbyist, territorial delegate to Congress Joseph M. Carey, the first two political obstacles had already been overcome. Republicans controlled both houses of Congress and the executive branch with Benjamin Harrison as President. Also, the states in line ahead of Wyoming had been admitted. Even so, other political hurdles had to be overcome.

Several complaints were raised, especially in the House of Representatives. "One congressman urged that Wyoming be denied statehood until the territories of Idaho, Nevada, and Arizona were able to organize." Others objected to provisions of the proposed constitution which would allow women to vote, require people to be able to read in order to vote, require compulsory education, and give alien property owners many of the privileges of citizen property owners.[42]

Congressman Barnes of Georgia raised two other objections besides women's suffrage. He argued that because Congress had not passed enabling legislation authorizing Wyoming to write a constitution, the territory had acted irregularly by going ahead with its constitution anyway. "Such a case," he argued, "is without precedent in American history." Barnes and others also said that the population in Wyoming was too small. After all, the argument went, "the fact that only 8,000 voted in the election for the adoption of the constitution indicated in itself a lack of popular support for the movement."[43]

Larson notes that since most of the objections were voiced by Democrats, the major complaint may have been partisan distress of admitting another Republican state, "but with Republicans in control of both houses of Congress, it would hardly do to argue publicly against adding a Republican state. So, they (Democrats) talked unconvincingly about the evils of woman suffrage."[44]

Responding to these criticisms was delegate Carey. On March 26, 1890, Carey made a lengthy, impassioned speech on behalf of Wyoming. In it he refuted the major criticisms aired by the various congressional opponents. He said, for example, that partisan differences between Republicans and Democrats should not be an issue, and explained that the turnout was low in the vote to ratify the constitution because nearly everybody was for it and because voters tend not to turn out for constitutional elections. By today's standards, or any for that matter, Carey laid it on pretty thick. He said that the population was twice what it actually was (over 100,000, he said), and exaggerated the area's vast agricultural, mineral and human resources. Even so, his speech served its purpose. In spite of attempts by opponents to delay and amend the Wyoming statehood legislation, the measure passed the House of Representatives, 139 to 127, with 63 not voting.[45]

Celebrating the Forty-fourth State

Passage in the House on March 26, 1890 was followed three months later by a 29 to 18 vote in the Senate. The forty-fourth state was admitted with President Harrison's signature on July 10, 1890.

Long noted for their partying instincts, the people of Wyoming did not let their chance to celebrate pass by unobserved. News of passage in the House:

. . . brought a great outburst of cheering in Wyoming towns. Church bells, train whistles, fire bells, cowbells, and trumpets sounded in Cheyenne. All the bunting in town was displayed. A spontaneous parade of men and women marched to Governor Warren's. . . . He congratulated the people, especially the ladies. That evening a huge bonfire of packing boxes blazed at the corner of Seventeenth and Ferguson (Carey), after which a crowd filled the opera house to hear speeches.[46]

When word of passage in the Senate reached Wyoming, "again there was an impromptu parade in Cheyenne, with 'Clanging Bells, Shrieking Whistles, Incessant Yelling'." Following President Harrison's signing the bill into law on July 10, the third celebration was touched off. "There were the usual bells and whistles, accompanied this time by firecrackers and bombs, 'and the yelling was ear-splitting and incessant'." In Laramie, there was a "forty-four-gun salute"; in Rock Springs "cannon boomed"; the celebration in Douglas was "louder than ever." "A dispatch from Rawlins announced that "Rawlins Town is wild," and another from Buffalo said that 'the great north is delighted'." The official celebration, the fourth in a series of five, was in Cheyenne on July 23, 1890. Five thousand people observed a two-mile parade and participated

National Guard in Statehood Parade, 1890. Also showing the G.A.R. marching. Looking west on 16th Street with Warren Mercantile Company in the background. Cheyenne, Wyoming. Wyoming State Archives, Museums and Historical Department, University of Wyoming.

in festivities which "lacked the spontaneity and wild shrieking of the first three celebrations." The fifth celebration occurred three days later when Carey and his family returned to Cheyenne from Washington. Again, there was a parade, music, and a speech, followed . . . by a Republican caucus in the Hoffman brothers' saloon." Clearly, Wyoming was "drunk" on statehood![47]

The Equality State

As already shown, women's suffrage (i.e., right to vote) was an issue at the first territorial legislature (1869), and the statehood convention (1889), and at other times as well (such as the 1871 attempt to rescind their right to vote, ratification of the 19th Amendment, and ratification and later attempts to rescind ratification of the Equal Rights Amendment in the 1970's). Although women's right to vote is taken for granted today, Wyoming was a trend-setter at the time. While this is probably not Wyoming's most significant historical act, it is something that the state can point to with pride. As such, the women's movement has firm roots in Wyoming's past. Here was a "new" state, with relatively few people and unlimited challenges facing them at every turn. In the midst of all these obstacles, here were the region's leaders

thinking of, and pioneering in, civil rights. While women had been allowed to vote in isolated eastern school board elections, Wyoming was the first state or nation in the world to recognize men and women as voting equals. Truly, this is a role that looms large in the state's history and is a major aspect of Wyo-

Mrs. Louisa Ann Swain (nee Gardner), first woman to vote in Wyoming Territory and the first woman in the world to vote on political equality with men. Born August 1801 at Norfold, VA. (Taken about 1865) Courtesy of her son, Mr. A. P. Swain. Wyoming State Archives, Museums and Historical Department, University of Wyoming.

WIZARD OF ID by permission of Johnny Hart and Field Enterprises, Inc.

ming's heritage. Consider, then, exactly what the first territorial legislature did, how it happened, and who deserves credit.

Earlier, reference was made to Friday, November 12, 1869, when council (senate) President William H. Bright introduced a resolution to the first territorial legislature. While the session passed other bills dealing with women (e.g., one prohibited sex discrimination in teachers' pay, another protected married women's rights to own property), Bright's bill was the one that made history. It read:

FEMALE SUFFRAGE
Chapter 31
AN ACT TO GRANT TO THE WOMEN OF WYOMING TERRITORY THE RIGHT OF SUFFRAGE AND TO HOLD OFFICE
Be it enacted by the council and House of Representatives of the Territory of Wyoming:
Sec. 1. That every woman of the age of twenty-one years, residing in this territory, may at every election to be holden under the laws thereof, cast her vote. And her rights to the elective franchise and to hold office shall be the same under the election laws of the territory, as those of electors.
Sec. 2. This act shall take effect and be in force from and after its passage.

Notice, the act gave every woman, age 21, not only the right to vote, but the right to hold office as well.

But, why? Why did Wyoming become the first to pass such a law? Historians have found several possibilities. For one thing, the conditions were right. As mentioned, women could vote in isolated local elections in the East, suffragettes such as national leader Susan B. Anthony were active and attracting attention throughout the East and Middle West, and in 1856 a similar bill had passed one house of the Nebraska territorial legislature. So, it was going to happen somewhere. Wyoming legislators "had the option of jumping in at the head of the parade or of watching it pass by."[48] Particularly, Wyoming legislators expected

that the Utah legislature, which was to meet in the weeks after the Wyoming session began, would pass the legislation, which it did in February, 1870.

There were several other reasons for the law's passage, as well. There was a scarcity of women in the new territory, for example. The 1870 survey would later show that there were six men for every woman in the territory at the time of passage. Some legislators, then, probably supported the bill because there were so few women about to join the electorate. Also, western legislators probably viewed this as a great public relations opportunity. This was the common explanation in the 1870's and 1880's for Wyoming's action. Dr. Larson writes:

The *Cheyenne Leader,* for instance, said when the act was adopted, 'We now expect at once quite an immigration of ladies to Wyoming,' and added in March, 1870, that it was 'nothing more or less than a shrewd advertising dodge. A cunning device to obtain for Wyoming a widespread notoriety.'[49]

In addition, others may have voted for passage simply because they thought that it was the right thing to do. After all, blacks had been given the right to vote by the Fifteenth Amendment to the U.S. Constitution. Delegates, such as Bright, are thought to have believed that their wives should have the same right. Bright was influenced by his lovely, young, suffragette wife. On April 28, 1870, the *Cheyenne Leader* quoted a racist remark from a legislator who said that if minorities should be able to vote, "we will ring in the women, too." The delegate, however, apparently did not view the action in the positive light in which Bright saw it.[50]

Finally, there is a possibility that women's suffrage was passed as a joke. In her thesis analyzing the history of women's suffrage in Wyoming, Miriam Chapman paraphrases the *Cheyenne Leader,* saying, "Wyoming had adopted petticoat government for the same reason that Barnum brought forward the Fege Mermaid. . . ."[51] And, an article which appeared in the *Wyoming Tribune* on October 8, 1870 states this theory bluntly:

Once, during the session, amid the greatest hilarity, and after the presentation of various funny amendments and in full expectation of gubernatorial veto, an act was passed Enfranchising the Women of Wyoming. The bill, however, was approved, became a law, and the youngest territory placed in the van of progress. . . . How strange that a movement destined to purify the muddy pool of politics . . . should have originated in a joke. . . . All honor to them, say we, to Wyoming's first legislature!

Dr. Larson, by the way, believes that the article was written by Edward M. Lee, who was secretary of the territory in 1869. The joke theory says that the Democratic legislature passed the bill in jest, certain that Republican Governor John Campbell would veto it, but that rather than be known as the man who killed it, he signed it even though he opposed it at the time.[52]

It seems, then, that we cannot say definitely why the legislature passed the bill. The joke possibility is just one of several explanations and we do not know whether it was any more important than the others. If it was passed as a joke, though, it sure shoots holes in the earlier "idealistic" comments about how Wyoming was a pace-setter. But the full answer simply is not known.

Another difficult question to answer is who the primary moving force was in bringing about the act. Or, put differently, who deserves the credit for this act that Wyoming is so proud of? There are several claims. At various times, for example, Mrs. Bright (wife of the man who introduced the bill), J. H. Hayford (editor of the *Laramie Sentinel* and a Republican leader), and secretary Edward M. Lee, have each been advanced as the author of the bill. Lee's claim is based on the belief of some that Bright, not having introduced any bills

during the session, sought Lee's advise about something to introduce. Lee, the position says, suggested the suffrage bill and even wrote it for Bright. By this version, Lee was the driving force; Bright is merely seen as a politician who wanted *something* to introduce. In her detailed study, Chapman concludes that while no one person deserves sole credit, "the strongest bid for authorship is that of E. M. Lee. . . ."[53]

Professor Larson disagrees. He, too, notes that there are several claims to the authorship which are valid in varying degrees. But, the professor believes "the evidence warrants giving major credit for woman suffrage in Wyoming to William H. Bright." After all, this position argues, Bright wrote the bill, introduced it, debated and lobbied for it, and the accounts and histories which were written at the time gave credit to him. In 1889, a movement began to "nudge Bright from the center of the stage," replacing him with Mrs. Esther Morris. Mrs. Morris was a large woman in her middle fifties who had served eight-and-a-half months as a justice of the peace in South Pass City in 1870. The 1889 drive to give Mrs. Morris credit was started by her son, who owned the *Cheyenne Sun* newspaper. He began referring to his mother in the paper as the "Mother of Woman Suffrage." Others, including influential historian Grace Raymond Hebard (who until that time gave Bright and Morris equal credit), joined Mrs. Morris's sponsors.

Mrs. Morris's case was based on a position later outlined by H. G. Nickerson, in a letter to the Lander newspaper (Wyoming *State Journal,* published in 1919). By Nickerson's account, Mrs. Morris was a leader of the women's movement who sought and received a pledge by Bright and Nickerson that whoever won their race for the territorial legislature would introduce the bill. Bright won and introduced the bill. Mrs. Morris, then, is

Mrs. Esther Morris, credited as the author of women's suffrage in Wyoming. Wyoming State Archives, Museums and Historical Department, University of Wyoming.

of characters.[54] Finally, in a letter to the National Woman Suffrage Association's Convention, "Mrs. Morris gives all the credit for the bill to the men."[55] So, the issue of who should receive credit for pioneering Wyoming women's right to vote is confusing. Quite likely, all the people mentioned deserve some degree of credit.[56]

With this historic beginning, women have gone on to play important roles in the state's history. The first woman governor in the United States was elected in Wyoming in 1924. Mrs. Nellie Tayloe Ross, whose husband was governor until his death a month before he was to stand for reelection, was nominated to fill the resulting vacancy on the Dem-

Poster from the reelection campaign of Mrs. Nellie Tayloe Ross, first woman governor in the United States. Wyoming State Archives, Museums and Historical Department, University of Wyoming.

seen as the primary force in the women's movement. This account was repeated in pamphlets and histories after 1919, and was increasingly accepted as accurate. The movement on behalf of Mrs. Morris culminated in her being selected in 1955 as the state's outstanding citizen. Her statue was erected in Washington, D.C. and in Cheyenne.

But, again, one might question whether she actually deserves this high praise. After all, she campaigned for no public office, for herself or anyone else, wrote nothing for publication, made no major public addresses during the period, probably was not in Cheyenne in 1869, and was never mentioned in Governor Campbell's thorough diary. Thus, Larson believes that the evidence indicates that Mrs. Morris was one of several people in the suffrage cast ocratic ticket. Mrs. Ross accepted the nomination, declining to campaign (she said that she represented the principles of her husband), and was elected. Although another women, "Ma" Ferguson (Mrs. Miriam A. Ferguson), was elected governor of Texas on the same day, Mrs. Ross was sworn in nearly three weeks before the Texan. Another first for Wyoming!

Again, this is not to overplay the issue. After all, a year after the territorial legislature passed the women's suffrage measure, it attempted to repeal the new law. Governor Campbell, however, vetoed the legislature's attempt to kill the right of women to vote. Think of that: territorial legislators in what was to become the Equality State trying to reverse their earlier historic action! Then again, there was considerable sentiment against women's rights at the consitutional convention in 1889.[57] And after the state ratified the Equal Rights Amendments, two attempts were made to rescind (or reverse) the earlier approval, in 1977 and 1978. Clearly, there have been notable instances in the Equality State of less than equitable treatment. But, notice, each of the examples above failed. In each of these instances, the heritage of the Equality State was upheld.

NOTES

1. James A. Michener, *Centennial* (New York: Random House, 1974), pp. 186–187.
2. T. A. Larson, *Wyoming: A Bicentennial History* (New York: W. W. Norton, 1977), p. 39.
3. T. A. Larson, *History of Wyoming* (Lincoln: University of Nebraska Press, 1965), p. 9.
4. Ibid., pp. 10–11.
5. The Pacific Railway Acts of 1862 and 1864 gave the U.P. $27 million in loans (6 percent interest for 30 years), which were repaid. The loans were based on a formula which awarded $16,000, $32,000, or $48,000 depending upon the terrain. More importantly for Wyoming

history, the railroads were awarded the odd numbered sections of land in a 40 mile strip (20 miles on each side) along the tracks. Accordingly, the U.P. came to own 4,582,520 acres, plus mineral rights, in Wyoming alone.
6. See Grenville M. Dodge, How We Built the Union Pacific Railway, Senate Document 447, 61st Cong., 2d sess., 1917.
7. Larson, *History of Wyoming,* p. 39.
8. Churches were active in these communities, as were theater and music groups, etc.
9. Larson, *History of Wyoming,* p. 37. Also, for a more thorough treatment of the issues outlined in this section, see Larson, pp. 36–63 or any of a number of other works including, John Carson, "Union Pacific: Hell on Wheels," *Press of the Territorian* and Robert W. Fogel, *Union Pacific Railroad* (Baltimore: John Hopkins Press). For a treatment of the U.P. as a political agent at the end of this period, see Marie M. Frazer, "Some Phases of the History of the Union Pacific Railroad in Wyoming" (Masters thesis, University of Wyoming, 1927).
10. Lewis L. Gould, *Wyoming: A Political History, 1868–1896* (New Haven: Yale Univ. Press, 1968), p. 1.
11. Ibid., p. 2
12. Velma Linford, *Wyoming: Frontier State* (Denver: Old West Publishing Co., 1947), p. 210.
13. C. G. Coutant, "History of Wyoming, written by C. G. Coutant, Pioneer Historian, and Heretofore Unpublished," *Annals of Wyoming* 12 (1940):323–327.
14. Larson, *History of Wyoming,* p. 65.
15. The bill had been introduced on February 13, 1868 by Illinois Senator Richard Yates.
16. There are several excellent books and articles dealing with the territorial campaign. For example, see Gould, pp. 1–22 and Larson, *History of Wyoming,* pp. 64–94. Also, see J. K. Jeffrey, *The Territory of Wyoming* (Laramie: Daily Sentinel Print, 1874).
17. Linford, p. 212.
18. Other appointments included W. T. Jones of Indiana and John W. Kingman of New Hampshire as associate court justices and Church Howe of Massachusetts as U.S. Marshal.
19. Among the anti-U.P. bills were acts guaranteeing widows and heirs of U.P. employees killed on U.P. property the right to sue the

railroad whether the death occurred while at work or not; the legislature prohibited "yellow dog" contracts; also, county tax collectors were authorized to seize U.P. property when the railroad refused to pay its taxes.

20. Gould, pp. 26–32 and Larson, *History of Wyoming,* pp. 73–78.
21. Gould, p. 106.
22. *Wyoming Blue Book,* gen. ed. Virginia Trenholm, 3 vols. (Cheyenne: Wyoming State Archives and Historical Department, 1974), 2:463–464.
23. See Larson, *History of Wyoming,* pp. 292–293.
24. *Wyoming Blue Book,* 2:463.
25. Gould, pp. 49–50.
26. *Wyoming: From Territorial Days to the Present,* ed. Frances Birkhead Beard, 3 vols. (New York: American Historical Society, 1933), 1:427–428; also, Larson, *History of Wyoming* pp. 236–237.
27. C. G. Coutant, "History of Wyoming, written by C. G. Coutant, and Heretofore Unpublished," *Annals of Wyoming* 13 (July 1941): 196–198.
28. Larson, *History of Wyoming,* pp. 236–238.
29. J. M. Carey was particularly effective in persuading county commissioners to act. For a thorough discussion, see Gould, p. 111.
30. *Wyoming Blue Book,* 2:495.
31. *Laramie Daily Boomerang,* 4 June 1889.
32. *Wyoming: From Territorial Days to Present,* pp. 430–431.
33. Gould, pp. 111–113.
34. *Wyoming Blue Book,* 2:541–557.
35. Larson, *History of Wyoming,* p. 245.
36. Ibid., p. 246.
37. People who had voted previously were assured their right to vote, regardless of whether they could read. This provision of the constitution is no longer in effect.
38. See Kirkpatrick vs. Pressler 394 U.S. 526 (1969).
39. This section is paraphrased from Larson's excellent discussion in *History of Wyoming,* pp. 247–256. Also, see Henry J. Peterson, *The Constitutional Convention of Wyoming* (Laramie: University of Wyoming, 1940).
40. Gould, p. 113, quoting F. W. Warren in a letter to J. M. Carey, Feb. 26, 1890, Warren Papers and Warren in a letter to W. Van Devanter, Nov. 13, 1890, Van Devanter Papers.
41. *Wyoming: From Territorial Days to the Present,* p. 427.
42. Linford, pp. 312–313.
43. *Wyoming: From Territorial Days to the Present,* p. 427.
44. Larson, *History of Wyoming,* pp. 258–259.
45. For Carey's speech see *Wyoming Blue Book,* 1:573–613.
46. Larson, *History of Wyoming,* p. 259. Larson's accounts are taken from local newspapers.
47. Ibid., pp. 259–261. Also, for a treatment of other political issues of this period, see Gould, pp. 108–136.
48. Larson, *History of Wyoming,* p. 80.
49. Ibid.
50. Miriam Gantz Chapman, "The Story of Woman Suffrage in Wyoming, 1869–1890" (Masters thesis, University of Wyoming, 1952), pp. 54–57.
51. Ibid., p. 57.
52. Ibid., pp. 60–61.
53. Ibid., pp. 67–68.
54. The list includes Bright, Morris, Mrs. Bright, Lee, Hanford, Governor Campbell, Mrs. M. E. Post, Redelia Bates, Anna Dickinson, J. W. Kingman, Mrs. M. B. Arnold, Mrs. Seth Paine.
55. Chapman, p. 68.
56. Larson, *History of Wyoming,* pp. 89–94; also, see Chapman, pp. 62–68.
57. Linford, pp. 223–224.

CHAPTER
TWO

Political Parties and Elections

Definition of "Political Party"

Political scientists generally disagree upon a universal definition of a political party. Most agree that they are in varying degrees organized and decentralized combinations of people who usually share some ideological beliefs of right and wrong which lead them to try to elect members to governmental, decision-making positions of influence.

This is not as complicated as it might sound. Parties are obviously made up of people. For the most part, the members share certain beliefs about their community, state, and nation. These common beliefs, for example, may be anything from local issues (what should be taught in the schools?) to international issues (how should the U.S. "fight" communism?). We find, then, that one party tends to be a little more liberal while the other tends to be a little more conservative on *many* (but not all) issues. Also, political parties are organized so that votes, campaigns, and money can be coordinated to improve or facilitate political influence. After all, 90,000 individuals acting alone would have little political clout. But 90,000 Wyomingites organized into a political party, with some members working actively while others support them with their votes, constitute a pow-

erful political force. Finally, political parties tend to be decentralized. In America, there are no truly national parties. Rather, the national parties are loose associations of *state* parties. While there is a national Democratic party, at least in name, it is made up of the Democratic parties of Alabama, New York and the others. These state organizations, with their different philosophies (and the differences between Democrats from Alabama and New York are great!), leaders, money, and candidates come together every four years to temporarily work for their party's presidential nominee. Thus, sustaining or long-term political power lies in the various state parties. And the state parties, after all, are but combinations of county, city, and town organizations. In most states, the party structures divide up the cities and towns even further into smaller wards and precincts. Clearly, political power in America is decentralized.[1]

In an overall sense, then, a political party is "a group of individuals, often having some measure of ideological agreement, who organize to win elections, operate government, and determine public policy. . . . Unlike parties in most countries, power in American political parties is highly decentralized."[2]

23

Sidebar 2-1
Early Wyoming Elections

by T. A. Larson
(Former University of Wyoming Professor of History, Member of Wyoming House of Representatives)

No doubt certain reprehensible practices were prevalent in Wyoming and elsewhere in the days before the Australian ballot was adopted in 1890. After the 1882 election the *Cheyenne Sun* had reported frauds by both parties—emigrants being taken from trains to vote; men voting more than once, using assumed names; fifteen-year-old girls voting; and men publicly buying votes at the Seventeenth Street polling place.

Charles A. Guernsey, who was elected to the House in 1884 and to the Senate in 1886, has published a description of some of the unusual features of Wyoming elections as he observed them in Laramie County before the Australian ballot brought changes [Charles A. Guernsey,

Wyoming Cowboy Days (New York: Putnam, 1936), pp. 97–102]. After the party conventions, enterprising individuals of both parties printed tickets, selecting candidates from the major tickets. Each person, society, lodge, union, or company printing such a ticket claimed to control a certain number of votes. A candidate could get on such a ticket by paying the ticket sponsor so much for each vote the sponsor claimed to control, or in some cases on merit alone if the sponsor approved him. Such printed tickets were accepted at the polls. Guernsey recalled that in 1884, he paid the Union Pacific master mechanic for the four hundred votes he claimed to control.

Reprinted from *History of Wyoming,* Second Edition, revised by T. A. Larson by permission of University of Nebraska Press
Copyright © 1965, 1978 by the University of Nebraska Press.

Background-Political Party History in Wyoming

The Early Years. Although the early affair with the Democratic party was short-lived, Wyoming was a Democratic state in its earliest years. At the first territorial election in 1869, for instance, 23 positions were contested; the Democrats won every position in an election in which "there were no serious disturbances, only the usual drinking and rowdyism, on election day"[3] (See Sidebar 2-1). In the election for congressional delegate, the only race voted for throughout the territory, Democrat Stephen F. Nuckolls defeated his Republican opponent, W. W. Corlett, 3,331 to 1,963.

As mentioned before, the early Democratic dominance was only a passing fancy. The Republicans took advantage of several openings offered by their opponents. One reason for the Democrats' decline was that they weren't as well organized as their Grand Old Party (or GOP, a nickname for the Republican party) opponents. When Democratic President Grover Cleveland took office in 1885, for example, he had difficulty finding a qualified Democrat who was willing to accept appointment as Governor of Wyoming Territory.[4] When an appointment was made (George W. Baxter), it was withdrawn after 45 days in the midst of a scandal.[5] Because of these events—being unable to replace GOP Governor Warren for over a year and a half and having their choice for governor resign after only a month and a half—the Democrats were severely embarrassed. The embarrassment further undercut popular support of the Democrats.

Another reason for the Democrats' decline was their lack of able leaders, like Warren and Carey. Democratic Governor Thomas Moonlight (1887 to 1889), for example, alienated most large ranching and farming interests while splitting the Democrats themselves. It seems, then, that "the Democrats had no leader comparable to Warren and Carey, who stood head and shoulders above all other Wyoming politicians."[6]

Finally, there were policy differences other than agricultural ones which hurt the Democrats. In particular, the Republican stand supporting high tariffs appealed to many people in Wyoming. Thus, by the time of the first election after passage of statehood in 1890, the GOP had firmly established its control. In that election, for example, Republican candidates won all state offices by comfortable margins, control of the state senate by a 13 to three margin, and the house by 26 to seven.[7]

Populism and the Warren Machine. American history is filled with periods of reform. Indeed, American history can, in part, be read as a series of responses to social, economic, and political abuses. Some view the women's movement of the 1970's, for example, as a reform movement borne out of generations of a subservient status. Going farther back, the civil rights movement of the 1960's, unionism of the 1940's, child labor and antitrust movements at the turn of the century, and the Civil War anti-slavery drive were each reform movements to correct existing abuses.

Beginning in the middle 1890's, America entered a period of wide unrest. In the decades after the Civil War, the economy boomed. These years of industrialization led to stark abuses in an age of plenty. Child labor, poor wages, unsafe working conditions, corporate monopolies, and political machines and bosses were common. The reformers, who covered the entire political spectrum (including Republicans, Democrats, independents, socialists), came to be called Progressives or Populists. Their ranks included the LaFollettes of Wisconsin, William Jennings Bryan, Teddy

Roosevelt, and in some senses, Woodrow Wilson. In Wyoming, the Progressives were led by Joseph M. Carey.[8] This period was one of the most interesting in Wyoming's political history.

To fully appreciate Carey's role in the Progressive era, a little background is necessary. As has been mentioned repeatedly, Carey and Francis E. Warren were the outstanding leaders of the statehood movement. For their efforts, Carey and Warren were elected as Wyoming's first United States Senators in 1890.[9] Both in their middle 40's, they were seemingly at the height of brilliant political careers. After a brief political setback in 1892, Warren was reelected to a vacant senate seat in 1895.[10] Carey, however, was defeated in 1895. Carey's removal touched off a political feud between Carey and Warren which lasted at least until 1918.

Carey's defeat stemmed from several factors, including his opposition to the free coinage of silver[11] and alleged involvement in the Johnson County War.[12] But more important to the history of Wyoming's political parties, Carey was defeated in part by Warren's successful lobbying.

Among the state's Republicans, there was considerable opposition to sending two Cheyenne men to the Senate. Whether motivated by anti-Cheyenne jealousy or a sincere concern for statewide representation, many Republicans thought that either Warren or Carey had to go (both were from Cheyenne). Warren rallied his friends—including Edward A. Slack (Republican editor of the *Cheyenne Sun* newspaper), James H. Hayford (GOP editor of the *Laramie Sentinel*), and Willis Van Devanter (future Chief Justice of the Wyoming Supreme Court)—to convince Republican legislators to back Warren. By 1896, the leadership battle was complete; Warren had won control of Wyoming's strongest political party, the

Grand Old Party. Warren signaled Carey's final defeat in letters to Van Devanter in April, 1896:

With things looking as they do now and with the walloping you are giving Carey all the rats and mice, yes, and monkeys, too, will leave the sinking ship.

. . . now when we come to cut around him, leaving nothing of him from last fall's election, and then not leave even a grease spot of him in this last fight you can rest assured he will not cause much trouble for some time to come in the way of opposing or being able to influence any formidable number of votes.[13]

Carey was unforgiving. For over 20 years the Warren-Carey feud continued.[14]

Warren used his position of leadership to build a political machine. Political machines are "well-entrenched party organization(s) headed by a boss or small group of autocratic leaders." Machines in American history have maintained power through thorough organization, patronage (giving out government jobs), satisfying personal needs (helping supporters' children get admitted to colleges, or into apprenticeship programs), dominating nomination procedures, and sometimes the use of corruption. While political machines were common at local and state levels in the nineteenth century, they have generally declined in the twentieth century due to a variety of reforms (direct primaries, civil service, and election law reforms).[15]

Senator Warren's machine was built upon several props. His influence was largely due to the number of government projects that he brought to the state. Through his membership on, and ultimately chairmanship of, the powerful Appropriations and Military Affairs Committees, Warren brought literally millions of government dollars to Wyoming (especially for irrigation and reclamation projects). Also, "throughout the whole of Warren's career his political connections made the task of getting favors less hard than might

When Senator Warren of Wyoming celebrated his 82nd birthday, a giant cake was served at the capital in his honor. The Wyoming senator, who has served 34 years in the senate and who is its oldest member, is seen between Senator Dill of Washington and Robert Baumgartener, a chef. Wyoming State Archives, Museums and Historical Department, University of Wyoming.

otherwise have been the case."[16] Warren himself noted that his personal friendships with Presidents McKinley and Teddy Roosevelt, and working relationship with President Taft, translated into programs (and money!) for Wyoming. One student of Wyoming's political history notes that while the Senator was conservative in most every sense, he didn't mind government "intervention" when it meant getting money for Wyoming. He explains that, "The federal government poured millions of dollars into Wyoming in the period that Warren was a senator, and he never thought of it as paternalism or an unwarranted extension of government power."[17]

Besides using his patronage powers to his political advantage (especially when it came to Post Office positions), Warren strengthened his machine through what is today called constituency service. "At all times he strove to fulfill even the slightest and most unimportant requests that were made of him by his constituents." Accordingly, he "helped hundreds of Wyoming war veterans to secure disability pensions. . . ," making certain in each case that the recipient's local newspaper was informed. He utilized this access to the voters to the utmost, responding promptly to requests as varied as "requests for garden seeds, for war trophies, (and) for tickets to Washington social events. . . ." These personal touches, which "must have numbered well into the thousands," plus the Wyoming projects he steered through Congress, were the cornerstones of the Warren machine's strength.[18]

Other props of the machine were favorable treatment by the "predominantly Republican press," which generally assured him of complimentary press coverage;[19] and his "absolute loyalty to party. . . . Throughout his whole public career, Warren remained the purest of Republicans."[20] Unshakable party loyalty, after all, is essential to machine politics.

As with most other political machines, Warren and his machine were frequently accused of improprieties. Throughout his career, for example, Warren was repeatedly confronted with the charge that he had illegally fenced government land. Questions were even raised about how he had obtained his land. And during his Senate years, there were charges that he improperly and illegally had

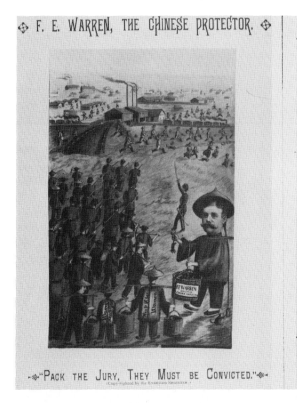

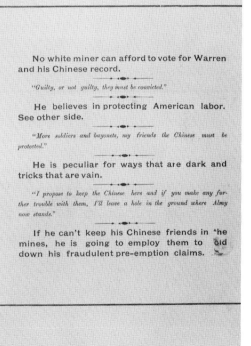

Early campaign material attacking Senator Francis E. Warren for allegedly supporting the use of Chinese laborers in Wyoming mines, fraudulent pre-emption claims, and other trickery. The campaign material shows the low level of some aspects of early politics in Wyoming. Wyoming State Archives, Museums and Historical Department, University of Wyoming.

people on his office payroll (his son, who was attending Harvard, was allegedly on the office payroll), had leased his own buildings to the government, and that he had used his influence to secure an electricity contract at Ft. Russell (now Ft. Warren near Cheyenne) for a company in which he had a personal interest. These charges led to regional and even national articles on the Warren machine. Typical of these was a 1905 series in the *Denver Post*. "The theme of the series was that the Warren group controlled a political machine that kept the State of Wyoming completely under its thumb." While the fencing charges may have had basis in fact, Warren was generally exonerated from the others.[21]

In the midst of the Warren machine era in the first decades of the twentieth century, the Populist-Progressive movement arrived in Wyoming. But unlike in the more populous states, "the Wyoming Progressives were not responding to an overwhelming new economic or social order. Neither industrialization nor urbanization had made an impact on the state."[22] Thus, the movement in this state was not intended to get women and kids out of sweat shops, or make plants safe for workers, or improve living conditions in urban ghettos. Rather:

the Wyoming progressives embraced only a part of the national progressive program. Direct democracy was the key which would break the machine control, and, in the words of Carey, 'bring to the state energetic men and women ready to contribute to the upbuilding of the state which has so much to do in the way of development of its resources. Other progressive Republicans who refused to join the new party or who affiliated only briefly . . . were concerned with reforms for the same purpose—updating Wyoming.[23]

Clearly, the progressive movement sought to "defeat" Warren's political machine.

The movement also served individual political purposes. Carey, out of a position of po-

litical leadership since 1896, used the call for reform "in his bid for a return to a position of importance in state politics."[24] Indeed, Carey seized the moment by seeking the Republican gubernatorial nomination in 1910. Denied the nomination by the Warren machine, he announced as an independent candidate. Then he abruptly switched parties again, winning the governor's office as a Democrat in 1910. As governor, he failed to decisively organize an opposition party capable of defeating the War-

Campaign poster of the progressive minded Robert D. Carey, governor from 1919-1923. Wyoming State Archives, Museums and Historical Department, University of Wyoming.

ren machine. Even so, Governor Carey and following administrations achieved several of the reforms they sought, including a direct primary, Corrupt Practices Act, secret ballot, commission government for cities, workmen's compensation, non-partisan judiciary, labor legislation, and a utilities commission, for example.[25]

All in all, the Populist-Progressive movement in Wyoming was more interesting than long-lasting. Made up of a flexible coalition of progressive Republicans, Democrats, independents and socialists, the progressive movement achieved significant reforms, elected three governors (J. M Carey in 1910, John B. Kendrick in 1914, and J. M.'s son Robert Carey in 1918) and a United States Senator (John B. Kendrick in 1919). When the movement had run its course, however, it had

achieved some—but not all—of its objectives, and the Warren group was still in power. Even so, the period is notable if for no other reason than for being one of those relatively rare eras in Wyoming history when the Republicans faced serious challenges from their opponents.

Next Half Century. As the Great Depression approached, Wyoming was again firmly under Republican control. For a conservative state with agricultural interests and a prestigious Republican senator who had brought millions of dollars to the state, this was quite natural. Except for sporadic losses in races for governor and the U.S. Senate, Republicans unquestionably held the reins of state government until the Franklin Roosevelt years of the 1930's and early 1940's. In 1934, in the midst of the early Roosevelt triumphs, the Democrats swept the state. For two terms (1934 and

President Harry Truman campaigning with Wyoming Senators Joseph O'Mahoney and Lester Hunt. Truman is wearing glasses; Hunt is to the left; O'Mahoney is next on the left. Except for a two-year interruption, O'Mahoney represented Wyoming in the U.S. Senate from 1933 to 1961. Wyoming State Archives, Museums and Historical Department, University of Wyoming.

1936), the Democrats controlled both houses of the state legislature, for the only time in Wyoming history.

With the passing of the Roosevelt era, Wyoming returned to the Republican column. With notable exceptions, the Grand Old Party dominated state government through the 1960's. The most significant exception was in 1964, when President Johnson's defeat of Republican presidential nominee Barry Goldwater helped Democrats win several offices, including control of the state senate. Consistent with traditional political patterns, the Democratic gains were short-lived. In 1966, the Republicans once again swept the state, with Stan Hathaway (governor) and Cliff Hansen (U.S. Senate) heading the ticket.

The Party Balance Today

As is evident from the foregoing section, Wyoming's Republican tradition is alive and well at the outset of the 1980's. By practically any measure, Wyoming politics is dominated by the GOP.

Austin Ranney, a prominent political scientist, has computed the number of elections won in each state by major party candidates between 1961 and 1978. In his formula, a score of 1.0 would mean that every election in the state during the 18 year period was won by the Democratic candidate; .0 would mean that every election was won by the Republican candidate, and .5 would be the score if each party won half of the elections. Noting that Republicans occupied the governor's mansion during 12 of those 18 years, and were in the majority in the house for 16 of the 18 years and were never in the minority in the senate during the period, Ranney computes Wyoming's index score at 0.320. He goes on to conclude that during this period Wyoming was not a competitive two-party state, in the ordinary sense. Rather, he places Wyoming in

a category with Idaho (0.345), Colorado (0.339), Kansas (0.338), South Dakota (0.337), and Vermont (0.331), which are under the dominance of a "Republican majority." While Ranney is careful to point out that Democrats are fully capable of challenging Republicans at particular times and in particular races (indeed, Democrats usually win in Sweetwater County and often have the advantage in Uinta, Albany and Carbon Counties), his index concludes that the GOP was more successful in Wyoming than in any other state in the union between 1961 and 1978.[26]

B.C. by permission of Johnny Hart and Field Enterprises, Inc.

It is, of course, not surprising that Wyoming is generally a Republican state. As shown above, the Democrats dominated during the early territorial period after 1869, but their decline was well under way by statehood in 1890. Embarrassed by its lack of strong party leadership, dragging its feet on statehood, and generally languishing in disorganization, the Democratic party at the end of the nineteenth century set the precedent for its minority status.

This tradition has continued throughout Wyoming's history. Whereas the state's electorate has voted for Democratic presidential candidates in nine of 23 elections (through 1980) and for Democratic gubernatorial candidates 12 of 27 times, Democratic candidates have won only one race for state treasurer, three for state auditor, five races for secretary of state, and five campaigns for superintendent of public instruction, *throughout the state's history* (See Table 2.1). This, coupled with

Table 2.1. Party Affiliation of Successful Candidates for National, State Elective Offices, and State Legislature, in Wyoming, 1890–1980

Year	President	U.S. Senate	U.S. House	Governor	Secretary of State	State Auditor	State Treasurer	Supt. of Pub. Inst.	State Legislature			
									Senate		House	
									Dem.	Rep.	Dem.	Rep.
1890		RR	R	R	R	R	R	R	3	13	7	26
1892	D		D	D					5	11	16	12[1]
1894		RR	R	R	R	R	R	R	4	14	2	34[1]
1896	D		D						4	14[1]	11	23[1]
1898		R	R	R	R	R	R	R	6	13	3	35
1900	R	R	R						2	16[1]	2	34[1]
1902			R	R	R	R	R	R	2	21	4	46
1904	R	R	R	R			R		3	20	3	47
1906		R	R	R	R	R	R	R	2	21	5	45
1908	R		R						3	24	7	49
1910		R	R	D	D	R	R	D	6	21	25	31
1912	D	R	R						8	19	28	29
1914			R	D	D	R	R	R	9	18	15	42
1916	D	D[2]	R						11	16	25	32
1918		R	R	R	R	R	R	R	10	17	11	43
1920	R		R						3	22	1	53
1922		D	R	D	R	R	R	R	5	20	23	37
1924	R	R	R	D					11	16	23	39
1926			R	R	R	R	R	R	12	15	17	45
1928	R	D	R						10	17	11	51
1930		R	R	R	R	R	R	R	6	21	26	36
1932	D		R	D					12	15	42	20
1934		D	D	D	D	D	D	D	14	13	38	18
1936	D	D	D						16	11	38	18

Table 2.1—*Continued*

Year	President	U.S. Senate	U.S. House	Governor	Secretary of State	State Auditor	State Treasurer	Supt. of Pub. Inst.	State Legislature			
									Senate		House	
									Dem.	Rep.	Dem.	Rep.
1938			R	R	D	D	R	R	11	16	19	37
1940	D	D	D						11	16	28	28
1942		R	R	D	R	D	R	R	10	17	17	39
1944	R		R						6	21	20	36
1946		D	R	D	R	R	R	R	7	20	10	46
1948	D	D	R						9	18	28	28
1950			R	R	R	R	R	R	10	17	17	39
1952	R	R	R				R		6	21	11	45
1954		D	R	R	R	R	R	D	8	19	24	32
1956	R		R						11	16	26	30
1958		D	R	D	D	R	R	D	11	16	30	26
1960	R	R	R						10	17	21	35
1962		R	R	R	R	R	R	R	11	16	19	37
1964	D	D	D						12	13	34	27
1966		R	R	R	R	R	R	R	12	18	27	34
1968	R		R						12	18	16	45
1970		D	D	R	R	R	R	R	11	19	20	40[1]
1972	R	R	D						13	17	17	44[1]
1974			D	D	R	R	R	R	15	15	29	32
1976	R	R	D						12	18	29	32
1978		R	R	D	R	R	R	D	11	19	20	42
1980	R		R						11	19	23	39

SOURCES: *Wyoming Historical Blue Book,* ed. by Virginia Cole Trenholm (Cheyenne, Wyo.: Pioneer Printing and Stationery Co., 1974), Volumes I–III; *Wyoming Official Directory and Election Returns,* Wyoming Secretary of State, 1944–1978; and *Government and Politics of Wyoming* by John B. Richard, Dubuque, Iowa: Kendall/Hunt Publishing Company, 1974).

1. In 1896 and 1900 there was one third-party member in the Wyoming Senate. In the House of Representatives there were five third-party members in 1892, one in 1894, four in 1896, four in 1900, one in 1970, one in 1972, one in 1974 and one in 1976.

2. First election in which Wyoming's U.S. Senator was elected by the people. Prior to this change brought about by adoption of the 17th Amendment to the U.S. Constitution in 1913, senators were appointed by the state legislatures.

the seemingly permanent Republican control of the state legislature (Democrats have controlled both houses for only four years of the state's history), shows the degree of Republican control. A recent paper analyzing the 1978 election in Wyoming summarizes the Republican advantage nicely. U.W. Professor Oliver Walter explains:

Although attractive Democratic candidates and an issue such as environmental protection can cause occasional deviation, Wyoming is a very Republican state. Historically, the Democrats have been competitive in presidential, gubernatorial, and senatorial elections. But they have won less than one-quarter of the congressional and non-gubernatorial elective offices. The Democrats have controlled the Wyoming House of Representatives only five times since 1890 and the State Senate only two times. Using the Ranney index of party competition . . . Wyoming has the strongest Republican majority in the United States and [a larger proportion of] registered Republicans than in any state requiring party registration (48.7 percent).[27]

This Republican dominance is, of course, a direct measure of public preferences, as attested to by Professor Walter's reference to voter registration in Wyoming. As of 1979, there were 98,000 registered Republicans (48.7 percent), 78,600 Democrats (39.1 percent), and 24,500 unaffiliated (12.1 percent) voters in the state. This is an important numerical advantage for the Grand Old Party. Considering that national voting studies show that Republicans are more likely than Democrats to actually vote, the advantage may be

even greater than the figures indicate. Indeed, as Professor Walter shows in detail in Sidebar 2–2, this is the case in Wyoming.

Wyoming Republicans have another numerical advantage over the Democrats—the ability to raise campaign contributions. While it is a generalization, it is nevertheless true that Republicans find it much easier to raise campaign funds than their Democratic counterparts. Essentially, this is because Republican conservatism appeals to equally conservative business and agricultural organizations. Democrats, on the other hand, usually receive the larger portion of the contributions by organized labor. Labor contributions, however, tend to be significantly smaller than those by the business community in Wyoming.

Sidebar 2–2
The Normal Vote

by Dr. Oliver Walter
(Professor of Political Science, University of Wyoming)

The Republican advantage in Wyoming is not solely due to a greater number of Wyoming residents who register or identify with the GOP. Unfortunately for the Democrats, the Republicans have two other advantages: They are less likely to vote for a candidate of the other party and they are more likely to go to the polls on election day. Among persons who strongly identify with either the Republican or the Democratic parties, strong Republicans are seven percent more likely to vote than strong Democrats and three percent more likely to vote for a candidate of their own party than the Democrats. The Republicans have even a greater advantage among weak party identifiers. The chances of a weak Republican going to the polls is eight percent greater than a weak Democrat and the chances of voting for a candidate of one's own party is six percent greater among the Republicans. An additional advantage for the

state's Republicans is the five percent greater likelihood that independents will vote Republican than Democratic.

Thus the Republicans have a threefold advantage in the state of Wyoming. There are more Republicans, they are more likely to participate in elections and they are more likely to vote for Republicans than Democrats are to vote for Democrats. If all three factors are taken into account, a statewide GOP candidate can expect to receive over 56 percent of the vote. Only when Democrats run attractive personalities such as Teno Roncalio or when they favor extremely popular issues positions such as the increased severance tax, can the Democrats have a chance at gaining office. Wyoming Republicans may win with lack-luster candidates and by supporting positions not popular with the majority. The same cannot be said for the Democrats.

Makeup of the Political Parties in Wyoming—A Few Comparisons

During the period of anti-Viet Nam War demonstrations in the late 1960's and early 1970's, it was common to hear the charge that the major American political parties were just alike; tweedledum and tweedledee, they were called. In fact, that allegation crops up even today. Although the parties and their members are undoubtedly similar in many ways (the similarities probably outnumber the differences several times over), important differences are also to be found.

Examination of Platforms. One way to discover some of the differences between the two parties is to compare their party platforms. A "platform" is "a statement of principles and objectives espoused by a party or a candidate that is used during a campaign to win support from voters."[28] In other words, a party's platform is its official statement of what its members (more exactly, the party's *active* members) believe or represent. There are, of course, always a few members who do not support particular portions—called planks—of their party's platform. Thus, it is appropriate to think of a party platform as a somewhat theoretical statement of beliefs by the party's activist majority. Parties generally try to implement some of their planks, but leave others for the future. It is also useful to recognize that platforms are "time bound." A party principle of today may change when the party writes a new platform two years later, as is the case in Wyoming (platforms in Wyoming are written at the party conventions held every other year).

Sidebar 2-3 summarizes the party positions, as stated in their platforms written between 1976 and 1980. A straight comparison of 1980 platforms is not possible because the 1980 Democratic platform is a brief, philosophical overview of party positions. This platform is an experiment which lacks the specifics of past platforms. Accordingly, the 1976, 1978, and 1980 GOP platforms are contrasted with the 1976 and 1978 Democratic platforms.

Sidebar 2-3
Republican and Democratic Platforms Compared

(Excerpts from the 1976–78–80 platforms)

Republican Positions	Democratic Positions
Role of Government	
. . . the federal government has continuously legislated more power to itself at the expense of state and local governments and . . . the federal government has grown remote from its citizens demonstrating little sensitivity to local concerns . . . endorses and promotes an immediate and continuing reduction in the size of the federal government and that federal statutes which interfere with states' rights be repealed (1980) . . . urges that our elected representatives work toward the curtailment of the continuing de-	. . . support endeavors to lessen unreasonable and unnecessary federal and state restrictions on business, particularly small business, and to provide adequate preference for state contractors in the construction of state and local government projects. . . . Constant vigilance to prevent invasion of privacy by public and private agencies, including such invasions as no-knock laws, preventive detention, wire-tapping, and releasing credit reports without the permission of the individual involved. . . . Wyoming, one of the

Republican Positions

struction of the free enterprise system that made this country great . . . supports the elimination of unneeded governmental programs and the streamlining of programs that are necessary . . . alarmed at the continual encroachment in our daily lives by regulatory agencies and their executive personnel, none of whom were subject to the elective process, we strongly support legislative action that would bring those political or social incursions into our lives under more direct control of the will of the people (1978) . . . strongly believes in and supports personal freedom, personal responsibility and greater protection of individual rights (1976).

Democratic Positions *[WANTS LEGISLATURE TO SPEND MORE MONEY]*

wealthiest states in the union, is one of the lowest in the amount spent per capita on human services. Therefore, we encourage the state legislature to more adequately fund community human service programs (such as) health services, youth services, senior citizens, mental health, developmental disabilities, and drug and alcohol abuse programs . . . support strengthening of state and local programs to protect children from abuse and/or neglect, to aid dependent children and to provide day-care homes and centers . . . support programs to maintain the well-being of our senior citizens through increased government support of health care, meals, transportation, utility and cost relief, and increased state supplementation of supplemental security income (1978).

Economy and Taxation

The current disastrous inflation and illness in our economy is due to 25 years of excessive federal spending and ill-conceived programs instituted by a Democrat(ic)-controlled Congress, more recently compounded by a misguided, inept, vacillating Democrat(ic) president . . . inflation can and must be reduced . . . (favor) the establishment of a responsible, lower balanced budget, achieved through lower total spending and less taxation, and a constitutional amendment tying total federal spending to a percentage of Gross National Product except in a determined case of national emergency. Place an emphasis on putting private investment capitol into the private production sector of our economy with proper tax changes complete with a consistent control on credit, rather than taxing away the private citizen's initiative and incentive to save and invest in the private sector. . . . Finally recognize that government competition with, and over-regulation of, the private sector of our economy with our own citizen's hard earned money and capital destroys our individual productivity, initiatives and willingness to work for and help ourselves and our fellow Americans . . . believes in the responsible reduction of federal, state, and local taxes whenever possible . . . continuing the favorable tax climate in Wyoming by enacting tax increases only when clearly defined needs for additional revenue are identified (1980).

. . . support a vigorous program to provide employment opportunities for all, including public service employment if necessary, with particular attention to the needs of youth and minority groups, in which unemployment is a national scandal; to protect incomes from inflation; to guarantee that the burdens and gains of economic adjustment and progress be fairly shared. . . . Whereas we wish to more fairly distribute the tax burden, we . . . support elimination of the sales tax on retail food other than meals prepared in restaurants and quick food establishments, a truly progressive federal income tax, including the elimination of tax loopholes; . . . support a tax system which provides revenue by taxing the natural resources of Wyoming as they are developed rather than continually increasing the level of personal property taxes, a system which bears most heavily on the poor, the disabled, and the elderly, and the formation of an equitable plan for the distribution of funds so derived (1978). . . . We point to the fact that Wyoming has the most regressive personal tax structure in the Rocky Mountain Region and the fourth most regressive in the United States. The reason for this is that Wyoming's present tax structure is dependent on Wyoming's people, rather than Wyoming's wealth. We urge a fair increase in the severance tax on appropriate minerals and coal with one-half of that amount going to the Permanent

[AGAIN WANTS TO SPEND MORE MONEY]

[REVISE TAX STRUCTURE]

Republican Positions

Democratic Positions

Mineral Trust Fund . . . favor distribution of mineral tax revenues to meet the "front end" money needs of designated impact areas, to meet urgent short-term capital needs for all Wyoming communities and to meet long-term income needs when minerals are depleted (1976).

Foreign Affairs

Whereas . . . the Carter Administration has failed to support those new weapon systems, programs, and personnel requirements capable of providing a strong national defense . . . the Soviet Union has gained military pre-eminence and surpassed the United States in most major military capabilities . . . the Republican Party of Wyoming opposes the Salt II treaties . . . support(s) a vastly improved defense posture, such as registration of men, and increased military preparedness to restore the United States as the military authority of the world . . . recognizes Taiwan as an independent friendly nation . . . the Carter Administration . . . has lost the confidence and respect of our allies and jeopardized the free world and our national freedoms . . . the U.S. (should) develop a realistic and practical bipartisan foreign policy . . . (and) reduce foreign aid . . . (and) that legislation establish that an attack on our military or diplomatic installations or personnel abroad be considered an act of war (1980) . . . we detest the actions of the Carter Administration in forcing and coercing the ratification of the Panama Canal Treaty (1978).

Whereas the world is still far short of a lasting peace, and . . . violations of human rights still occur in countries throughout the world, we . . . support continued emphasis on human rights and a strong effort to aid developing countries by means of assistance exclusively earmarked for educational, nutritional and economic development of the people; strong efforts to negotiate with the great powers to resist the burgeoning arms race throughout the world, which negates any effort to bring about harmonious relations among the people of the world (1978). We believe in a firm commitment to the basic principles and goals of the United Nations, opposing illegitimate intervention by the U.S. in affairs of other countries, greater caution in the sales of military arms and equipment . . . and to oppose further funding of the B–1 bomber (1976).

Disadvantaged, Minorities, and Equality

. . . supports effective quality education and services for the handicapped . . . salutes the senior citizens . . . as outstanding contributors to our society and supports efforts to recognize and deal with their particular concerns (1978).

. . . support increased legislation designed to secure the rights of all minority groups . . . ; endorse . . . the Equal Rights Amendment to the U.S. Constitution (and) the appointment of more women to State boards and commissions and the hiring of more women in administrative positions at all governmental levels. We recognize the inequities within our society. We support the efforts of minorities to protect and promote their cultural heritage. We must continue our unceasing effort of pushing for civil rights and the elimination of all forms of discrimination . . . recommend that mandatory retirement be abolished. . . (1978). We support and endorse the American Indian and other

Republican Positions

Democratic Positions

minorities in their efforts to protect and promote their heritage and to achieve equality of opportunity . . . urge the legislature to adequately finance the Fair Employment Practices Commission and give it more adequate powers of investigation and enforcement . . . support a Fair Housing Agency to prevent discrimination in housing . . . (1976).

Energy and Environment

. . . strongly endorses the protection of states' rights, local identification of needs and local solutions of impact problems of the states of energy origin . . . demands the repeal of the Federal Excise Tax on oil now erroneously called the "Windfall Profits Tax." . . . favors rapid development of alternate energy sources and . . . development of natural and synthetic energy sources through the provisions of tax incentives (for the private sector) (1980) . . . seek the repeal or modification of the national 55 MPH speed limit at the earliest possible time . . . strongly opposed to the creation of additional primitive and wilderness areas to further withdrawals of federal lands from multiple use by the federal government within . . . Wyoming (1978).

"Quality growth" requires a sensible balance between industrial, economic and population expansion and the protection of our environment. . . . We support a balanced program of conservation, ambitious development of historic energy sources and renewable sources of energy; the right of . . . Wyoming to adopt environmental standards which are more stringent than federal minimum standards; sufficient funding of the Dept. of Environmental Quality, Industrial Siting Council and other environmental regulatory agencies . . . ; a go-slow approach to development of nuclear generation facilities in Wyoming and support only if warranted by power demand within the state; prohibiting storage of imported radioactive wastes in Wyoming (and) stringent control of hazardous wastes including uranium wastes (1978).

Water and Agriculture

. . . recognizes and supports the (state's) constitutional ownership and jurisdiction of water within its boundaries . . . deplores the continuous attempt by the Carter administration to impose its control over Wyoming's water . . . (1980). State and privately owned water rights should be protected . . . advocates the limitation of undue federal control of production and marketing methods; intensive development of foreign markets for American agricultural products; reduction of imports . . . recognizes that . . . agriculture is not the root cause of food cost inflation and should not . . . be condemned as such by the government or media . . . firmly opposes any effort by the federal executive branch to delegate, confer or in any way transfer any . . . responsibilities . . . from the Dept. of Agriculture to any other executive branch . . . department . . . supports legislation to repeal the 160 acre limitation provisions of the 1902 reclamation laws (1978).

. . . support a National Water Policy which is the product of a commission appointed by the State Governors and subject to ratification by the individual state legislatures . . . support improvement of all agricultural educational facilities at the College of Agriculture, U.W. . . . support agriculture policy allowing . . . agriproducers to work with the Secretary of Agriculture . . . support a stronger educational program directed toward the American public of the true facts regarding agricultural production and prices . . . support the exportation of agriproduce and the expansion of foreign markets for American agriculture . . . support a reduction in the importation of foreign agri-products when American farmers can provide these products . . . (Favor) prohibiting the use of Wyoming water for the purpose of exporting coal in the form of a slurry (1978).

Republican Positions

Democratic Positions

Labor

. . . recognizes with pride the role of labor in Wyoming. We support equal rights and opportunity for all working people to receive a fair return for their efforts and proper recognition for their work (1980). The Republican party has ably represented the interests of the working people . . . by providing a business climate that offers excellent job opportunities and the lowest unemployment rate of all 50 states . . . pledges its efforts to continue to promote high employment and further improve the earning capabilities of our working people (1976) . . . vigorously supports the principle of Right-to-Work in . . . Wyoming and shall defend the retention of 14–B of the Taft-Hartley Act (1978).

We support the repeal of the so-called Right-to-Work Law and Section 14b of the Taft-Hartley Act which hinders many Wyoming workers from securing just and fair employment and treatment . . . further support improved laws for Wyoming's workers such as adequate Workers' Compensation which would give immediate and equitable compensation for injury plus additional remedies for employer negligence; adequate Unemployment Insurance; the right to bargain collectively in both the public and private sectors . . . minimum wage . . . protection against the use of polygraph tests as a condition of or continuation of employment; adequate funding for enforcement of the Wyoming Occupational Health and Safety Act . . . support legislation that would reform and liberalize the Hatch Act(s) . . . (1978).

Education

. . . supports a method of funding public schools which is equitable for all citizens in this state, does not lower standards to just an average, but which raises all schools to the highest quality education possible, and allows local school districts control in determining and meeting the needs of their communities (1980) . . . commits itself to an improved competency assurance system in primary and secondary schools to ascertain that reasonable levels of proficiency are attained (1978) . . . recommend increased attention to basic educational skills and the virtues of the American way of life including required instruction on the governments of the U.S. and Wyoming and the free enterprise system . . . continuation of . . . cooperative efforts between the University and community colleges . . . (1976).

. . . endorses the . . . development of a state plan of educational finances that would provide the children of every school district with adequate and comparable programs and facilities; support . . . continuing adult education, vocational education and equal opportunities for education of the handicapped and developmentally disabled; increased educational opportunity through student grants, low-cost student loans, and work-study programs; right of educators at all levels to negotiate collectively; passage of a Professional Practices Act that would require public school teachers to be responsible for certification and decertification of those in the profession (1978).

Health and Insurance

. . . believes that issues involving insurance and insurance regulations, including those related to no-fault insurance and medical malpractice insurance, should be resolved by the states and not by the federal government (1976).

. . . support national health insurance which is comprehensive, preventative and which provides continuity (1978). State funding to fully match federal funds to improve the physical and mental health of Wyoming citizens of all ages. . . . A state medical care program for isolated rural areas . . . Medicare which will pay the total cost of medical bills incurred by retired citizens . . . (1976).

The excerpted platforms show several characteristics of the major parties in Wyoming and tell us something of platform writing itself. To begin with, the platforms are obviously political documents, because they use dramatic and exaggerated language. The 1980 Republican platform, for example, says that President Carter has been ". . . a misguided, inept, vacillating Democrat president" whose policies have "been based upon amateurism" which "has . . . jeopardized the free world and our national freedoms." Language such as this is quite common in politics and political documents. The party that is out of power, whether Republican or Democratic, always charges that the other party is leading the city, state, or nation down the path to disaster. Likewise, both platforms assure that each is the only party that is truly on the side of justice, peace, and prosperity. The use of such language is understandable. After all, one of the purposes of a platform is to make it easier for the party's candidates to win elections.

Beyond mere rhetoric, platforms also convey certain themes about their authors. As is evident in Sidebar 2–3, Wyoming's Republican party is opposed to the federal government's playing an active role in everyday aspects of society. This is not to say that Wyoming's Republican platform opposes all federal activity. Rather, it is to say that Republican platforms in recent years have repeatedly endorsed "an immediate and continuing reduction in the size of the federal government. . . elimination of unneeded governmental programs and the streamlining of programs that are necessary. . . ." The platform says Republicans are "alarmed at the continual encroachment in our daily lives by regulatory agencies. . . ."

When government involvement is appropriate in a particular area, the Republican platform stresses state involvement. States'

rights, then, is a second major theme of GOP platforms in Wyoming. The 1980 plank on energy is typical. It says that Republicans strongly endorse the protection of states' rights, local identification of needs and local solutions of impact problems of the states of energy origin. . . ." The plank on water makes the same point. In recent years, the federal government has initiated measures to create a national water policy, suggesting national control of water. The Republican platform "deplores the continuous attempt . . . to impose . . . control over Wyoming's water . . . State and privately owned water rights should be protected."

The third theme, which is implicit in the first two, is the party's emphasis on the importance of an unencumbered free enterprise economic system. The platform "urges that our elected representatives work toward the curtailment of the continuing destruction of the free enterprise system that made this country great." Likewise, "the Republican party opposes direct competition by the federal government or any state government with private enterprise." These planks are expressions of, and reinforced by, the close ties between the Republican party and the corporate sector of the economy.

Another major theme of the GOP platform in Wyoming is the emphasis on less government spending and taxation. Republicans favor "the establishment of a responsible, lower balanced budget, achieved through lower total spending and less taxation. . . ." The platform supports the proposal to amend the U.S. Constitution "tieing total federal spending to a percentage of Gross National Product except in a determined case of national emergency."

The one major exception to the spending cuts by the GOP in Wyoming is in the area of national defense. Planks calling for a strong military are the fifth major theme of recent Republican platforms. Charging the foreign policy of the recent Democratic president with "amateurism and unrealistic premises," and concluding that "the Soviet Union has gained military preeminence and surpassed the United States in most major military capabilities, "the Republican document calls for a "vastly improved defense posture, such as registration of men, and increased military preparedness to restore the United States as the military authority of the world." Other planks call for a reduction in foreign aid and "that legislation establish that an attack on our military or diplomatic installations or personnel abroad be considered an act of war." The strong military posture is apparent in each of these excerpts.

The sixth major theme of recent Republican platforms is the extent to which the party downplays specific social issues like civil rights, sexual equality, and affirmative action. The point here is not that the Republican party in Wyoming is opposed to civil rights, sexual equality, or affirmative action. Rather, the absence of these issues is consistent with conservative philosophy, which sees such matters as secondary to the reduction of government involvement and spending. Although the GOP platform has broadly worded statements in support of the elderly, a call for education of the handicapped, and "support (of) equal rights and opportunity for all working people to receive a fair return for their efforts . . . ," the 1976–80 platforms do not discuss minority rights, women's rights or the Equal Rights Amendment, or affirmative action. The point is that the noticeable absence of these issues from recent platforms implies that these concerns are of a relatively low priority within the GOP.

In contrast with the Republican platform, recent Democratic platforms have devoted considerable attention to social issues involving the poor, racial minorities, the women's movement (and the Equal Rights Amendment), children, the handicapped and the elderly. The 1978 platform, for example, "support(s) increased legislation designed to secure the rights of all minority groups . . . endorse(s) the Equal Rights Amendment . . ." and calls for "Medicare which will pay the total cost of medical bills incurred by retired citizens . . . ," government funding of day-care facilities for children with working parents, and creation of a state agency "to prevent discrimination in housing. . . ." The considerable attention devoted to social issues is one of the major themes of Democratic platforms in Wyoming.

Another major Democratic theme is the support for organized labor. Whereas the Republican platforms "recognize with pride the role of labor in Wyoming," Democratic platforms go further. The Democratic documents "support the repeal of the so-called Right-to-Work Law and repeal of Section 14b of the Taft-Hartley Act which hinders many Wyoming workers from securing just and fair employment and treatment . . . ," endorse the right of all workers "to bargain collectively in both the public and private sectors . . . ," and call for "adequate funding . . . of the Wyoming Occupational Health and Safety Act. Therefore, just as Republican platforms express a pro-business bent, Democratic platforms have a pro-labor theme. Once again, while this does not mean that Wyoming Republicans are particularly anti-labor, nor that Wyoming Democrats are particularly anti-big business, their priorities are quite apparent.

Party differences regarding support for (GOP platform position), or opposition to (Democratic platform position), "right-to-work" is perhaps the major example of this theme. Section 14(b) of the Labor-Management Relations Act of 1947 (also called the Taft-Hartley Act) allows states to pass laws which prohibit making union membership a qualification for employment. Accordingly, workers in the approximately 20 "right-to-work" states are not obligated to join or pay dues to a union as a condition for keeping their jobs. Proponents say that the right of free association is a basic liberty. Opponents say these laws are attempts to lessen union membership, thereby weakening labor's bargaining position.

The third theme in recent Democratic platforms is their less emphatic (i.e. more moderate) position on military spending and different approach to foreign affairs. Unlike their counterparts, authors of the Democratic platforms endorse "a strong effort to aid developing countries by means of assistance exclusively earmarked for educational, nutritional and economic development of the people . . . (and) strong efforts to negotiate with the great powers to resist the burgeoning arms race. . . ." Other Democratic planks oppose "illegitimate intervention by the U.S. in affairs of other countries . . . and oppose . . . the B-1 bomber."

The two remaining major themes that are evident in the Democratic platforms overlap considerably. One of these themes is a more active role for the federal government. Although Democratic platforms, like Republican platforms, call for the handling of many programs at the state level, they still give the federal government more latitude than their GOP counterparts. Federal water policy is perhaps the best example. While the Republican platforms emphatically contend that managing water is a state matter, the Democrats "support a National Water Policy which is the product of a commission appointed by the State Governors and subject to ratification by the individual state legislatures. . . ." In other words, on this issue the GOP platform says that water management is a matter for state jurisdiction; the Democratic platform says that once the states have set the parameters of the issue, national management is appropriate. If that example is inadequate (and it might be, because involvement of the federal government is merely implied in the Democratic plank), consider the issue of national health insurance. The Republican platform "believes that issues involving insurance . . . should be resolved by the states and not by the federal government"; the Democratic platform "supports national health insurance which is comprehensive, preventative and which provides continuity." Although this example might also be faulted (the GOP plank makes no mention of national health insurance), the point is still quite valid—Democratic platforms in Wyoming emphasize state handling of problems, but envision a rather active role for the federal government in many policy areas.

The fifth major theme of the Democratic platforms is less emphasis upon holding down government spending. This is not to say that Wyoming Democrats are big spenders; after all, they, too, pledge the elimination of waste and unnecessary programs. The difference is that the Republican platform says it more often, louder, and with greater depth of conviction. While it is admittedly an oversimplification, the Republican platform stresses cutting back, while the Democratic platform wants to manage public funds better while doing more. This theme is evident at both the national and state levels. Regarding state programs, the Democratic platform says, for example, "Wyoming is one of the wealthiest states in the union, is one of the lowest in the amount spent per capita on human services. Therefore, we encourage the state legislature to more adequately fund community human services, youth services, senior citizens, mental health, developmental disabilities, and drug and alcohol abuse programs . . . support strengthening of state and local programs to protect children from abuse and/or neglect, to aid dependent children and to provide day-care homes and centers . . . support programs to maintain the well-being of our senior citizens through increased government support of health care, meals, transportation, utility and cost relief, and increased state supplementation of supplemental security income."

This discussion shows that when their platforms are taken literally (a risky business, at best), the two major political parties in Wyoming have somewhat different philosophies. In reality, there are important differences. The Republican platform—with its emphasis on reduced federal spending, reduced government involvement at all levels, greater personal responsibility, and increased military spending—is quite conservative by practically any definition. The Democratic platform—with emphasis on social matters, state involvement preferred over federal involvement but with little overall federal "withdrawal" from most policy areas, negotiations with our adversaries, and balanced military spending—is quite moderate by most standards. Do not lose sight of the fact, however, that these are indeed political documents. As such, they are subject to both hyperbole and a bit of hyper-"bull."

Demographic Differences of Members. There are, of course, other ways to probe for differences between the two parties besides looking at their platforms. One might speculate, for instance, that if the platform differences outlined above show actual differences between the parties, different types of people would be attracted to them. One way to explore the parties further, then, is to turn to public opinion polls.

Looking at data from the Center for Government Research's 1978 statewide survey,[29]

" I'M REPUBLICAN, MY HUSBAND'S DEMOCRAT, AND FIDO'S RADICAL. "

Reprinted by permission of the Chicago Tribune-New York News Syndicate, Inc.

several minor differences between party members are detectable. Using very broad definitions of Republican and Democrat (respondents who said they are "strong," "weak," or "lean" toward Republicans are combined in the Republican category, for example),[30] slight differences are apparent in terms of levels of education. As seen in Table 2.2, approximately 10.1 percent of Wyoming's Republicans dropped out of school before graduating from high school, compared with 18.8 percent of the Democrats in the state. While the figures in the table must be viewed cautiously (opinion polls are subject to sampling errors[31] and most of these figures are quite similar), there are nevertheless indications that Wyoming Republicans are *slightly* better educated than their Democratic counterparts. Notice, for example, that 57.1 percent of the Republicans surveyed have spent time in college

Table 2.2*. Highest Year of Education Completed by Wyoming Republicans and Democrats (Number Surveyed = 849)

Political Party	Level of Education					
	Less Than High School Degree	High School Degree	Some College	College Degree	Graduate or Professional School	Total
Republican (N = 465)	10.1%	32.7%	27.7%	20.4%	9.0%	99.9%
Democratic (N = 384)	18.8%	41.1%	18.8%	12.0%	9.3%	100.0%

*This is called a "crosstabulation." It means that 849 people were surveyed in Wyoming; 465 said they are, or lean, toward the Republicans, while 384 said they are, or lean, toward the Democrats. The figures indicate that 10.1% of the Republicans did not finish high school; 32.7% of the Republicans did finish high school, but did not enter college (meaning 32.7% got through high school but went no further); 27.7% of the Republicans entered college but did not graduate (the assumption also is that they finished high school as well); 20.4% of the Republicans graduated from college; and 9% more of Wyoming's Republicans have finished their education by going to graduate school. Statistically, it is unlikely that these are the exact percentages for *all* the Republicans in Wyoming (since only 465 out of thousands were surveyed). But it is likely that these figures are *very close* to being accurate.

(combining the "some college," "college degree," and "graduate or professional school" responses), compared with only 40.1 percent of the Democrats. This is a small, but significant, difference.

Another minor difference exists in terms of total family income. In 1978, about one-quarter of the members of both parties had annual family incomes of below $12,000. The only noticeable difference was among people in the highest income category. Of all the Republicans surveyed, 26 percent had annual family incomes of over $27,000, compared with only 11 percent of the Democrats. Once again, though, these figures should be viewed with caution. It would not be accurate, for example, to conclude from these figures that Republicans are richer than Democrats. After all, a $27,000 family income does not mean great wealth, even in 1978; besides, there are other ways besides annual income to determine wealth. But, the figures do indicate (as other studies show of the nation at large) that Wyoming people with higher incomes tend to identify with the Republicans. Considering the long-standing GOP ties with the business community (particularly big business), this is as

expected. Finally, although it is somewhat skewed by the fact that there are more Republicans than Democrats in Wyoming, the point is made further by the fact that 64 percent of all the upper income respondents identify with the GOP; only 24 percent were Democrats.

A more pronounced difference between party members than either level of education or income has to do with affiliation with labor unions. Since the time of Franklin Roosevelt in the early 1930's, unions have been a bastion of Democratic support. As seen in the Democratic platforms, the labor-Democratic party ties are found even in non-industrial Wyoming. As shown in Table 2.3, Wyoming's union members prefer the Democratic party

Table 2.3. Partisan Identification of Wyoming Union Members (1978)
(Approximate Number Surveyed = 60)

Democrats	49%
Republicans	24%
Independents and Other	27%
	100%

over the Republican party by approximately two to one. Although the two to one ratio is based upon a small number of respondents, it is supported by other figures—15 percent of all the surveyed Democrats are members of at least one labor union, compared to a six percent GOP affiliation rate. These seemingly low percentages—only seven percent of all the people surveyed in this state belong to a union—also show just how small Wyoming's union population is.

Although there are other differences that might be raised (nationally, for example, Catholics are more likely to be Democrats than are Protestants), the education, income and union patterns are less than dramatic. While this is not to downplay the sometimes subtle, other times expected, differences between Wyoming Republicans and Democrats, it is to say that the party members are quite homogeneous overall. In that sense, Wyoming's two parties are very similar.

At first glance, the similarities between Republicans and Democrats seem to tell us little about Wyoming politics. Actually, the opposite is the case—the homogeneous nature of Wyoming's political parties tells us that to the extent that the parties are different in this state, they are generally different in ways other than their members' backgrounds (or at least those mentioned). This is important not just for Wyoming parties, but as one of the state's defining characteristics (see the discussion on political culture in Chapter 7).

Ideological (Liberal-Conservative) Differences. Although there do not appear to be stark differences (subtle, yes; stark, no) between Wyoming Republicans and Democrats in terms of their personal backgrounds, the previous discussion of platforms shows that the activist members of the parties have discernible ideological perspectives. Accordingly, the question then arises whether mass party members share the perspectives of their activist counterparts. In other words, do the thousands of Wyoming Republicans differ from the thousands of Wyoming Democrats in terms of liberal, moderate, and conservative ideologies?

Bearing in mind that conservatives tend to favor limited government activity and spending, states' rights, and a strong military posture, and that liberals emphasize the positive use of government to correct social problems, protection of the environment, and avoidance of Cold War military postures (see Chapter 7 for a thorough discussion of these concepts), the figures in Table 2.4 show that there are indeed ideological differences between the two parties' mass memberships. The table shows how Wyoming's Republicans and Democrats labeled themselves in the 1978 statewide survey.

First, the Democratic party is roughly twice as liberal as the Republican party—29 percent of the Democrats say they are liberal compared with 15 percent of the Republicans. Likewise, Democratic survey respondents said they are the more moderate party, 44 percent

Table 2.4. Political Party Identification (Republican-Democrat) by Political Ideology (Liberal-Moderate-Conservative)

Party Identification	Political Ideology								
	Extremely Liberal	Liberal	Slightly Liberal	Moderate	Slightly Conservative	Conservative	Extremely Conservative	Total	Number Surveyed
Republican	.4	2.6	12.3	25.8	24.9	31.5	2.4	99.9	454
Democratic	1.9	8.5	18.4	43.5	14.7	12.3	.8	100.1	375

to 26 percent. Interestingly, a majority of the Republicans identify themselves as conservatives. Long-noted as the more conservative party nationally, Republicans in Wyoming clearly fit the bill. In fact, conservatives are twice as common in the Republican party (59 percent) than among their Democratic opponents (28 percent). Another trend here is how "balanced" the Democratic party is—29 percent liberal, 44 percent moderate, and 28 percent conservative—compared with the Republicans. As mentioned, the conservative wing of the Grand Old Party is clearly the majority—15 percent liberal, 26 percent moderate, and 59 percent conservative. In a state where 41 percent of the entire population describe themselves as conservative, this often gives the Republicans the advantage (the state as a whole describes itself as 21 percent liberal, 35 percent moderate, and 41 percent conservative).

So far the comparison of Republicans and Democrats has been according to their self-perceptions as liberals and conservatives. Table 2.5 shows party positions on a number of issues in which liberals and conservatives and/or Democrats and Republicans might dis-agree. The table shows that Republicans are more likely to favor government tax cuts, an increase in military spending, and are more oriented toward business than the Democrats. Likewise, Democratic respondents spoke up more often in defense of Wyoming's environment, against the Right-to-Work Law, and with less enthusiasm for business.

Two points are evident in Table 2.5. First, people in both parties are quite conservative about federal spending and national defense. This is as expected—Wyoming is a conservative state. Second, subtle differences between the parties are apparent. Both parties are conservative on federal spending and defense, but Republicans are more enthusiastic; significant portions of both parties give the environment priority over development, but Democrats are more enthusiastic; a large block of each party wants to keep the Right-to-Work Law, the Republicans are more enthusiastic; both parties prefer not to give the business sector tax breaks at the expense of middle and lower income groups, but Democrats are more enthusiastic. Clearly, subtle differences on these issues, and presumably others, exist between the members of Wyoming's major political

Table 2.5. Selected Issue Positions by Party Identification

Statement:	Party Identification—% in Agreement	
	Republicans (N = approx. 450)	Democrats (N = approx. 375)
The government in Washington should fight inflation by cutting goverment spending	84%	76%
Increasing the size of the U.S. defense budget	64%	53%
Giving priority to the protection of the environment even at the expense of limiting the development of Wyoming mineral resources	43%	52%
Retention of the state's Right-to-Work law	66%	47%
Providing tax relief for business and industry even if such relief might result in smaller tax cuts for middle and lower income groups	36%	26%

parties. And for the most part, the differences are in the same direction as the departures between the platforms.

Attitudes Toward Government. Political scientists use the term "political efficacy" to describe the degree to which people believe they control government. When people believe their public officials care what they think, that their votes make a difference, that government isn't so complicated that they can't understand what's going on, the link between the people and their government is intact. The people are then thought to be in control, working through their government officials. In Wyoming, however, there is an alarming counter-trend. Indeed, this may to some extent be the case throughout the nation. The 1978 statewide survey shows (Table 2.6) that a large segment of the state's population is inefficacious (i.e., believe that they have little or no say about what the government does). In the recent statewide survey, for example, nearly half of the respondents said that public officials don't care much what they think, and that outside of voting, they have no say about what the government does. Also, three-quarters indicated that politics and government are so complicated that they can't really understand what's going on. And 35 percent of the survey respondents agreed that they "don't have *any* say about what the government does."

In terms of statistical significance, we must be careful with comparisons in Table 2.6. As was discussed earlier regarding random survey data, there is always a chance of error. Even though over 450 Republicans were surveyed, it is always possible (about one chance in 20) that the survey sample was not typical of all the Republicans in Wyoming. That said, one important theme is evident from the table: Wyoming Democrats are somewhat less confident that "the people" are in control of government. In each case (except perhaps that voting is the only way to influence government), Democrats were slightly more pessimistic regarding their influence over government and what the government does. Even so, it is worth noting again how negative members of both parties are. Clearly, government officials in Wyoming—and quite likely America as a whole—should take notice of this "credibility gap" between the rhetoric that insists that government is controlled by the people and the people's own doubt that their government listens to them.

Even so, the apparent difference in the degree of political efficacy (belief that government is responsive to the people) between the parties is probably not as large as Table 2.6 indicates. Respondents were asked, for example, how much of the time they "can trust the government in Washington to do what is

Table 2.6. People's Control of Government (or Lack Thereof) by Party Identification

Statement:	Party Identification—% In Agreement	
	Republicans (N = approx. 450)	Democrats (N = approx. 375)
I don't think public officials care much about what people like me think.	44%	53%
Voting is the only way that people like me can have any say about the way the government runs things.	47%	54%
People like me don't have any say about what the government does.	30%	43%
Sometimes politics and government seem so complicated that a person can't really understand what's going on.	74%	82%

right." The party response rates were basically the same. Republicans responded, 2.2 percent "all the time" (to do the right thing), 23.0 percent "most of the time," 69.1 percent "some of the time," and 5.7 percent "none of the time." Democrats responded, four percent "all," 25.7 percent "most," 64.7 percent "some," and 5.6 percent "none of the time." Perhaps this much can be said—there are party differences in the "confidence gap." That difference is not dramatic on the whole, and when only the government in Washington, D.C. is considered, the parties are equal in their feelings of political inefficacy.[32]

Summary. The discussion in this section may at first seem quite difficult. Actually, it is not as complicated as one might think. Although Republicans and Democrats are quite similar in Wyoming, this much can be said about their differences: recent Republican platforms have been conservative documents overall; Democratic platforms, though conservative themselves in many policy areas, tend to be more moderate; there are slight differences between party members in terms of their levels of education, income, and union affiliation; and although members of both parties agree overall on many policies, slight differences do exist on the *degree* to which various opinions are held.

Party Structure

The smallest, or most basic, political party unit is a precinct. Wyoming cities, for example, are divided into precincts inside their city limits. Each party has at least two representatives in each precinct (one committeeman and one committeewoman), assuming candidates for these volunteer positions can be found. It isn't always easy to fill these spots.

Generally, these men and women are party contacts at the "grassroots" (or local) level.

Some precinct committeemen and committeewomen are more active than others. The inactive keep the positions so they can feel like they are part of their party. Active precinct representatives, on the other hand, are a great asset to their party. They help in several ways—locating party members in their neighborhood, getting them to register, arranging rides to the polls on election day, making them aware of party meetings and rallies, and generating enthusiasm for the party. Even so, the picture of active and dedicated precinct workers devoting long days to the party is overstated. Typically, precinct committeemen and committeewomen are proud Republicans and Democrats who give a little time to their party, attend a meeting or rally now and then, talk a lot about politics, and generally enjoy their limited involvement. To many, it is similar to a hobby.[33]

The next level in the party structure is the county central committee. Both the Republican and Democratic parties have organizations in each county, consisting of the committeemen and committeewomen in the precincts in the county. These committees select someone to head the party's efforts as county chairman. Under the chairman's direction, members organize rallies, find candidates for office, coordinate and support the candidates' campaigns, raise and spend campaign money (buying advertising, for example), and elect a state committeeman and committeewoman to sit on the state central committee. The county chairman is crucial to the party structure. He or she is the driving force in the county organization. When a Republican or Democratic county organization is especially active, it is nearly always due to the efforts of an energetic chairman.

One of the most important activities of the county central committee is to call a county convention during the first 15 days of March (typically in, but not limited to, odd numbered years). Legally, delegates to the convention are supposed to be members of the county central committee (unless the party provides for an alternative method of electing delegates). While some county conventions are careful about who qualify as voting delegates, others are not so mindful. Nearly all county conventions welcome anyone who is an interested observer. These conventions are "grassroots" politics at their best. Besides giving members a chance to meet with friends in their party (and this social function is no unimportant aspect of political participation), county conventions also elect delegates to their party's state convention and draft a county platform. This is one way for people to have their opinions heard by their government, because resolutions that are passed at the county conventions go on for consideration at the party's state convention.[34]

Both major political parties have a state central committee, which meets (usually for one day) "during the first 15 days in December of odd numbered years. . . ." Each county central committee elects two people, one man and one woman, to represent it on the party's state central committee. Technically, the Republican and Democratic state central committees "run" or direct their parties. Actually, though, they elect a state chairman who is in charge, although his or her major actions must be approved by the central committee. The state chairman gives up a great deal of personal time to lead the party. The chairman's major functions are to encourage his party to organize and be active throughout the counties, coordinate and arrange the party's state convention, raise money, be a public relations spokesman, find and encourage the best candidates the party has to offer, and be available to help the party's officeholders in the ways they determine beneficial. While the chairmen are not paid a salary for their labors, they generally receive free publicity; state chairmen sometimes use the office as a stepping stone to advance their own political careers. The state chairman of today may be a candidate of tomorrow.[35]

Finally, each party holds a state convention "on the second Saturday in May of even numbered years." Delegates and alternates to the state conventions are elected at the various county conventions. For counties that are a long way from the convention site (which varies year by year; there are no permanent convention sites), electing state convention delegates is often a matter of finding someone who is willing and able to attend. These are typically festive affairs. Party enthusiasts from throughout the state meet at their respective conventions to renew old friendships, reaffirm their political beliefs, and generally "celebrate" their politics. This is treating the conventions somewhat romantically, but that's part of it. There are always a fair share of cocktail parties and banquets. In fact, in 1978 the Democrats even had a disco party.

In terms of business, conventions held during presidential election years nominate their party's candidates for the electoral college (three men or women from each party who will cast Wyoming's presidential votes if the party's candidate wins the popular vote), and select delegates to represent the party at its national convention. Most of the convention's time, however, is taken up with the party's platform. Both the Republican and Democratic state conventions go through their respective county platforms, combining some resolutions, defeating others, and passing still others. This way, both parties offer a statement of beliefs and principles (their platforms) to the voters. Even though platforms are usually ignored by the voters, and often ignored by some candidates, they nevertheless serve important ideological and symbolic functions for party members.

Elections and the Electoral Process

The Right to Vote. Few rights are more basic to a democracy than the right to vote. Suffrage, or the right to vote, applies to most adults today. It hasn't always been that way in the U.S. In earlier days, many Americans were prohibited from voting. The list used to be long. Until 1870, blacks and other non-whites didn't even have the symbolic right to vote. And, of course, it took minorities over ninety years to win meaning for their constitutional right to vote. Until 1920, women could not vote in most of America (Wyoming, of course, was a notable exception). Think of that; 1920 wasn't all that long ago! Until 1964, some poor people couldn't vote, and through 1965 some people who could not read were barred from the polls. And, until 1971, most young people 18 to 20 years old could not vote. Today, these limitations have generally been removed.

Wyoming is typical of the other states. In this state, any person may vote who meets four qualifications. First, he or she must be "a citizen of the United States." Also, he or she must "be at least 18 years of age on the day of the next election." Third, the voter must be "actually and physically a bona fide resident in Wyoming." Finally, he or she must register to be eligible.[36] To qualify as a resident, a person need only "actually or physically" be living in Wyoming; anything from buying a home to living in a dormitory suffices. This means, for example, that college students who register, are 18 years old, and are American citizens are eligible to vote while attending school in Wyoming. Registration must be done at least 30 days before the general election, but may be done the day of primary elections (registration is ordinarily done at the county or city clerk's office).[37] Accordingly, legal requirements which once kept blacks, women, 18 to 20 year-olds, the very poor, and people who can't read from voting are banned by various American laws. The result, as is the case in Wyoming, is that most adult Americans are eligible to vote.[38]

Considering that voting is such an open, relatively "easy" matter, one might expect that most Wyoming people would cast their ballots. As Professor Douglas Parrott points out, presidential elections since the 1930's have *typically* drawn about 60 percent of the eligible voters. Although the voting level may vary in any given presidential election, this means that of every 100 Americans who are eligible to vote in any particular presidential election, about 60 will actually cast their ballots. Wyomingites, however, consistently turn out at the polls at higher rates than most Americans. As Professor Parrott shows, in a typical presidential election (assuming there is such a thing), Wyoming voters will turn out in numbers four to 12 percent higher than the national figures. He goes on to show that Wyomingites vote and participate in other political activities at higher rates than Americans in general, whether one compares Americans and Wyomingites according to their social class, age, education, sex, political party affiliation or occupation. He notes, for example, that in 1972, 83 percent of the nation's farmers who were eligible to vote actually did so, whereas in 1976, 99 percent of the Wyoming farmers who were eligible to vote did so.[39]

So, whether the national 60 percent voting rate is considered high or low (many observers think it is alarmingly low, particularly considering that the rate is poorer for state elections and even lower for local elections, where 25 to 30 percent of the eligible voters actually go to the polls), it is correct to note that the level is higher in Wyoming. This, of course, reflects Wyoming's patriotic, conservative ethic. In regions like Wyoming, voting is an important expression of citizen duty or responsibility.

Types of Wyoming Elections (Or, Today I'm Proud to Announce My Candidacy for the Office of Governor). Picture this: you're sitting around at home, complaining about politicians. "Maybe I ought to run for something. I could straighten the mess out," you say. "That's a good idea," your friend says. So you decide to run for governor. Let's trace your campaign.

First, notice what happened in the kitchen—you decided to run. Your friend agreed; he was supportive. But you made the decision. So it usually is in politics. Most candidates are self-starters. There are important instances, of course, of political candidates deciding to run in response to public pressure (Dwight Eisenhower, for example). And, the argument could even be made that all successful top level politicians are to some degree responding to public demand. Nevertheless, most politicians place themselves in the political limelight.

Next, you have to file for office. After checking the election code, you know what to do. If you were running for an office like city council, in which all candidates run against each other without party labels, you would fill out an application for the "nonpartisan" primary. But since you have decided to run for higher office, you fill out an application for nomination in the party primary, stating the office sought, swearing that you are a resident of Wyoming, a registered voter, and a registered Republican or Democrat (or third party). If you were running for a county office (sheriff, county clerk, country treasurer, or county assessor), you would fill out the forms in the office of the county clerk. But since you have decided to run for governor (or U.S. senator, House of Representatives, state representative or state senator, or any of the four statewide offices besides governor), you fill out forms with the secretary of state in Cheyenne.

You must file between 45 and 60 days before the primary election.

If you were running for the state legislature or county office, you would then have to pay a $10 filing fee. But since you have filed for governor, you must pay a $100 filing fee. You cannot run without paying the fee, and once it is paid, it will not be refunded.

After you have filed the application and paid the filing fee, you are officially a candidate. Notice, we are assuming that you are running as a Democrat or Republican. If you want to run as in independent, you may, but you have to get thousands of people to sign your petitions (five percent of the total number of votes cast in the most recent race for the U.S. House of Representatives) to run for a statewide office. To run as an independent for a county position, a candidate would need signatures on petitions equal to five percent of the previous congressional votes cast in that county.[40]

Next, the campaign gets into high gear. Because you realize that independent candidates seldom win, you have filed as a Republican or Democrat. However, suppose a few other men or women also filed for your party's nomination for governor. You have to beat them in the primary election to win the party's nomination. So, when your campaign began (a few months before the official filing), you raised a few hundred thousand dollars and hired somebody to create your image. Your "image maker" shows you what the voters want. After you have decided what the major issues are, your "image maker" tries to project you as the man (or woman) who best represents what the voters want. He does this through an advertising campaign. If the polls show that you are ahead of your opponents, you project an image of calm, responsible leadership. If the polls say you are behind, you will probably have to attack your opponents' positions. This, you hope, will show that you are

B.C. by permission of Johnny Hart and Field
Enterprises, Inc.

years, you face the first hurdle in your bid for the governor's mansion—the primary election. On that day, registered Democrats vote for their favorite candidate for each office. Registered Republicans do the same. But notice, in Wyoming *only* registered Democrats can vote in the Democratic primary, while *only* registered Republicans can vote in the Republican primary. This system, called a "closed primary," prohibits independents from voting in primary elections. This way, the rationale goes, we know that the Republican and Democratic nominees are the clear choices of their respective parties. In other states, which allow more flexible primary voting, members of one party sometimes vote in the other party's primary, hoping that if enough members of their party cross over, weak candidates will win the other party's nominations. Even though Wyoming laws are designed to prohibit this, some cross over happens in Wyoming because voters are allowed to change their party registration at the polls on primary election day. Also, voters who are not registered may register at the polls on the day of the primary.

After the primary votes are tallied, the man or woman with the most votes wins the party's nomination for the appropriate office. Thus, while your party may have had four candidates for governor before the primary, afterwards the party has only one nonimee.[41] In the example, you have won your party's nomination for governor. You then face the winner of the other party's primary in the general election. The winner of this election becomes governor.[42]

With your upset primary victory, the number of candidates was cut to two, you and the other party's nominee. Of course, there may be an independent candidate or even a minor third party candidate, but these are usually not important factors in Wyoming elections. For two months after the primary, you campaign as vigorously as possible. You stress suc-

dynamic and that your opponents are weak candidates. Your commercials may have you standing by a stream, riding a horse, talking quietly to the voters, or pounding a fist. But, as with new cars or a brand of mouthwash, to be successful, your campaign (and your image) needs to be properly packaged.

At this point, you have been campaigning full-time for approximately six to 10 months, including four months or more before the official filing. In early September (first Tuesday after the second Monday) of even-numbered cessful themes or issues from your primary election campaign and attack your opponent's weaknesses. If you are a Democrat, you probably have trouble raising campaign funds (unless you are an incumbent who is likely to win reelection). If you are a Republican, you will have to spend some time fund raising, but will find it a little easier. And, once again, your image maker will try to parlay the money into an effective advertising campaign.

In early November (first Tuesday after the first Monday) of every fourth even-numbered year, the general election is held. All registered voters, as discussed earlier in the chapter, are eligible to vote. Quite simply, the person with the most votes wins the office, whether he or she has a majority (over 50 percent of the votes cast for that office) or a plurality (more votes than any other candidate, but less than 50 percent of the votes, as when third party candidates take a part of the vote). In your case, the voters once again confirmed your confidence in the democratic system. You have won an overwhelming victory. In political terms, it's a landslide! Two months later, on the first Monday in January, you and all other winners from the general election take office.

There you have it. Follow those steps carefully and you will not only understand something about Wyoming elections, you will also have an outline for your gubernatorial campaign. Of course, several hundred other potential candidates may be making similar plans.[43]

Keep one last point in mind. Primary and general elections take place during each even-numbered year. While the race for governor happens every four years (1978, 1982, and so on), state representatives and the member of the U.S. House of Representatives are elected every two years (1978, 1980, 1982 . . .), and U.S. Senators are elected every six years (one senator in 1976, 1982, and so on and the other senator in 1978, 1984 . . .). The periodic elec-

tion of other government officials, from city council to president, means that political buffs get to practice their trade (or hobby, as the case may be) every two years. For the professionals, it really never ends.

Presidential Elections in Wyoming

While most Wyoming voters cast their ballots during presidential election years, many apparently do not understand how presidents are elected. The discussion below summarizes presidential elections from Wyoming's standpoint.

Presidential campaigns of today are long and expensive matters. If our successful governor in the example above runs for president, he (or she) had better be prepared to commit up to two years of time and several million dollars. After a demanding series of state presidential primaries and caucus-conventions, and after the national conventions every fourth summer, the Republican and Democratic parties have each selected their party's candidates. After the candidates put in ten more weeks of active campaigning, the voters go to the polls and either pull a lever, punch a card, or mark an "X" on a ballot next to the name of the candidate they prefer. But the candidate with the most popular votes (meaning the millions of votes cast by individual Americans throughout the nation) is not necessarily the winner. He usually is, but not always. Instead, the candidate who wins in the electoral college voting wins the office. Tracing the electoral college voting in this state will help us to understand how the electoral college process works.

Earlier in this chapter, you read that Wyoming's electors are selected at the state political conventions. This is the first major step in the electoral process for Wyoming. At both the Republican and Democratic conventions, committees are appointed to select their parties' nominees for the electoral college (in May of every fourth even-numbered year). They select active members of their party whom they would like to honor. Selection as an elector, after all, is an honor. The state conventions then vote on, or ratify, the committee's choices. These names—three Democrats and three Republicans—are then filed with the Wyoming secretary of state. Both parties nominate three people for the electoral college because a state's representation in the college equals its representation in Congress.[44] Since Wyoming has two U.S. Senators and one member of the House of Representatives, it gets three votes in the electoral college.

On the day of the general election, voters cast their ballots for their presidential preferences. The candidate who wins the state's popular vote wins that state's electoral votes. In 1980, for example, Wyoming voters preferred Ronald Reagan over Jimmy Carter. Because Reagan was the Republican nominee, the Republican electors had won in Wyoming. After the state canvassing board confirms which candidate has won the state's popular vote, the governor issues a certificate to each of the appropriate electors. The certificates confirm their election and instruct them to meet with the governor in the office of the secretary of state at noon on a day in early December (the Monday following the second Wednesday).

At this meeting, the three electors cast their official electoral ballots for the office of president. In most states, the electors are merely on their honor to vote for the person who won the state's popular vote. Because there have been instances of electors breaking their pledges, political scientists are often concerned that the electors might someday cause a constitutional crisis.[45] Consider this scenario: Candidate Smith narrowly defeats candidate Jones in the nation's popular vote and is supposed to win in the electoral college by five votes, but three of the electors who were on their honor to vote for Smith change their minds and cast their official ballots for Jones. The loss of three votes by Smith and the addition of three to Jones means that Jones will win in the electoral college by one vote. Think of that. Smith wins the popular vote and is supposed to win in the electoral college. But *three* people in this hypothetical example will throw the whole country into an uproar, a real constitutional crisis which will almost certainly end up before the Supreme Court. To guard against Wyoming's electors breaking their honor-bound pledges, our state is one of those which legally requires electors to vote according to their state's popular vote.[46]

Wyoming's electoral votes are then sent to Washington, D.C. The votes from all the states are opened on January 6 before both houses of Congress. The winner is then officially announced, and takes office at noon on January 20. Out of 538 votes cast in the electoral college, the winner must get 270, a clear majority.[47]

Notes

1. For a discussion of "state oriented" political parties see Hugh A. Bone, *American Politics and the Party System,* 3d ed. (New York: McGraw-Hill, 1965), pp. 648–655.
2. Jack C. Plano and Milton Greenberg, *The American Political Dictionary,* 4th ed. (Hinsdale, Illinois: Dryden Press, 1976), p. 134.
3. T. A. Larson, *History of Wyoming* (Lincoln: University of Nebraska Press, 1965), pp. 71–72. The positions filled were: one delegate to Congress, nine members of the Territorial Council, or upper house, and 13 members of the Territorial House of Representatives.
4. As discussed in the first chapter, territorial governors were appointed by the President. When opposition parties gained control of the White House, they made new appointments to terri-

torial positions. Cleveland, a Democrat, attempted to replace Republican President Arthur's territorial officials.

5. Baxter, it was charged, had illegally fenced government land, thus depriving public use of open range. Baxter had done the fencing, but was vindicated by a later court ruling.

6. Larson, p. 238.

7. Ibid., pp. 238 and 265.

8. Other progressive leaders in Wyoming were Henry Breitenstein, Shakespeare E. Sealy and L. C. Tidball.

9. Keep in mind that U.S. Senators were elected or appointed by the state legislatures until ratification of the 17th Amendment to the U.S. Constitution. Carey was elected on the first ballot, Warren on the seventh. Warren resigned as governor (after serving only six weeks) to accept the senate position.

10. Warren, himself, had failed reelection in 1892, leaving Wyoming with only one senator in the interval between 1893–95. By 1895, Warren had mended his fences and won reelection.

11. In the 1890's, most western states favored moving away from the "hard" money gold standard to silver. This, they believed, would make more money available, helping poor farmers and the working class. Also, western states believed a shift to silver would be a boom to silver mining in western states. Believing it in the nation's interest to oppose regional silver concerns, Carey supported the gold standard against most other westerners.

12. In the 1880's, large ranch operators repeatedly clashed with owners of small ranches. The large operators were troubled, they said, by continual cattle thefts by the small operators. In 1892 a party of 50 owners and managers of large operations and hired gunmen from Texas rode north near Buffalo to "eliminate" some of the troublemakers. While a few people were killed, the invaders were put down. It was subsequently charged that Carey (and Warren) had sponsored the "invasion." This is explained in more detail in Chapter 3.

13. Lewis L. Gould, *Wyoming: A Political History, 1868–1896* (New Haven, Conn: Yale, 1968), p. 242 quoting Governor Warren in a letter to Willis Van Devanter, April 20, 1896, Warren Papers and a letter to Van Devanter, April 23, 1896, Van Devanter Papers.

14. See Larson, pp. 284–293, Gould, pp. 118–119, 125, 236, 241 and 244, and theses in the University of Wyoming Library, Laramie, Wyoming, by Robert Jones, Wesley Bowen, Walter Samson, George Paulson, and Thomas Kruger.

15. Plano and Greenberg, p. 134.

16. Walter L. Samson, Jr., "The Political Career of Senator Francis E. Warren, 1920–1929" (Masters thesis, University of Wyoming), pp. 57–58.

17. Ibid., p. 83.

18. Ibid., pp. 63–72.

19. Ibid., p. 67.

20. Ibid., p. 85.

21. Robert F. Franklin, "The Political Career of Senator Francis E. Warren, 1902–1912" (Masters thesis, University of Wyoming), pp. 131–140.

22. Betsy Ross Peters, "Joseph M. Carey and the Progressive Movement in Wyoming" (Masters thesis, University of Wyoming), p. 259.

23. Ibid., p. 260.

24. Ibid.

25. Ibid., pp. 260–264.

26. Austin Ranney, "Parties in State Politics," in *Politics in the American States,* eds. Herbert Jacob and Kenneth N. Vines, 3d ed. (Boston: Little, Brown, 1976), p. 61.

27. For an analysis of the 1978 Wyoming election, see Oliver Walter, "Politics in the 1970's: A Review," (Laramie: Center for Government Research, 1978), p. 4.

28. Plano and Greenberg, pp. 132–133.

29. The Center for Government Research is associated with the Department of Political Science, University of Wyoming, Laramie, Wyoming. It is part of U.W.'s Institute of Policy Research.

30. Admittedly, there are problems with combining Republicans and Democrats in this fashion. After all, a respondent who says he is a strong Republican is different than one who says he is an independent who leans Republican. Recognizing this discrepancy, the broad categories are used for two major reasons. First, this material is intended as an introduction to the subject for beginning students. As such, broad, general approaches, which are probably easier to understand, are particularly appropriate. Second, studies indicate that many people who say that they are independents who lean toward one particular party are actually more partisan voters than they admit. To some

voters, being an independent is a badge of pride which is often forgotten in the voting booth.

31. In a statistical sense, these figures mean that if all of the Wyoming Republicans and Democrats were surveyed, there would be a 95% chance that the figures used in these tables would be within a few percentage points (usually between three and nine, depending upon the number of people in the sample and how close to the middle, i.e. 40 to 60 percent range, the figures are) of the "real world" figures.

32. In fact, three-quarters of both parties believe that the federal government wastes "a lot" of the money we pay in taxes.

33. See the 1979 Wyoming Election Code, Sections 22–4–101, 22–4–102, and 22–5–204.

34. Ibid., Sections 22–4–101 through 22–4–107.

35. Ibid., Sections 22–4–108 through 22–4–120.

36. Ibid., Chapter 3.

37. To determine residency qualifications, the county clerk may consider the applicant's occupation and location of employment, location of vehicle registration and driver's license, property owned, etc.

38. The following are the most important amendments, laws and court rulings: Right to vote not to be denied on account of race, color, or previous condition of servitude (15th Amendment to U.S. Constitution, ratified 1870); women's right to vote (19th Amendment, 1920); Grandfather clauses, which granted the right to vote to persons whose ancestors had voted prior to 1867, thereby disenfranchising blacks (Guinn vs. U.S., 1915); blacks were given the legal right to vote in primary elections (Texas white primary cases, particularly Smith vs. Allwright, 1944); poll taxes, whereby people must pay to vote are banned (24th Amendment, 1964); being required to read in order to vote is no longer legal in areas where literacy led to discrimination (Voting Rights Acts of 1965, 1970, 1975); 18-year-olds have the right to vote (26th Amendment, 1971).

39. Douglas Parrott, "Political Participation in the United States and Wyoming," *Learning Modules on Wyoming Politics,* funded through a grant from the National Science Foundation, Local Course Improvement Program, Grant No. (SER77–03819) (Laramie: Center for Government Research, September, 1977), pp. 11–33.

40. See the 1979 Wyoming Election Code, Article 2.

41. Nonpartisan elections are different. Typically, the two top vote-getters face each other in the November election. All registered voters are eligible to vote in nonpartisan primaries, regardless of their affiliation or independence.

42. See the 1979 Wyoming Election Code, Article 2.

43. Ibid.

44. Every state is represented by two U.S. Senators and one member of the House of Representatives (for approximately every 500,000 population). The census is taken every 10 years to measure any changes in population.

45. See the 1979 Wyoming Election Code, Sections 22–19–101 through 22–19–119.

46. There are several examples of electors breaking their pledges. In 1976, for example, one elector who was pledged to Ford voted for Reagan. In 1960, 15 southern electors pledged to John Kennedy actually voted for conservative Senator Harry F. Byrd.

47. If no candidate receives a majority, the House of Representatives elects the President from among the top three electoral college vote-getters, with each state getting one vote. The vice-president is selected by a majority of the 100 senators.

CHAPTER

THREE

Interest Groups

Interest Groups Defined

Suppose you are an avid snowmobiler, a real winter freak. Then you pick up a newspaper and read that snowmobiles have been banned from all state parks. "An outrage!" you say. But what can be done? As president of your local club, you call a meeting. Then you hear that there is to be a statewide meeting of snowmobile clubs. Your club votes to send you. So off you go. At the statewide meeting, it is agreed to form a Wyoming Snowmobilers Association (WSA) and that representatives of the WSA will go to Cheyenne when the legislature meets the next month. Since your club has joined the WSA, and because you are a persuasive person, the association asks you to go to Cheyenne on behalf of the new association. The association has assigned you and a few others to go tell the legislators why snowmobilers should be allowed on the state land where they have been banned. You have been selected to lobby on behalf of your interest group. Accordingly, you are a lobbyist.

If your organization is serious about winning on the issue, it will have to rally a whole lobby campaign, including persuading the public that you are right, doing research that supports your position, convincing members and the public to contact their legislators, and perhaps even "wining and dining" individual legislators. This obviously involves money, or-

ganization, and dedication. But the key is still the people who represent, or lobby for, the group or association.

A lobbyist, then, is someone who represents his or her group (whether a recreation association of businesses, unions, environmentalists, farmers and ranchers, teachers, firemen, other government employees, or college students) to government, particularly legislators, bureaucrats, and the chief executive (whether President or Governor). Or, the lobbyist might represent no one other than himself, although that is normally not the case. In the example above, the Wyoming Snowmobile Association is an interest group. It might also be called a pressure group, a lobby group, or a special interest group. The association is a group of people who share a common interest—being allowed to snowmobile on government land. They have combined in numbers, probably pooled some money, and have sent their representatives off to convince the "powers that be" to let them snowmobile.

Notice the elements of the interest group—common or shared beliefs, organization, money, and an attempt to influence government decision-makers. Actually, the element of "competition" might be added, because when the snowmobile lobbyists get to Cheyenne and ask to talk to their first legislator, lobbyists for environmental groups will probably tell him not to listen. And, of course, there will almost certainly be competition among the various viewpoints within any particular association. The point is that organized pressure groups on one side of an issue cause people on the other side to organize as well.[1]

The Notion of "Pluralism"

If you were asked how our democracy functions, or who runs things in this nation or state, what would you say? Most of your life you have been told that the people elect public officials who listen to all sides of an issue and then decide the issue by passing or defeating legislation. People who have this common perception are called "pluralists" because they accept the notion that our state and nation are run through competitive, legitimate institutions which represent their members or constituents. Politics is seen as a huge arena filled with people, like the snowmobile lobbyist above, who represent their organization's mass membership. The lobbyists are like gladiators doing battle (within the law). Their weapons are facts, arguments, subtle distortions, media and public influence, emotionalism and political clout. The theory assumes that the "gladiator" with the best argument will usually win. In other words, politicians listen to all of the lobbyist arguments, select the wisest policies, and make them law. Because a) lobbyists represent the people in their groups, and b) practically all ideas or positions are repre-

sented by groups, and c) politicans themselves are selected by and representative of the people, pluralists say that government policies generally come from the people (through these representatives). Thus, pluralists say that "the people" run Wyoming and America.[2]

It is beyond the scope of this text to investigate the merits of pluralism; that is for you to decide.[3] The point, however, is that if a person accepts the validity of pluralism, interest groups are an essential vehicle for expression of the public will. Yes, this is putting it in romantic terms, but if the pluralist premise is accepted, the romanticism is appropriate.

The Good and Bad of Interest Groups

There is an old Victor Mature movie in which the leading character and the heroine typically fall in love. When she finds out his occupation, she breaks off with him because he has a corrupt, dishonorable occupation. Mature spends the rest of the movie trying to win her back. In the end, he wins his fair lady only by quitting his job. He was a lobbyist.

Is this view of lobbyists accurate, or fair? Generally not. Even though their reputations were once poor, lobbyists perform an important function in America. Says a congressman:

A lot of people seem to think that lobbying is a bad thing. I think that is one misconception which still

WIZARD OF ID by permission of Johnny Hart and Field Enterprises, Inc.

needs to be corrected as far as the general public is concerned. Lobbying is an essential part of representative government, and it needs to be encouraged and appreciated. [Lobbyists] are frequently a source of information. If they come to your offices and explain a program or factors contributing to the need for legislation, you get a better understanding of the problems and the answers to them . . . they can teach you what an issue is all about, and you can make your own decision. There can be bad lobbying . . . of course, but basically lobbying is a good thing.[4]

As the congressman notes, lobby groups perform a service for legislators by providing information, detailed studies, and explanations of legislation and issues. While the congressman was referring to national legislators, his point is at least as applicable in Wyoming.

As will be seen in the next chapter (Sidebar 4–1), Wyoming has been faulted for not providing adequate research facilities and resources for legislators. Although improvements have been made in recent years, legislators sometimes have trouble finding the answers to all of their questions, even today. Besides being able to look to the Legislative Service Office (which performs a great deal of research), where else can these legislators turn for the information they need? Often they turn to the interest groups. Lobbyists are usually happy to find the answers for legislators. After all, the larger interest groups have both the facilities to prepare studies (staffs, expertise, time) and the desire to do so. By providing the information, the lobbyists get a chance to put their views before the legislator and even to "color" or interpret the facts to their advantage. Even so, legislators normally think of interest group involvement in generating information and research as a service and an overall benefit to our political system. One state legislator puts it this way:

Lobbyists are a vital part of the legislative process. Without them to explain, you couldn't get a clear picture of the situation. They can study and present the issues concisely—the average legislator has no time or inclination to do it, and wouldn't understand bills or issues without them. A professional lobbyist in ten minutes can explain what it would take a member two hours to wade through just reading bills. Both sides come around to you, so you can balance off all one-sided presentations (and they're all one-sided). A definite function is performed by lobbyists.[5]

A second broad benefit that our system enjoys from interest groups is more philosophical. It relates to the earlier romantic notion of pluralism. As you have read, pluralism assumes that "the people" run our nation and states through competitive institutions which represent their members. This view, then, sees interest groups as one of the important ways that the people tell their government what to do. When a lobbyist for the Teamsters attempts to persuade a legislator how to vote on a bill, for example, he isn't representing himself. Rather, he is seen as the mouthpiece for the hundreds of people who are in the Teamsters Union in Wyoming. This view says that it's as if the individual Teamster members were speaking to their legislators.

But this is not to say that everything is peaches and cream with interest group involvement in politics. They have a negative presence as well. Historically, for example, interest groups have lent an element of corruption to politics. While this is particularly true of early American history, it has not been a major factor in Wyoming. Although there were political overtones in the Johnson County War and Credit Mobilier scandals, the state has not had interest group-government corruption in the usual sense.[6] When Illinois Secretary of State Paul Powell died several years ago, for example, hundreds of thousands of dollars in race track stock was found in shoeboxes in his closet. Investigators subsequently determined that Powell and former Governor Otto Kerner (then a federal judge) had been "bought off" by racing interests. No political scandals of these proportions have been uncovered in Wyoming, but the potential is always there, nevertheless.

The second drawback or negative aspect of interest groups deals with pluralism again. If the positive view is that interest groups represent their members, thus enabling government to do what the people want, what happens to the people who aren't represented? The negative aspect says, "Sure, agriculture, unions, energy and minerals, environmentalists, educators, and bureaucrats are represented. They're organized. But what about all the migrant workers, native Indians, children, consumers, and students? Who represents them? Nobody. Oh, sure there may be a token social worker or student who lobbies now and then, but they have no money, no organization, and no political clout." If the benefit is that interest groups represent "the people" and keep government in touch with the people, the drawback is that in Wyoming (and elsewhere) some people aren't represented well or even at all. That is a failing of our democratic system because it means that a segment of "the people" have little or no say in what the government does; they either aren't heard or aren't heard well.

Finally, some people are critical of the role of lobby groups because they see the ties between certain legislators and lobbyists becoming so strong that the legislators become representatives of the special interests rather than their constituencies. This is the chicken and egg syndrome; the question is which came first? Are certain legislators and lobbyists close because the lawmaker has lost sight of his constituency, or are they close because the constituency is so closely associated with that interest? Is there anything wrong with a legislator working closely with the Wyoming Farm Bureau when he represents a farming county? Of course not. Are there limits? Certainly.

Interest groups serve important practical and philosophical roles in Wyoming. In this state, they are active in and normally quite beneficial to state politics. But we should recognize that there are both positive and negative arguments about their roles.[7]

The Techniques of Lobbying

The process of persuading legislators to vote, think, act, and speak in a particular way is obviously challenging. To meet the challenge, lobbyists develop strategies within their resources. The larger lobbies, with more money, members, and organizational support, prepare broad-based lobby campaigns; smaller, poorer, and less organized groups must save their ammunition for the bigger volleys. These strategies include two major categories of lobby tactics—direct and indirect lobbying.

Direct lobbying is done face-to-face. When most people think of lobbying, they picture two or more people talking, one from an interest group and the other from the legislature. This is direct lobbying. It may occur anywhere from the halls of the capitol (special interest representatives talking to legislators in the "lobby" is how they became known as lobbyists), to a restaurant or golf course. It is commonly said of Wyoming that more legislating takes place at the Hitching Post Bar in Cheyenne than in either house of the state legislature. An exaggeration, it makes the point that much work takes place off the floor of the legislature. Former State Senator Ray Nott, a minister from Powell, tells the story that because he wouldn't drink with lobbyists, they often didn't know how to approach him. Until the post-Viet Nam and Watergate concern for ethics in government, lobbyists frequently bought legislators drinks and meals. But as Wyoming Farm Bureau lobbyist Doug Gibson says (see Sidebar 3–1), lobbyists buy lunch

Sidebar 3–1
Farm Bureau Lobbying Techniques

by Doug Gibson
(Director of Public Affairs and Chief Lobbyist)

Lobbying is essential in our representative democracy because it offers an ingredient—information—without which legislative bodies can't operate. It provides issue information on which legislators can base decisions.

Farm Bureau uses the lobbying process to present its position in an effort to achieve policy objectives. Farm Bureau develops a comprehensive lobbying plan for its legislative program which involves the state and county Farm Bureaus.

There are various lobbying techniques, but they may not prove effective unless an organization's members have developed a sound policy foundation. Farm Bureau has such a policy base.

One of the most effective techniques is constituency contacts with legislators before they go to Cheyenne. County Farm Bureaus are encouraged to conduct meetings with their legislators to briefly review issues the organization expects to support, oppose or seek modification.

Before the session state Farm Bureau leaders will secure sponsors for legislation the organization wants introduced. It also will seek bi-partisan support for these key bills.

When the legislature convenes the state Farm Bureau distributes facts sheets on issues of concern and interest with brief comments of its position on each. At the same time, Farm Bureau exchanges information with allies to see on what issues they agree and can work together to increase lobbying clout. Securing state agency support for or neutrality on Farm Bureau's position also proves helpful in many instances.

Farm Bureau analyzes all bills affecting agriculture and rural life. It follows numerous ones to final disposition. In doing so, contacts with legislators are critical. Farm Bureau may contact them at the House or Senate spending a few minutes explaining its position. If it's a complicated issue, Farm Bureau's lobbyists may invite a legislator(s) to discuss the topic over a meal. One can't buy a legislator's support and Farm Bureau doesn't try. However, it does use this method to present its perspective on a bill. Such meetings often result in greater understanding of a problem and persuasion to its position.

Farm Bureau contacts committee chairmen and committee members considering bills of importance to convey its position. It makes timely presentations before such committees. Such are oral comments or formally presented statements. It offers amendments to improve legislation or it explains why it supports or opposes a measure. Expert witnesses are used to testify at special public hearings. Written statements are submitted.

Constituency contacts during a session are also very important. Midway through the session Farm Bureau conducts a legislative conference for county leaders. Legislators and spouses are invited to a dinner at which county and state leaders discuss the issues with the lawmakers. At other times, in person contacts may be needed. If FB requests contacts on short notice, phone calls are used. If such contacts aren't possible, then telegrams may be utilized. If time permits, county leaders and members write letters urging appropriate action.

Sometimes another legislator is asked to help persuade a colleague to Farm Bureau's position. In some instances, an ally can better influence a lawmaker on a certain issue on which both organizations agree.

When legislation is up for full House or Senate consideration, Farm Bureau may have handouts distributed to lawmakers describing why a measure should or should not receive approval.

No matter what the issue Farm Bureau strives to be honest and sincere in its use of lobbying techniques. It avoids making any threat to a legislator's political future in seeking to achieve organizational policy objectives.

and the chance to be heard. They are not buying a vote. Today, Wyoming legislators seem more cautious about accepting a meal or a drink from a lobbyist. In fact, many Wyoming lobbyists say that they have self-imposed rules against direct lobbying of this kind except under unusual circumstances. Rather, such lobbyists say they visit bars to gather their own information and to socialize.

A Wisconsin legislator, referring to the common practice in his state of accepting dinner, drinks, and entertainment from lobbyists, says that some legislators voted to prohibit these favors in 1957 for reasons of ethics, but that more voted that way to improve their image with voters.[8] Whether for reasons of ethics or politics, Wyoming legislators are often watchful of these "freebies."

Indirect lobbying is an attempt to use public opinion to the pressure group's advantage. A legislator may say "no" to a lobbyist, but will he say "no" to his constituency? Will he say "no" if he gets 50 or 100 letters asking him to support a particular measure? Maybe, but it becomes more difficult. Both letter-writing and telegram campaigns are examples of indirect lobbying. During recent legislative sessions, the Wyoming Outdoor Council (an environmental lobby group) has run a "successful" telephone chain. Shortly before an important piece of environmental legislation comes up for a vote, Outdoor Council lobbyists in Cheyenne call assigned members (or sympathizers) in communities throughout the state. Each of these people call a few others on the chain, who in turn telephone others, and so on. At each level, people are told the issue, number of the bill, and are asked to send a telegram or telephone their legislators, requesting them to consider voting as the Council believes proper. This simple process results in a significant amount of pressure being placed on legislators to vote the way the interest group wants. It doesn't mean that all legislators comply. But they generally listen and consider the request. And the contacts probably persuade some undecided legislators. After all, nobody wants to take an unpopular voting record home for the next election.

Another technique of indirect lobbying involves use of the media. Why, for example, has the Wyoming Farm Bureau Federation occasionally sponsored television coverage of news events? Why does the Powder River Basin Resource Council pay for TV ads on rangeland and water? The Union Pacific tells us that they are "a million miles of history" in order to get more business, but it goes farther than that. In each instance, the agricultural, environmental and railroad concern is trying to persuade us to adhere to their point of view; they are indirectly lobbying the government. The more people they persuade to their side (or of their competence, creativity, or sincerity), the larger their public opinion base is. The larger that base is, the larger their "clout" will be with government officials.

Farm Bureau lobbyist Doug Gibson details the techniques used in the Bureau's lobby campaign (Sidebar 3–1). Notice the emphasis on direct lobbying. The Bureau encourages members to contact legislators in their home counties before the legislative session and to explain their positions on key agricultural issues. The Bureau's legislative team lobbies lawmakers individually when the session begins, through conversations, meals, presentations to committees, contacts with various committee chairmen and members, and a mid-session banquet. Notice, too, the Bureau's emphasis on lobbying the various legislative committees. This is understandable considering that legislative committees are critical to the success or failure of legislation. Thus, the Bureau not only talks with agriculture committee members, but offers to provide amendments (meaning research) and witnesses to explain its viewpoint. These tactics, and the others in the sidebar, plus an extensive indirect media campaign, have helped to make the Farm Bureau an important voice in the Wyoming legislature.

There are other important lobby techniques in addition to those mentioned in the sidebar. While it's not the function of interest groups to run candidates for office, many interest groups get involved through political action committee contributions to candidates and they often try to influence the selection of candidates. In fact, Wyoming legislators are often members of successful interest groups, particularly the Wyoming Stockgrowers, Farm Bureau, education groups such as the Wyoming Education Association, and labor unions.

Of all the various lobby tactics and techniques, research at both national and state levels suggests:

. . . direct-contact methods as most effective, indirect contacts as next most effective, and wining and dining legislators as least effective. In all settings where the matter has been subjected to any kind of careful inquiry, unethical lobbying techniques such as bribery were found to be regarded as very ineffective relative to other techniques. If it is the conventional wisdom that entertaining and bribing legislators are thought by American lobbyists to be effective persuasive methods, the evidence is heavily against it.[9]

Wyoming legislators support this conclusion. They rank personal discussions and presentations of the lobbyists' point-of-view, testimony given before legislative hearings, and contact by constituents who favor the lobbyists' position as the most effective lobbying techniques. They say that being entertained, receiving campaign contributions, and bribery are the least effective approaches.[10]

Laws on Lobbying

The laws which regulate lobbying are liberal in Wyoming. In other words, Wyoming

lobbyists are given a great deal of flexibility in their operations. Even so, there are some legal restrictions on them.

During each session all lobbyists must register with the Legislative Service Office. They are required to give their name and the name of any organization or persons that they will be representing. They also pay a small registration fee.[11] The applicable Wyoming statute defines a lobbyist as "any person, who, on behalf of any association, corporation, labor union or any interest other than personal, . . . is receiving expense reimbursement or compensation for his services as a lobbyist. . . ." Thus, anyone who represents any interest other than those that are personal, such as a corporation, association, or union, and who receives all or part of his expenses from the organization must register. Failure to register is a misdemeanor crime and is punishable by a fine of up to $200. Lobbyists must also wear badges which denote that they are "registered lobbyists." This is helpful to legislators who do not know all of the people who approach them. The list of registered lobbyists is distributed to the legislators. During the 1979 legislative session, there were 458 registered lobbyists.

The law doesn't make individual citizens register. The statute reads, "Nothing in the provisions of this act shall be construed to prohibit or infringe upon the right of a citizen as an individual to petition or to address written or oral communications to members of the legislature."[12] This means that citizens may contact legislators to express personal opinions without registering as long as they don't represent anyone else and aren't receiving money from outside sources. Really, it has to be that way. It would be undemocratic to have to register in order to talk to government officials. Indeed, it is a cornerstone of our political system that anyone has the right to contact his government officials as he wishes.

The registration law is designed to "open" the lobbying process a little. Legislators (and the public) are able to tell who is at a session, who they represent, and how many lobbyists a particular industry or point-of-view has at a session. This way, the theory goes, it's all open and aboveboard, and the public may be more knowledgeable about who and what the various lobby interests are.

Also, interest groups are limited with regard to political contributions in Wyoming. They may contribute to political candidates, but they must comply with the law in how they go about it. In this state, only individuals, political parties, and political action committees (called PAC's) may legally "contribute funds, other items of value or election assistance" to political candidates or parties. While organizations of all kinds ("including a corporation, partnership, trade union, professional association, or civic, fraternal or religious group") are barred from making direct political contributions, they may contribute through "educational programs" of political action committees.[13] Wyoming interest groups that want to contribute to candidates, then, form these PAC's with their own officers. The PAC's must report their expenditures to the Secretary of State.

The idea behind PAC's is that they allow broader participation of group members in giving out contributions. The theory is that by having a separate but affiliated organization to give out campaign assistance, those people in the organization at large who want to be politically active with time or money will be able to do so with less internal "control" of the resources by the interest group's officers. Also, the interest groups are thought to be more accountable in terms of obeying campaign laws because each PAC's officers are delegated that specific responsibility.

It is also worth noting that not all Wyoming interest groups have PAC's. Whereas the Wyoming Education Association has an active PAC, for example, the Wyoming Farm Bureau has none. Thus, the WEA contributes to political campaigns while the Farm Bureau does not. In one sense, nearly all interest groups aid some campaigns rather informally, because Wyoming law allows an interest group to "communicate directly with its own members on behalf of a particular candidate or political party." This allows interest groups to endorse candidates or to speak well of particular candidates in organization material which is available to members. Still, these are limited forms of aid. But we need not feel sorry for the Farm Bureau or the other interest groups that don't have PAC's. Any interest group may organize a political action committee, thereby enabling it to make contributions. There are no limitations on the amount of money that a political action committee may donate to a particular candidate or in a given election at the state level.[14]

Finally, lobbyists are obligated to act within the range of Wyoming criminal law. Violators are, of course, subject to criminal penalties. Specifically, for example, the state constitution prohibits the bribing of legislators. It reads:

Any person who shall directly or indirectly offer, give or promise any money or thing of value, testimonial, privilege or personal advantage, to any executive or judicial officer or member of the legislature, to influence him in the performance of any of his official duties shall be deemed guilty of bribery. . . .[15]

Lobby Pressures on the Governor

As mentioned earlier, when people think of lobbyists, they usually picture interest group representatives talking to legislators. But pressure groups also lobby executive branch officials, particularly the governor. This is

Sidebar 3–2
Governor Stan Hathaway (1967–1975)
On Interest Group Pressure on the Governor

Question: Did you ever have any surprising or unpleasant experiences with interest group or pressure group activity in your governorship, . . . that sort of thing?

Governor Hathaway: Well, there are at least 500 special interest groups in Wyoming. They're of different sizes, but everyone, of course, wants their particular endeavor to come out on top. I got off badly with the third house (i.e. lobbyists)—maybe it wasn't badly; if I had to do it over again, I'd do the same thing. You know a governor starts immediately with a legislative session. I was feeling my way, trying to get a hold of the job. I had a delegation of 15 lobbyists come in one day. They were mostly on the economic side—oil industry, stockmen, Farm Bureau, railroads, etcetera. They announced to me that they were quite unhappy with my message (the State of the State address). They were quite unhappy with the way I was handling the office. Some of them said they had contributed to my campaign and they expected results. They said they didn't think I represented the Republican party. And I said, "Well I've just spent eight months out talking to 150,000 people. I think I've got a pretty good idea of. . . . Besides, I'm not governor of just the Republicans, anyway." Then they said something that really infuriated me. They said "Well, if you continue on the path you're on, you have no political future." I stood up, pounded my desk, and said, "Don't ever come in here and threaten me with my political future. In the first place, I never expected to be Governor of Wyoming. But, I'm here and I'm going to do what I think is right while I'm here. And you'll get nowhere threatening me with my political future." They didn't come around the rest of that session. The next session they started to filter in as individuals but they never applied that group pressure on me again.

Question: Was that type of confrontation common or was it a little more subtle in most instances?

Governor Hathaway: Well, I didn't have any more confrontations like that. I don't know whether it was common before or not. But apparently I didn't fit the mold that these people thought I should fit.

understandable because lobby groups want certain things from the governor. They want his support on legislation that is important to their members; not just lip service, but enthusiastic support. They want him to sign these bills when they pass in the legislature, rather than veto them. The governor and the people who work for him often have the power to interpret portions of legislation when they execute the laws. These interpretations may help or harm particular interests, so lobbyists want the governor's help in interpreting legislation to their advantage. For these reasons and others, lobbyists concentrate their efforts on the governor as well as legislators.

In the summer of 1977, Professor John T. Hinckley interviewed four Wyoming governors—Milward Simpson, Clifford Hansen, Stan Hathaway, and Ed Herschler. As the governors told Professor Hinckley, interest groups typically approach governors in a professional manner. They are quick to add that this is the only approach that they were (or are) receptive to.

Sidebars 3–2 and 3–3 are Governor Hathaway and Herchler's reflections on abusive lobby tactics. While the governors credit most

Sidebar 3–3
Governor Ed Herschler (1975–1979–)
On Interest Group Pressure on the Governor

There is a lot of pressure applied both to the legislature and to the executive branch, I think. Some of the lobbying is very beneficial because actually, some of the lobbyists are able to give you insight on bills and the ramifications of things that perhaps an individual never thinks about. Even in my office, where I have people that are able to do research for me, we some-times completely overlook something. That (kind of lobbying) is very helpful. But by the same token, I have had special interest groups come in and not only lobby but threaten. So, my position is, "I'm sorry, but my feeling is that the program I have is for the best interest of the state, in my judgment, and I can't go along with you and I don't mind telling you."

lobby groups with ethical and tactful lobby approaches, each had other kinds of experiences. In these instances, the lobbyists challenged the governors. But by their accounts of these events, the governors believe the lobbyists hurt their causes far more than they helped them. Clearly, the governors were "turned-off" by the confrontations, and high pressure tactics. Thus, while these approaches are relatively rare, they do occur on occasion.

**Prominent Lobby Groups
in Wyoming History**

Several interest groups have played major roles in Wyoming's development. Time and again, the interest groups discussed below were (and often still are) at the center of important events in the state.

Union Pacific Railroad. Earlier mention was made that Wyoming was "opened" by the railroad. So it was. Before the railroad entered the region, very few white men or women lived here. As you should remember from Chapter 1, the mountain men were long gone by the late 1860's. The area was like a thoroughfare in the 1860's. Thousands of people travelled through, but few stayed. But the railroad

changed that. The railroad was a boon to the economy of the territory. It meant that railroad jobs would be created (particularly in Cheyenne and Laramie), goods could be shipped to and from the new towns, and people could come more easily. Also, the railroad improved the presence of the U.S. Army. Troops could be shipped more easily, as could be their supplies. As whites came, whether to live or merely travel through, more soldiers were needed.

For the area's new economic interests, this had two major benefits. First, it meant that the military would become a buyer for merchant and agricultural goods. This was an important prop for the economy. Second, the presence of the railroad made the defeat of the Indians only a matter of time. Because the railroad meant increases in the white population, military presence, and economic interests, a conflict with the Indian population was inevitable. Many settlers and businessmen thought that prosperity would come only after the Indians were "conquered." Thus, the railroad increased both the likelihood and ability of the Army to act against the Indians.

During this period, which began in the late 1860's, the Union Pacific was active in western politics. The U.P. had—and has today—a big stake in Wyoming. In order to convince the Union Pacific to build half of the transcontinental railroad, Congress gave the U.P. huge grants of land along the proposed track. All told, the U.P. received over 11 million acres of land, 4.5 million of which were in Wyoming.[16]

This "dominant economic position translated itself into political power for the Union Pacific. In the 1870's, the railroad intervened more openly and consistently in Wyoming politics than it would a decade later."[17] To an extent, the U.P. was active in politics for defensive reasons. Because individuals and groups that objected to U.P. policies often made political issues of them, the U.P. became active on some issues to counter its opponents.[18] And have no doubt, it had opponents. The first legislature, for example, passed several "anti-Union Pacific" laws, including measures requiring the railroad to provide for widows and heirs of employees who were killed by "a train or other company property," no longer allowing employees to sign away their rights to sue the U.P. upon taking a job with the railroad (called a "yellow dog" contract), and permitting county tax collectors to seize U.P. property for failure to pay taxes, to name a few.[19]

This, of course, is not to imply that the railroad had no political successes; its influence was great. The anti-U.P. measures just mentioned, with the exception of the ban on yellow dog contracts, were subsequently repealed by Congress "at the railroad's behest in the spring of 1870."[20] Also, the railroad was active in partisan politics, sometimes successfully, other times unsuccessfully. In response to railroad pressures on partisan politics, for example, territorial Governor John A. Campbell wrote:

. . . I do demand as a right that the Republicans of this Territory be permitted to manage their own affairs without this absurd interference on the part of Railroad officials who know nothing whatever concerning the political issues in this Territory and are using the influence of their positions to destroy the power which gave them any position whatever.[21]

While the Union Pacific's lobbying role has decreased since the territorial period, it was quite significant in the early years. This, of course, is not to conclude that the railroad has no influence today. It is politically involved and has influence, particularly along the tracks in the southern portion of the state, but to a lesser degree than was true a hundred years ago.

Wyoming Stockgrowers Association. If there has been a single most influential group in the state's history, it is the Wyoming Stockgrowers Association. Founded as the Laramie County Stockgrowers Association in 1873, the powerful organization was formed by cattlemen to voice agricultural, and ultimately ranching interests. In 1879, the association merged with other county associations and took its present name. From that beginning, the association's influence grew to dramatic levels. The political influence of this association was attested to by its ability to get the notorious Maverick Law of 1884 passed by the legislature. The law "gave the Wyoming Stock Growers Association full control of roundups in the territory and set up procedures for dealing with mavericks."[22] In other words, the association's influence was so great that the state legislature let it set the "laws" governing the roundup of stray cattle! And, remember, in their early history the Stockgrowers were no friends of smaller ranching operations (see Johnson County War discussion below).

This is not to say that the association's influence grew without ever losing a few issues or suffering its own embarrassments. As might be expected, there were ups and downs, periods of growth followed by brief periods of decline. But overall, its influence in the earliest period of territorial and state development was remarkable. During the early decades (and to a remarkable extent today), political leaders often were members of the association and community of large ranching interests. Dr. Richard, for example, notes that the Stockgrowers early influence was so great that:

During territorial and early statehood days, the stockgrowers were reputed by many to have been one of the most powerful organizations in the country, in some minds comparable to the powerful political machines of the big cities.[23]

The mention of "political machines" here is a reference to the Warren machine which was discussed in the previous chapter. Warren and his supporters were "boosters" of, and boosted by, the Stockgrowers. It is not unfair to conclude that the Stockgrowers were an important component of the Warren machine.

The power and arrogance of the Stockgrowers Association during this period are attested to by one of the more infamous events in American history and certainly the most bizzare series of events in state history—the Johnson County War. In the 1800's, the larger ranching operations in the territory were plagued with theft. With times being hard and cattle grazing over so much territory, small settlers occasionally helped themselves to some of the beef of the larger operators. Small operators and settlers often viewed these "isolated" acts as justice. They believed that the Maverick Law and subsequent "reforms" gave the large operators a near monopoly on rounding up stray cattle. Thus, they often thought that if the large ranchers lost a few head here and there, it all evened out in the end.

Frustrated with the courts, where the big interests found juries were often sympathetic with the "rustlers" and gave them lenient sentences or even failed to convict them, the large operators began taking the law into their own hands. In July, 1889, a group of the large operators caught and hanged two alleged rus-

tlers, James Averell and Ella Watson, near Independence Rock. The lynchings were controversial because Watson (Cattle Kate as she became known) was the only woman ever hanged in Wyoming, whether legally or illegally. Even though it was widely assumed that the men who had done the hanging were known,[24] no one was ever punished for the crime. The six cattlemen, who had been arrested, "were released after four known witnesses to the crime failed to appear before the grand jury."[25]

The conflict intensified in the following years. Finally, in 1891–1892, the Stockgrowers began planning what had been rumored for years, a "war" against the rustlers. Stockgrowers of high position (no one below foreman was allowed to take part) were joined in early April, 1892 by twenty-five hired guns from Texas. On April 5, 1892, approximately fifty "invaders" headed north from Cheyenne to Casper by train, then on to sites near Buffalo, in Johnson County. It is unknown exactly how many small ranchers (or rustlers) the band was after. The accounts vary, estimating that the invaders intended to kill 19 to 70 men, with many more to be driven from the territory. Nor is it completely certain who was involved in the conspiracy. Dr. Larson writes:

Positive conclusions are hard to come by, but the presumption seems justified that Union Pacific officials who furnished the special train knew the intentions of the expedition. It seems also that Acting Governor Amos Barber; Senator Warren (more doubtful); Cheyenne attorneys Willis Van Devanter and Hugo Donzelman; E. Z. Slack, editor of the *Cheyenne Sun;* Asa S. Mercer, editor of the *Northwestern Livestock Journal;* and most members of the Wyoming Stockgrowers Association were privy to the plan.

On their way north, the invaders stopped at the KC Ranch, approximately 83 miles north of Casper, where they believed several rustlers were. After nearly a day's battle, the invaders killed two "rustlers," Nick Ray and Nate Champion. The battle, in which the last "rustler" held off the more than 50 invaders for several hours, ended when "the invaders loaded a wagon with pitch, pine and hay, pushed it up to the cabin, set fire to it and the cabin, and shot Champion to death before he could run very far."

By then, the townspeople of Buffalo had heard of the invading "force." Having been warned that a superior band was prepared to defend Buffalo, the invaders moved to the friendly TA Ranch, 13 miles south of Buffalo. After fortifying the ranch as much as they could, the invaders were attacked by more than 200 well-armed small cattleman and allies from the Buffalo area.

Made aware of the situation, Acting Governor Barber telegraphed President Benjamin Harrison for federal troops to stop the battle. On April 13, 1889, federal troops from Fort McKinney (near Buffalo) stopped the battle and took the invaders to the fort for their own protection and to answer for the deaths of Ray and Champion. Surprisingly, no one was killed at the TA Ranch shootout, although two of the invading Texans subsequently died of gangrene caused by their wounds.

The invaders' attorneys were successful in getting the trial scheduled for Cheyenne, where public opinion was much more in their favor. The invaders pleaded not guilty to murder charges in August, 1892. Friends of the invaders then had the two witnesses to the Ray-Champion killings taken east and concealed, so the prosecuting attorneys couldn't find them. When the judge ordered the defendants released on bond in late August, the Texans returned to their state, "pausing only to enjoy a farewell party featuring champagne." After two delays, the inept county prosecutor moved that the charges be dropped, which they were. No one was ever tried for the two murders.

The Johnson County War and related issues were long-argued, emotional concerns in the state and the war had long-lasting consequences. Senator Warren, for example, was repeatedly charged by his opponents with having helped direct this arrogant big rancher attack on the plain folk. The charges, however, weren't proven and didn't significantly hurt his career. Also, Buffalo area residents destroyed or stole much of the property and possessions that some invaders had owned in the region around Buffalo. While some invaders claimed that the operation was a success because it forced some of the rustlers to leave the territory, there is no evidence that the invasion inspired them to leave.[26]

Even though the Johnson County War caused a decline in the prestige of the Wyoming Stockgrowers Association, it shows the "power bent" of its leaders at the time and their high level support among leaders of the day.

Wyoming Woolgrowers Association. Wyoming witnessed a long range war during the first decade of the twentieth century (1900's). While sheep had always been in Wyoming, the state was nevertheless dominated by the cattle industry. But at the turn of the century more sheep were brought to the state. As the sheep population increased, grazing pressures on government land grew. Cattlemen said that they had the longer right to the use of government land and that sheep "destroyed" the grass; sheepmen countered that they had every legal right to the use of open range and that grass grew back after being grazed by sheep.

As a result of these differences and the sometimes difficult economic situation of cattlemen during the period, the years saw considerable violence. Because sheep herders often worked alone, they were easy targets. Between 1897 and 1909 the cattle-sheep conflict resulted in the deaths of 15 men and a boy (mostly sheep people), and perhaps 10,000 sheep.[27] To combat attacks by cattlemen and to increase their lobbying power in Cheyenne and Washington, woolgrowers organized the Wyoming Woolgrowers Association in April, 1905. As the industry grew, the association and its influence grew.

Violence against sheepmen climaxed in 1909 when 15 or more masked raiders attacked and killed three sheepmen near Tensleep.[28] The Wyoming and National Woolgrowers Associations offered large sums of money to support the discovery and prosecution of the culprits. Five men were convicted and received sentences varying between three years and life.[29] This experience of vigorous organization and prosecution, as well as the Woolgrowers' hiring of detectives to investigate crimes against sheepmen or their property, generally ended the violence against woolgrowers.

From this beginning, the Woolgrowers Association extended its political influence both in the state and nationally. Members were active, for example, in lobbying against public leasing of federal land, which sheepmen believed would aid cattlemen, retard the state's growth, and result in much litigation. The state association's efforts were generally supported by Wyoming Congressman Frank M. Mondell, and Senators Clarence D. Clark and Francis E. Warren. In fact, Warren was even the president of the National Woolgrowers Association until 1908. The Woolgrowers have long been influential in state politics.[30]

Wyoming Farm Bureau Federation. The Farm Bureau has long been an active, well organized, highly influential representative of Wyoming agriculture. The same is true, though perhaps to a lesser extent, of the national organization and its dealings with Congress. Founded in 1920, the Wyoming Farm Bureau is the largest of the agricultural organizations in the state. In 1979, the Farm

Bureau had over 8,000 family memberships, or between 16,000 and 20,000 people. As briefly shown in Sidebar 3–1, the Farm Bureau has active county and local chapters which are often effective in lobbying legislators. Clearly, the Farm Bureau has a tradition of influence.

Wyoming Taxpayers Association. During the Great Depression of the 1920's, many Wyoming people were concerned with government spending. In 1932, the president of the Wyoming Stockgrowers Association invited representatives of various groups and the counties to organize an association to control government spending in Wyoming. The organization that came from that meeting, originally known as the Wyoming Tax League, "began at once to look for ways to reduce the cost of state and local government, looking forward to influencing the next legislature." Since then, the Taxpayers Association has been involved in numerous attempts to limit government spending, growth, and influence. In 1933, for example, Governor Leslie Miller read a special message to the legislature calling for a study of state budgeting and tax reforms and government reorganization. The message was prepared by the Taxpayers Association. The example shows both an aspect of the Association's issue concerns and their political prominence.[31]

The Others. There are obviously many other interest groups that have been influential over the course of Wyoming history. Among business organizations, the Wyoming Retail Merchants Association and the Chambers of Commerce have successfully lobbied for laws to the advantage of the state's business climate. Wyoming bankers and oil interests are also worth noting; they too have played significant roles in the state's political history.

Although there are many other organizations that might be mentioned, those discussed above certainly belong at the top of the list in terms of historical prominence in the state. Their modern day influences, which are great, are explored below in more detail.

"Types" of Wyoming Interest Groups

Categorizing interest groups is a risky business. Some categories, or types, are relatively clear. Agricultural lobbies, for instance, are pretty easy to pick out. While they have philosophical and political concerns that are broad at times, they focus their attention and are most active on agricultural issues, such as land, water, and air policies. Other groups are more difficult to categorize. Where, for example, should the Wyoming Police Protective Association be placed? As public employees, members are concerned about a range of issues regarding state employment practices. At the same time, the association has concerns in common with, but not limited to, private sector labor unions. It is also a professional law enforcement association, which broadens its interests even more. When you look at the categorizations which follow, keep in mind that while the individual interest groups in the various categories have much in common, they often differ in other ways.

Table 3.1 shows the categories of interest groups that registered for the 1979 legislative session. The table shows the categories, an example or examples when necessary, the number of specific interest groups registered in the category, and the number of people registered to represent the category. For example, the first line of the table says that one category of interest groups registered to lobby during the 1979 legislative session was banks. Six banking *organizations,* such as the Wyoming Bancorporation and the Farmer's State Bank of Burns, had representatives registered to lobby. The six banking organizations had 19 people in Cheyenne pleading their cause.

The table shows that 250 separate pressure groups had representatives lobbying the 1979 session of the state legislature. There were 458 people registered to lobby. Because some of the 458 people represented more than one association or organization, 500 "concerns" were represented. As you look at the lobby categories and numbers, keep in mind that they are based on the 1979 session alone. As issues are resolved, new ones arise. Accordingly, a group's representation changes; some sessions an interest might send several representatives, other times fewer or even none. One of the major issues during the 1979 session, for example, dealt with liquor law reform. The legislature considered changing the liquor licensing laws to make it easier for new restaurants and bars to open. People who already have liquor licenses generally opposed the reform. Their licenses have a value of their own because so few are available in the more populated counties. Some of the present license holders paid thousands of dollars for their right to sell liquor. They feared that if the legislature made it easy for other people to get licenses, their licenses would lose their present extra value and their business would decline because of the added competition. So, they sent nine lobbyists to argue against changes in the law. In fact, the fraternal clubs lobbied on the issue as well, meaning that ten organizations were represented by 14 people. Now that the issue is resolved (a compromise making it easier for restaurants to get licenses), the liquor lobby may be smaller in future sessions. The liquor lobby will not shrink, however, if similar reform measures are introduced, or liquor dealers fear a last-minute attempt at reform, or they attempt to make their own changes. To put it simply, organizations normally send several lobbyists when their vital interests are before the legislature and fewer when they are not.

Table 3.1. Interest Group Registrations 1979 Legislative Session

Category (Example)	Number of Individual Interest Groups In The Category	Number of Individual People in The Category
Banks (Wyo. Bancorporation, Farmer's State Bank of Burns)	6	19
Railroads (Union Pacific)	3	6
Recreation/Tourism (Wyo. State Snowmobilers Assoc., Wyo. Outfitters Assoc.)	3	9
Liquor (Wyo. Beer Distributors, Inc.)	6	9
Other Business (Wyo. Automobile Dealers Assoc., Motion Picture Assoc. of America, Wyo. Assoc. of Realtors, Old Faithful Life Insurance Co.)	57	86
Energy (Mining—Wyo. Mining Assoc.; Oil—Texaco, Inc.; Utilities—Black Hills Power and Light Co.; Miscellaneous Energy—Panhandle Eastern Pipeline Co.)	52	88
Agriculture (Wyo. Farm Bureau Fed., Wyo. Stockgrowers Assoc., Women Involved in Farm Economics)	14	37
Labor Unions (United Transportation Union, United Steelworkers of America)	6	32
Education (Wyo. Education Assoc., Assoc. Students of University of Wyo., Wyo. Assoc. of School Administrators)	11	32
Local Government (Wyo. Assoc. of Municipalities, City of Riverton, Wyo. County Commissioners Assoc.)	16	29
Medical/Health/Social Services (Wyo. Hospital Assoc., Wyo. Assoc. for Retarded Citizens, Wyo. Human Resources Confederation)	12	25
Citizen Groups (League of Women Voters, Wyo. Taxpayers Assoc., Common Cause, Wyo. Girl Scout Council)	7	24
Professionals (Wyo. State Bar Assoc., American Institute of Architects)	9	21
Police and Firemen (Wyo. Police Protective Assoc., Casper Fire Fighters Assoc., Lusk Police Dept.)	9	17
Aging/Senior Citizens (American Assoc. of Retired Persons)	3	16
Environment (Powder River Basin Resource Council, Wyo. Outdoor Council)	4	11
Political Reform (Wyo. Right to Life Committee, Wyo. Stop ERA, Nat'l. Org. for the Reform of Marijuana Laws)	5	9
Fraternal Clubs (Wyo. VFW)	4	5
Miscellaneous Groups and Individuals (Wyo. Highway Users Assoc., Aid Assoc. of Lutherans)	23	25
Totals	250	500

The proof of this can be seen in the number of energy lobbyists at the 1979 session. Energy lobbyists were everywhere. Some represented oil companies, others mining interests, utility companies, and pipeline outfits to name but a few. Why were there so many energy groups? The answer is that the legislative session considered a number of issues that are very important to the energy industry. Two of the energy issues, for example, involved the question of whether the legislature wanted to authorize a new pipeline to transport Wyoming coal to a plant outside the state (they finally left this one up to the governor). Legislators also discussed whether they wanted to increase the amount of taxes the energy companies pay for severing, or taking, minerals such as coal and oil from the ground in the state (they voted not to increase the severance tax in 1979; See Chapter 7).

In his book on Wyoming government, Dr. Richard combines the various lobby categories into five broad groups—agriculture, business, labor, professions, and miscellaneous. Although this is helpful, it is possible to be more precise. It is more accurate to think of 11 broad categories or types of lobby groups in the state. Each of these types has an identifiable interest in that state's economy, social or environmental makeup. Each has a broad popular following, organization and structure, varying amounts of money, dedication among both leaders and members, and a large "presence" in the legislative process. While certain of these categories have had more legislative successes than others in the past, each "type" is an active participant in the legislative process at the outset of the 80's.

One of the major interest group categories in Wyoming is agriculture. As has already been noted, the various agricultural groups have long and impressive histories in Wyoming politics. The Stockgrowers, Woolgrowers, and Farm Bureau are joined by lobbyists

representing smaller farm interests called the Rocky Mountain Farmers Union, as well as the Wyoming Weed and Pest Council, Teton County Ranchers For Agriculture, a couple of organizations concerned with agriculture's position with regard to water law, and Women Involved in Farm Economics (WIFE), to name but a few. Women Involved in Farm Economics is a new lobby of farm wives and women. During the 1979 session, it had 11 registered lobbyists, more than any other agricultural group, in Cheyenne. While the agricultural groups have had dramatic differences at times in the past (e.g., such as the range war at the turn of the century), they are closely allied today on most agricultural issues. Also, they are an important conservative alliance that often opposes government growth, programs, and "interference" and at times finds itself opposed to some of the labor and social lobbies.[32]

The second broad type of lobby groups are bureaucrats ("bureaucrat" is intended as a neutral term for government administrators) in state government. These people do not have to register with the Legislative Service Office so they are not listed in Table 3.1. Even so, state administrators can and do talk extensively with legislators about programs and policies that are sought. Of course, these lobbyists may not always be able to ally themselves on every issue. A program or policy that the Game and Fish Commission wants may not be sought by the Wyoming Travel Commission. When that happens, the agencies (or bureaucrats) may actually lobby against one another. But whether administrators represent their agencies alone or an alliance of agencies, they are influential voices. This is understandable because legislators are often inclined to accept their advice on issues. Because legislators meet only 20 or 40 days each year, they often respect the advice of the full-time administrators who work with issues and problems every day.

An example of bureaucratic lobbying took place in 1979. All agencies can agree on the need to raise salaries of state employees. In 1979, the Department of Administration and Fiscal Control (DAFC) computed that state employees lost a little over nine percent of their salaries to inflation over the ten-year period before 1979. Accordingly, DAFC officials "informally" contacted people in other state agencies such as the University of Wyoming and the Department of Economic Planning and Development, and "quasi-agencies" throughout the state like the community colleges, and asked them to do whatever lobbying they could to convince legislators to support a supplemental increase to make up for losses over the past decade. DAFC proposed the bill and had it introduced; agencies in Cheyenne used direct lobbying techniques; parties throughout the state used indirect tactics such as letters. The result was passage of a 4.5 percent increase over the normal annual salary increase for state employees. In other words, the state employees got half of what they wanted plus an understanding that they could ask for the other 4.5 percent the next year.

Another major interest group category is business. This type includes a wide spectrum of interests. Included are railroads, insurance companies, liquor dealers, retail and wholesale merchants, chambers of commerce, realtors, contractors, trucking companies, airlines, entertainment companies, funeral home operators, and many more. They are generally conservative and are interested in legislation to help business, such as state tax laws, policies on the regulation of business, and measures to stimulate economic growth. Again, while these lobbies frequently ally on major issues, they are occasionally unable to work together because of conflicting interests.

The fourth type of pressure groups represent citizen concerns and various reforms. These are organizations which form to represent the public's "best interest." Sometimes the groups are broad in approaching or interpreting the public good; other groups are more specific or narrow in their concerns. The League of Women Voters, Common Cause, Taxpayers Association, American Association of University Women, and the Civil Liberties Union are all citizen groups which have broad perspectives. While broad citizen lobbies such as the League of Women Voters may become involved in a number of issues, others, such as the National Abortion Rights Action League, National Right to Life, National Organization for the Reform of Marijuana Laws, Wyoming Coalition for the Equal Rights Amendment, and Wyoming Stop ERA, have a more limited perspective. This category includes both liberal and conservative groups. Accordingly, they often oppose one another on issues. The two abortion organizations, for instance, represent completely opposite and often emotional positions. Even so, they all share in their desire to represent citizens, either in a broad or narrow sense. While some of these groups are of a permanent nature, others are temporary associations. When the Equal Rights Amendment issue is resolved, the two ERA groups may cease to exist; their members may move on to other concerns.

The fifth interest group category includes the education lobbies. The most active of these lobbies are the Wyoming Education Association (the WEA represents 6,000 Wyoming teachers, mostly between kindergarten and twelfth grade), the University of Wyoming, and Casper College. As the teacher movement grows nationally, Wyoming teachers have joined in the trend toward increasing teacher involvement in politics. In fact, the WEA is active in supporting political candidates with contributions and in encouraging people with "pro-education, pro-teacher" perspectives to seek office. Other education lobbyists represent individual schools and school districts, the Wyoming Association of School Administrators, Wyoming School Board Association, and the community colleges. While the various groups share a common belief in the need to support education, they often work at counterpurposes; they are not highly unified. Their differences are understandable, because teachers and school boards sometimes (or even "often") oppose one another on education priorities, such as whether teachers and school boards should negotiate teacher salaries in a labor-management setting. Other educational splits and jealousies exist between the public school personnel and higher education officials such as those at the University of Wyoming; community colleges and the University of Wyoming; wealthy school districts and poor school districts, etc.

Another major category of interest groups is made up of energy companies and concerns. As Wyoming's involvement in the nation's energy needs has increased in the 70's, the presence of energy lobbies has been more pronounced. Today, energy interests are numerous in the legislature. Examples include the Wyoming Mining Association, Wyoming Coal Information Committee, Petroleum Association of Wyoming, Pacific Power and Light Company, and Stauffer Chemical Company of Wyoming. These organizations typically work together to protect or improve their positions on such matters as taxation and environmental standards.

The seventh type are environmental groups. The Powder River Basin Resource Council, the Wilderness Society, Wyoming Outdoor Council, and National Audubon Society all had representatives at the 1979 session. Since the 1960's, environmental groups have become very common in Wyoming politics. Today, they are relatively small in membership, but

make up for their numbers with thorough organization and leadership dedication. While most lobbyists have their expenses paid and receive a salary from their organizations, for example, environmental lobbyists usually get only token support. Because these groups receive only donations, they cannot pay large salaries. This means that environmental lobbyists are normally quite dedicated people.

Environmental groups are primarily concerned with protecting the state's natural resources. In recent years, they have scored a number of legislative victories, including the creation of the Industrial Siting Council and air standards legislation. Because they have a somewhat progressive or moderately liberal bent, environmentalists often find themselves opposing conservative coalitions in general and energy companies specifically. Environmentalists, for example, generally support an increase in state taxes on energy operations. The two sides tangled on the taxation issue in both 1977 and 1979. In 1977, the environmentalists won; in 1979 the mineral interests were successful. The stage is set for this issue in the 80's.

The eighth interest group category in Wyoming is organized labor, including the United Steelworkers of America, United Mineworkers of America, Brotherhood of Locomotive Engineers, American Federation of Labor and Congress of Industrial Organizations (AFL-CIO) and others. They are concerned with a variety of labor-oriented issues, such as worker safety, wages, security, and negotiating rights. As shown in the next section, organized labor is generally less influential in Wyoming than its business and agricultural counterparts.

Another of the major interest group categories is local government. In a system based upon federalism, local governments get their powers from their state government (See Chapter 7). Also, many town, city, and county projects are funded with state money. Thus, representatives of the cities and counties lobby the legislature for money, tax advantages, and other policies of benefit to their city, town, or county (such as obtaining water). During the 1979 legislative session, for example, the Wyoming Association of Municipalities had seven registered lobbyists. They were joined by two each from Laramie, Casper, Riverton, and Cheyenne, and one each from Gillette, Glenrock, Powell, Cody, and Green River, plus various county representatives.

The next type of interest groups in Wyoming are the various professional associations, such as the Wyoming State Bar Association, Wyoming Engineering Society, Laramie County Pharmaceutical Association, American Institute of Architects, and others. These organizations normally take narrow approaches to lobbying, concentrating on their own professional concerns while often ignoring other issues that are outside of their profession. Representatives of the Bar Association, for example, concentrate lobbying on matters such as judicial procedures, seldom getting into social or administrative issues that are unrelated to the legal profession.

The final major interest group category covers the broad social concerns. These people represent the state's numerous programs dealing with health, social service, senior citizens, and others. Nearly all of these interests have a State of Wyoming "connection." Some are state agencies, others are local programs that are supported with state money. They all share a belief in the importance of doing more for Wyoming citizens, particularly the disadvantaged. When these socially oriented groups are not "fighting" one another for the same money, they are often supportive of, and sympathetic with, one another. Examples of interest groups in this category include the Wyoming Health Care Association, Southeast Wyoming Mental Health Center, Wyoming

Epilepsy Foundation, Wyoming Hospital Association, and the National Retired Teachers Association. While the social concerns are always a topic during the legislative session, they were particularly well represented in 1979 because a measure to reorganize the state Department of Health and Social Services was considered. Thus, representatives for the specific interests were out lobbying to protect their vested interests.

There are, of course, numerous other lobby groups which do not fit in the above categories. These are miscellaneous smaller groups which do not meet the definition of the larger categories. Again, remember that categorizing these groups is quite subjective. The groups listed above are the major types of interest groups from the author's perspective. Clearly, these categories are not cast in concrete. Keep in mind, for example, that agriculture and energy are also businesses. Thus, some people might combine them. The point, then, is that the above categories are organized interests with various amounts of money, leadership, and dedication which have either a common lobby interest or issue perspective. Thinking of them in categories helps us to understand their similarities and differences.

Most Influential Lobby Groups

As has already been seen, interest groups have different strengths and legislative advantages. Some have more members, others have more money. Some have more prestige, others have more dedication. Some are better organized, and others have a greater historical presence. These differences mean that some pressure groups are more effective than others. But which ones? Which interest groups are most and least influential in Wyoming?

To answer that question, three surveys were taken in 1979. One of the surveys, done in

Table 3.2. Most Influential Wyoming Interest Groups as Perceived by Wyoming Lobbyists (175 lobbyists surveyed with multiple responses)

Interest Group	Number Naming It Among the Most Influential	Percentage of Total	Interest Group	Number Naming It Among the Most Influential	Percentage of Total
Mining	84	15.5	Wyoming Taxpayers Assoc.	6	1.1
Oil	69	12.7	Common Cause	1	.2
Gas	30	5.5	*Total Citizen Groups		
Energy	15	2.7	Responses	7	1.3
Coal	14	2.6	State Government	3	.6
Utilities	10	1.8	Governor	2	.4
Uranium	2	.4	Public Employees	1	.2
*Total *Energy/Mineral*			*Total *State Government*		
Responses	224	41.2	Responses	6	1.2
Wyoming Stockgrowers/			Local Government	26	4.8
Ranchers	35	6.3	Wyoming Assn. of		
Agriculture/Farm	48	8.8	Municipalities	1	.2
Wyoming Farm Bureau	13	2.4	*Total *Local Government*		
Wyoming Woolgrowers	2	.4	Responses	27	5.0
*Total *Agricultural*			Environmentalists	17	3.1
Responses	98	17.9	Organized Labor	10	1.8
Liquor	37	6.8	Transportation	7	1.3
Truckers	18	3.3	Wyoming Bar Association	6	1.1
Railroads (especially U.P.)	18	3.3	Stan Hathaway Law Firm	2	.4
Banks	5	.9	Firemen	1	.2
Contractors	2	.4	Land Barons	1	.2
Motels/Tourism	2	.4	Wyoming Pyrotechnical		
Mountain Bell	1	.2	Assoc.	1	.2
Realtors	1	.2	Water	1	.2
*Total *Business*			Medical	1	.2
Responses	84	15.5	Anti-Labor	1	.2
University of Wyoming	19	3.5	Senior Citizens	1	.2
Wyoming Educ. Assoc./			Individuals	1	.2
Education	18	3.3	Pre-School Directors	1	.2
Teachers	9	1.7	*Total *Other* Responses	51	9.5
*Total *Education*					
Responses	46	8.5			

Totals: 543 Responses = 100.1%

preparation for this text, polled 175 lobbyists on their opinions of the three overall most influential pressure groups in Wyoming. Each of the 175 lobbyists was registered for the 1979 session; most had also lobbied at previous legislative sessions as well. While the lobbyists undoubtedly had the 1979 session in mind at the time of the survey, the question asked for an overall assessment of the most influential groups. Table 3.2 gives a thorough listing of the lobbyist responses. Also, the author surveyed 73 legislators who had served between 1975 and 1979. They, too, were asked to specify the three most influential Wyoming lobbies. These answers are shown in Table 3.3. Professor Oliver Walter of the University of Wyoming also directed a 1979 student survey of 83 legislators (out of 92 possible) who served in the 1979 session. These figures are included in Table 3.3.

The three surveys provide three perspectives of lobby influence in the state—an overall assessment by lobbyists, an overall assessment

Table 3.3. Wyoming Legislators Assess the Influential Interest Groups

Most Influential Interest Groups in 1979 Session (Based on U.W. survey of present legislators in 1979)

Interest Group	Number of Responses	Percentage of Survey
Mineral Lobby	40	31.5
Texas Eastern	2	1.6
*Total *Energy/ Minerals*	42	33.1%
Liquor	12	9.4
Truckers Assoc.	10	7.9
Railroads	4	3.1
Bankers	2	1.6
Industry	1	.8
Contractors Assoc.	1	.8
*Total *Business*	30	23.6%
Wyo. Educ. Assoc.	10	7.9
U. of Wyo.	8	6.3
*Total *Education*	18	14.2%
State Employees	8	6.3
Dept. of Agriculture	5	3.9
*Total *State Gov't.*	13	10.2%
Wyo. Farm Bureau	4	3.1
Ranchers	3	2.4
*Total *Agriculture*	7	5.5%
Wyo. Assn. of Municipalities	5	3.9
Senior Citizens	3	2.4
Wyo. Taxpayers Assn.	3	2.4
Outdoor Council	3	2.4
League of Women Voters	2	1.6
Wyo. Engineering Soc.	1	.8
Total	127	100.1%
Minerals	29	11.6
Oil	22	8.8
Gas	11	4.4
Coal	2	.8
Utilities	2	.8
Energy	2	.8
*Total *Energy/ Minerals*	68	27.2%

Most Influential Interest Groups—Overall (Based on the author's survey of legislators who served between 1975-79)

Interest Group	Number of Responses	Percentage of Survey
Education	31	12.4
Teachers	8	3.2
U. of Wyo.	8	3.2
Community Colleges	1	.4
*Total *Education*	48	19.2%
Liquor	17	6.8
Trucking Assoc.	10	4.0
Railroads	9	3.6
Banking	4	1.6
Insurance	2	.8
Private Enterprise	1	.4
*Total *Business*	43	17.2%
Agriculture	8	3.2
Wyo. Stockgrowers Assn.	7	2.8
Wyo. Farm Bureau	7	2.8
Ranching	6	2.4
Wyo. Woolgrowers Assn.	2	.8
*Total *Agriculture*	30	12.0%
Public Employees	14	5.6
Governor	1	.4
Dept. Admin & Fiscal Control	1	.4
*Total *State Gov't*	16	6.4%
Local Government	14	5.6
Labor	11	4.4
Environmentalists	11	4.4
Senior Citizens	3	1.2
Right to Life	2	.8
Bar Assoc.	1	.4
Wyo. Taxpayers Assoc.	1	.4
League of Women Voters	1	.4
Anti-Water Develop.	1	.4
Total	250	100.0%

The U.W. survey questioned 83 legislators from the 1979 session. The author's survey (administered through Northwest Community College) questioned 73 legislators from sessions between 1975-79. Both surveys asked the legislators to list the two (U.W.) or three (NWCC) most influential interest groups. Responses to the U.W. survey dealt solely with the 1979 session; the NWCC survey asked about overall lobby-group influence.

Table 3.4. Overall Comparison on Most Influential Interest Groups

Lobby	Survey of 175 Lobbyists On Most Influential Overall	Survey of 83 Legislators from 1979 Session on Influence In 1979 Session	Survey of 73 Legislators from 1975–79 Sessions on Overall Influence
Energy / Minerals	41.2%	33.1%	27.2%
Business	15.5	23.6	17.2
Education	8.5	14.2	19.2
Agriculture	17.9	5.5	12.0
State Government	1.2	10.2	6.4
Organized Labor	1.8	0	4.4
Local Government	4.8	3.9	5.6
Environmentalists	3.1	2.4	4.4
Social Concerns	.4	2.4	1.2
Citizen Representation / Reform	1.3	4.0	1.6
Professions	1.1	.8	.4
Other	3.3	0	.4
Totals	100.1%	100.1%	100.0%

by legislators, and a legislative assessment of specific influence in the 1979 session. Because the surveys asked respondents to give their opinions with no prompting by the questionnaire (called "open ended questions"), the responses cover a wide range. In Table 3.2, for example, lobbyists gave several energy responses, including mining, coal and energy. Because these responses are different, but so closely related, totals are given by the various categories. This is an important factor to keep in mind when looking at the detailed responses in Tables 3.2 and 3.3. To take another example from 3.2, only 13 respondents listed the Farm Bureau by name. However, 48 lobbyists gave broader answers of "agriculture" or "farmers/ farming." The exact responses are included in the table to allow for overlapping answers such as these. Table 3.4 compares the answers from the three surveys by category. If Tables 3.2 and 3.3 seem difficult don't worry, Table 3.4 is an easy comparison of the responses; 3.2 and 3.3 show the specific answers which make up the categories listed in 3.4.

What Does It Mean? Several patterns are apparent in these figures. The foremost pattern is the influence of four lobby concerns— energy and mineral companies, education, agriculture, and other business interests.

As the decade of the 1980's begins, the presence of the energy and mineral companies is both obvious and understandable. Wyoming is an energy and mineral rich state in an energy conscious era. Think of it as a logical progression. Wyoming is blessed with vast energy resources, which the nation so badly needs. However, energy companies may extract those resources only by operating within the "rules" as determined by the Wyoming legislature (and the U.S. Congress). Considering the tremendous stakes that are involved, it is only natural that energy and mineral companies do what they can to keep their taxes down, get access to water, or keep pollution standards at levels they can work with. To obtain these advantageous policies they, like other interests, try to influence the "rules" before they are set. Indeed, this is the very essence of lobbying. Thus, it is not surprising that 41 percent of the lobbyists surveyed recognized energy/minerals companies as among the most influential lobbies in the state. Considering that most respondents gave three answers, the 41 percent is particularly high. The data also show that the legislators and lobbyists consider mining (particularly coal) and oil interests to be the most successful segment of the larger category (see Table 3.3).

That the other most influential Wyoming lobbies are business, education, and agriculture, is consistent with much that has already been seen. These four interests have a number of legislative advantages. To begin with, their various associations (e.g. Wyoming Mining Association, Wyoming Education Associations, Chambers of Commerce, oil companies, Stockgrowers, Farm Bureau) tend to be well organized with plentiful funding. These advantages enable them to send the most manpower to represent them before the legislature. Literally, they send small armies of lobbyists to "guide" the legislators. The business lobby (combining "other business" with the banking, liquor, and railroad lobbies in Table 3.1) had 120 lobbyists registered for the 1979 session. Think of it. If they all attended the session, there were more business lobbyists than there were legislators (there are 92 legislators)! While this line of reasoning is an exaggeration—all 120 did not attend the session, some who did attend stayed for only a few hours (often to merely put in a good word or two for a specific bill, rather than some abstract pro-business position), and the number of lobbyists present does not mean automatic success—it emphasizes a point which is accurate: the most successful or influential interest groups typically have large lobbyist representations.

These four lobby categories have at least two other advantages. First, each has a large public following. Huge segments of the Wy-

oming populace make their living in business, agriculture, energy/minerals, and education (or have school-aged children). If a legislator in this state gets the reputation of not being sympathetic with agriculture, for example, his tenure in the legislature may be short. Second, the interests have significant representations among the legislators themselves. Of the 92 legislators elected to the 1979 and 1980 sessions, 28 listed either ranching or agriculture as their occupation. The legislature included 17 members of the Wyoming Farm Bureau, 16 affiliates of the Wyoming Stockgrowers Association, five Wyoming Woolgrowers, and one member of the Farmer's Union (several of the farmer/rancher legislators were in both the Farm Bureau and Stockgrowers Association). Clearly, farmers and ranchers are well represented in the legislature. Twenty-three legislators at the 1979–80 sessions were businessmen involved in everything from real estate to liquor to trucking. In addition, 12 legislators served as part-time officers in banks or savings institutions, and 21 were members of local chambers of commerce. Business is well represented. Eleven legislators either were or had been (prior to retirement) educators in the public schools, community colleges, or University of Wyoming. Some were teachers, others administrators. Another nine legislators were affiliated with education in a secondary capacity, such as community college trustees. And eight legislators either worked for, or in conjunction with, utility or energy companies. Likewise, education and energy are well represented in the Wyoming legislature.

These particular lobby groups are likely to receive more empathy, understanding, and even interest than other pressure groups. The 28 rancher/farmer legislators could not help but be sympathetic to the agricultural lobby. Both understand and appreciate agricultural problems and concerns. Indeed, those concerns are a part of these legislators' lives and perspectives. And remember, the lobbyists and legislators, in varying degree, both represent *people* who are engaged in agriculture. Their working together, from the pluralist perspective, is but an example of how our democracy functions.[33]

The Influence of Labor. Wyoming's labor unions are organized, represent significant numbers of people, and have money and dedicated leaders. But as is seen in Table 3.4, few lobbyists or legislators believe that organized labor is particularly influential in the Wyoming legislature. There are several reasons for this.

As Chapter One and Seven show, Wyoming is a fiercely "independent" state. Wyoming's roots trace to people who either succeeded or failed on their own merits. Even to early settlers who received government aid in the form of land, water and railroad grants and assistance, the difference between prosperity and failure was essentially a matter of individual hard work, imagination, and good fortune. Call it "independence" or "rugged individualism," Wyoming's heritage prides itself on individual achievement. To such people, labor unions are nonessential. In this ethic, a man is seen as "making it" on his own. Unions may be helpful, but they are not seen as essential. This ethic has been unchallenged by massive industrial abuse, as eastern areas witnessed in the decades around the turn of the century.

Another reason why organized labor has not equaled the legislative influence of energy, agriculture, education, and business is that it does not have the overwhelming public support which the others seem to have. In a statewide poll taken in 1976, for example, 79 percent of the 1,090 residents surveyed said they thought positively of Wyoming agriculture, while fewer than six percent had negative feelings. Think of that, 16 people felt good about Wyoming agriculture for every one who had neg-

ative impressions of the industry. Likewise, the public had positive impressions of the state's oil and coal industries, 70 percent to 9.8 percent, or seven to one. Public support of labor unions was somewhat muddled, however; 38.7 percent of the survey respondents said they had positive feelings toward Wyoming labor unions, but another 30 percent felt negative. In other words, people in Wyoming approved of their state's agriculture 16 to one, oil and coal seven to one, and labor unions by only four to three. This divided public support does not give labor the somewhat automatic "ear" of legislators that agriculture, energy, and presumably business, enjoy.[34]

A third major reason for labor's less dramatic influence in the legislature stems from the state's "right-to-work" law. Responding to pressure to pull the "reins" in on organized labor, Congress passed the Taft-Hartley Law in 1947. The law (Section 14B), as mentioned earlier, allows states to prohibit unions from compelling people to join a union against their will. In states which have these laws, workers cannot lose a job for refusing to join a union (in other words, "union shops" are banned in these states). In 1963, Wyoming joined the wave of western and southern states which passed these measures, called "right-to-work" laws. While the right-to-work law protects rights of individual choice, it also decreases the strength of organized labor. Because workers who are not in the union will receive the same benefits as those who are union members at a particular work place, the tendency is for some people to save the cost of the union dues by not joining. Over a few years, the union may come to represent a minority of the workers on that job; management then will normally stop negotiating with union representatives and the union is in a weak position. When this sort of thing happens statewide, organized labor loses membership, organization strength, money, and prestige. These factors translate to decreased influence with the legislature.

Finally, another legislative disadvantage labor experiences is the willingness of other powerful lobbies to work against it. When the legislature passed the Right-to-Work Law in 1963, for example, the Wyoming Farm Bureau Federation, Associated General Contractors of Wyoming, Wyoming Trucking Association, Wyoming Stockgrowers Association, Wyoming Retail Merchants Association, and the Wyoming Grange all lobbied against the unions and for the bill.[35] It is not at all uncommon for conservative alliances like these to oppose unions in Wyoming politics or elsewhere. The great prestige and influence of some of the more conservative groups, then, also decreases the effectiveness of organized labor in Wyoming.

This, of course, is not to say that organized labor is so weak that it is not an important factor in state affairs. This is far from the case. Labor lobbyists are as active, dedicated, and plentiful (32 registered in 1979) as are representatives of most interest groups. Organized labor also has a number of sympathetic legislators who work closely with union lobbyists. But even considering labor's strengths, it is nevertheless true that labor is generally a minority voice in the legislature. In fact, it is sometimes suggested that organized labor's influence in the legislature has declined since 1964 when labor narrowly lost a bid to repeal the right-to-work statute.

Legislative Receptiveness of Lobbyists

In order to succeed in their lobbying efforts, interest group representatives must have the chance to present their ideas to legislators and the legislators must be responsive. This does not mean that the legislators have to do what the lobbyists want. Rather, it means that lobbyists can't represent their organizations unless the legislators will listen to them and consider their ideas with open minds.

To discover how receptive legislators are to lobbyists in Wyoming, 175 lobbyists were asked the questions shown in Table 3.5. The table shows that Wyoming state legislators are

Table 3.5. Lobbyist Opinions on Legislator Responsiveness to Them Personally, to Their Ideas and by Political Party

How Receptive Are the State Legislators to You *Personally*?

29.7%	Very receptive. They almost all are willing to listen to what I have to say.
66.9%	Generally receptive. Most are willing to listen to what I have to say.
3.4%	Generally aren't receptive. Few are willing to listen to what I have to say.
0%	Completely unreceptive to me personally. Typically, they don't want to hear what I have to say.

100.0%
175 Survey Responses

How Receptive Are the State Legislators to Your *Ideas*?

11.2%	Very receptive. Overall, I believe most legislators are willing to consider my ideas and are frequently persuaded by them.
58.2%	Generally receptive. Many legislators, perhaps more than half, can be persuaded by my arguments.
30.6%	Generally aren't receptive. Many legislators don't really consider my ideas; their minds are often made up already.
0%	Completely unreceptive to my ideas. Frankly, most of the time I'm "spinning my wheels." The legislators are not very openminded to my ideas.

100.0%
170 Survey Responses

Which Political Party is More Receptive to Your Efforts?

28.2%	Republicans
22.9%	Democrats
48.8%	No difference

99.9%
170 Survey Responses

quite receptive to lobbyists personally. In other words, lobbyists feel that the legislators treat them well. Only 3.4 percent of the lobbyists felt otherwise.

Most of the interest group representatives also said that legislators are receptive to their ideas. However, 30.6 percent said that this is not true. Lobbyists for the labor unions were the most negative on the question, seven of the nine who completed the survey said, "Many legislators don't really consider my ideas, their minds are often made up already." While only three environmental and three reform lobbyists completed the questionnaire, two of each type answered this question negatively. One must be cautious, however, about drawing definite conclusions from such small numbers of survey respondents. Still, the indicators are that at least a few labor, environmental, and reform groups in this state find it somewhat difficult to discuss their ideas with many legislators. This is supported by the low ranking that these three groups received in terms of overall influence in the legislature.

If environmentalists find many legislators to be somewhat closed-minded, we might expect the energy/mining lobby to say just the opposite, because environmentalists and energy/mining representatives often oppose each other on legislation. Lobbyists for the energy and mining companies do indeed have a different view; 17 of 19 surveyed said that legislators are receptive to their ideas. Likewise, lobbyists for agriculture (12 of 15) and health/medicine (6 of 7) were positive regarding legislator responsiveness to their ideas. Most of the other lobby groups were somewhat divided on the issue. Typically, they said legislators were responsive to their ideas by roughly two to one. This was the case with lobbyists for the local governments, education, senior citizens, the professions and citizen groups.

Overall, lobbyists think that legislators are receptive to them in Wyoming. There are, of course, notable exceptions.

Table 3.5 also shows that lobbyists as a whole are not dealing solely with one political party. While the Republican party ordinarily controls the state legislature, most interest groups try to lobby both parties. It makes sense; there are votes on both sides of the aisle. Even so, several lobby groups have a better rapport, or relationship, with one particular party. The strongest alliances are between the labor unions and Democrats, and between energy/mining interests and the Republicans. Of nine union lobbyists, eight have closer ties to the Democratic party, one said there is no difference; 15 energy and mining lobbyists find the GOP more receptive; one said the Democrats are more receptive, and three find the parties equally receptive. These two "alliances" are not unusual. The Democrats, you will remember from the previous chapter, have long ties with labor. In fact, union rank-and-file have been an important component of the Democratic party since the Great Depression. Likewise, Republican political ties with energy and mining companies are quite strong.

Overall Legislative Assessment of Lobbyists

Overall, Wyoming legislators give lobbyists high marks. Table 3.6 shows the legislative responses to a series of questions designed to "characterize" or describe the role of lobbyists and lobbying as an element in the state political system. The table shows that 13 of the legislators who were surveyed believe that lobbyists as a group are extremely honest, 34 say lobbyists are quite honest, 14 slightly honest, and only one legislator responded that interest group officials are dishonest overall. By nearly the same ratio, Wyoming legislators find that the information that they receive from lobbyists is accurate; only three of 68 legislators

Table 3.6. Legislators' Overall Characterization of Wyoming Lobbyists
(In actual number of responses, not percentages)

Lobbyist Characteristic:	Extremely	Quite	Slightly	No Opinion	Slightly	Quite	Extremely	
Honest	13	34	14	4	0	1	0	Dishonest
Provide Accurate Information	13	34	13	5	2	1	0	Provide Inaccurate Information
Intelligent	12	27	17	7	2	0	0	Unintelligent
Positive Influence Overall	5	28	21	9	3	1	0	Negative Influence Overall
Not Overly Influential	2	7	16	15	17	6	1	Overly Influential

who answered the question said that lobbyists generally provide inaccurate information. This is important when one stops to realize that legislators so often rely upon lobbyists for information. Likewise, legislators characterize Wyoming lobbyists as quite intelligent; only two legislators disagree. While it is difficult to generalize too much from these findings, it is fair to say that Wyoming's legislators hold lobbyists in general in high regard in terms of honesty, intelligence, and as providers of accurate information.

Table 3.6 also points out the high overall marks given to state lobbyists. As shown, only four legislators (out of 67) believe that lobby groups are a negative influence overall in Wyoming. While the legislators are divided on the question of whether interest groups are overly influential in the state, they clearly recognize their role as positive overall. In fact, the University of Wyoming survey of Wyoming legislators, which was referred to earlier, found that 91.6 percent of our state legislators believe that lobbyists help the legislative process, especially as a source of information.

These high marks speak well of the legislative process in the state. Our democracy, as was discussed earlier, is based on the assumption that the people run the government. For this to be true, the institutions that connect the public with their leaders must work hon-

estly and legitimately. For that reason, nearly everyone would agree that elections must be run fairly and above board. It is for the same reason that interest groups in America and Wyoming are important. If the pluralist view is correct, then lobbyists must be honest and intelligent and provide accurate information. When they do these things in an honest, ethical manner, pluralists can conclude that interest groups are another of the important links between the people and their government. At least in the case of Wyoming, the link seems to be intact.

Notes

1. Most texts on American government and the legislative process include sections on interest groups. See, for example, Malcolm E. Jewell and Samuel C. Patterson, *The Legislative Process in the United States,* 3d ed. (New York: Random House, 1977), pp. 279–301.

2. Theodore J. Lowi, *The End of Liberalism* (New York: W. W. Norton, 1969), pp. 68–72.

3. Much has been written exploring elitist theories. For an example, see G. William Domhoff, *Who Rules America?* (Englewood Cliffs, New Jersey: Prentice-Hall, 1967). For articles on a more "radical" theory, see Stephen Earl Bennett, "Modes of Resolution of a 'Belief Dilemma' in the Ideology of the John Birch Society," *American Journal of Politics,* 33

(August, 1971):735–772; Tim R. Miller, "Teaching Political Science with the Help of the John Birch Society," *New Directions in Teaching,* 7 (Fall, 1980):22–28, and John Robison, *Proofs of a Conspiracy* (Belmont, Mass: West Islands, 1967). This is a John Birch Society reprinting of a book originally written in 1798.

4. Charles L. Clapp, *The Congressman: His Work As He Sees It* (Washington, D.C., 1963), pp. 162–163.

5. John C. Wahlke et al., *The Legislative System* (New York, 1962), p. 338.

6. For a somewhat humorous discussion of the "types" of corruptions see *Plunkett of Tammany Hall,* comp. and ed. William L. Riordon (New York: E. P. Dutton & Co., Inc., 1963) and Michael Parenti, "Corruption As An American Way of Life," *Democracy for the Few,* 2d ed. (New York: St. Martins, 1977), pp. 232–234.

7. For a brief discussion of the benefits and drawbacks of lobbying see Robert Sherrill, *Why They Call It Politics,* 3d ed. (New York: Harcourt, Brace, Jovanovich, 1979), pp. 248–265 and Malcolm E. Jewell and Samuel C. Patterson, *The Legislative Process in the United States,* 3d ed. (New York: Random House, 1977), pp. 293–299.

8. Samuel C. Patterson, "The Role of the Deviant in the State Legislative System: The Wisconsin Assembly," *Western Political Quarterly* 14 (1961):465–466.

9. Jewell and Patterson, pp. 290–291.

10. From a survey of 83 legislators from the 1979 legislative session, conducted by Dr. Oliver Walter and his students, Department of Political Science, University of Wyoming, 1979.

11. In 1979, the registration fee was $2.00.

12. Wyoming Statutes, 1957, 28–70.25 through 28–70.28, as amended.

13. Corporations may also provide funds directly to elected officials in return for services provided to the corporation. Often, for example, honorarium fees are offered in return for a speech.

14. The material in this section is from Wyoming Statutes, 1957, 22–25.101 through 22–25.102, as amended.

15. Wyoming Constitution, art. 3, sec. 43.

16. The Pacific Railway Acts of 1862 and 1864 gave the Union Pacific Railroad (building west from Missouri) and the Central Pacific Railroad (building east from California) the odd-numbered sections of land, including mineral rights, for 20 miles on each side of the tracks. In addition to this subsidy, the railroads received government loans and assurances of government business.

17. Lewis L. Gould, *Wyoming: A Political History, 1868–1896* (New Haven, Conn: Yale, 1968), p. 12.

18. Ibid.

19. T. A. Larson, *History of Wyoming* (Lincoln: University of Nebraska Press, 1965), pp. 77–78.

20. Gould, p. 26.

21. For a discussion of the whole issue, see Gould, pp. 40–41, quoting Gov. John A. Campbell in a letter to George Pullman, July 21, 1872, T. E. Sickels to Campbell, July 31, 1872, Campbell Papers; *Leader,* Aug. 13, 17 and 18, 1872.

22. Larson, p. 184.

23. John B. Richard, *Government and Politics of Wyoming,* 3d ed. (Dubuque, Iowa: Kendall-Hunt, 1974), p. 33.

24. Dr. Larson quotes the coroner's jury as reporting that Watson and Averell "came to their deaths by being hanged by the neck at the hands of A. J. Bothwell, Tom Sun, John Durbin, R. M. Galbraith, Bob Connor, E. McLain, and an unknown man."

25. Larson, p. 270.

26. Quotations in this account are from Larson, pp. 268–286; many other accounts of these events have been written including Jack R. Gage, *The Johnson County War* (Flintlock Publishing Co., 1967); Charles Bingham Penrose, "The Johnson County War" (Masters thesis, University of Wyoming, 1939); *The Johnson County War,* a rare reprint from the *Buffalo Bulletin* (Evanston, Illinois: Branding Iron Press, 1955).

27. Larson, p. 372. For other accounts that are even more dramatic, see Harold E. Briggs, *Frontiers of the Northwest* (New York: Appleton-Century, 1940).

28. The three men were Joe Allemand, Joe Emge, and Joe Lazier.

29. The five men were George Sabin, M. A. Alexander, Thomas Dixon, Herbert Brink, and Ed F. Eaton.

30. Larson, pp. 369–372; see also Henry G. Troutwein, "History of the Wyoming Woolgrowers

Association 1905–15" (Masters thesis, University of Wyoming, 1964).

31. Larson, pp. 462–464.

32. It is also worth noting how the various lobby coalitions sometimes formalize their ties. For example, the various agricultural groups have banded themselves into the Agriculture Unity Group. Likewise, business groups have formed the Wyoming Council for Economic Development (now named the Wyoming Council on Business and Industry). Memberships in the various alliances often overlap. The Farm Bureau, Stockgrowers, and Woolgrowers, for example, belong to both of these groups.

33. "Lawmakers of Wyoming: Forty-Fifth Legislature, 1979–1980," a biographical pamphlet distributed by the Wyoming Trucking Association.

34. From a 1976 Election Survey, conducted by the Government Research Bureau, University of Wyoming, 1976.

35. Larson, p. 537.

CHAPTER
FOUR

The Legislature

Constitutional Provisions and Background

As in other states, the Wyoming legislature plays a vigorous role in Wyoming politics. This has been the case since the founding of the territory in 1869. Often major issues and actions have sprung from the legislature. In fact, early legislatures were responsible for, or played leadership roles in, some of Wyoming's most notable events. Passage of women's suffrage is an example; going ahead with the statehood drive is another. In many ways, the Wyoming legislature is unique. Unlike many states, which have full or nearly full-time politician legislators, Wyoming has a part-time legislature of citizen lawmakers. While this may sound somewhat "romantic,"

Wyoming State Capitol Building, from the south, 1913. Wyoming State Archives, Museums and Historical Department, University of Wyoming.

it is one of the most unique aspects of Wyoming politics. As everywhere, Wyoming has its political "climbers" who see government service as a chance to advance themselves. But they are tempered by the notion of individual citizens who meet periodically to do public service. Yes, many legislators have ulterior motives which are sometimes self-serving. But they are checked by an aura (or atmosphere) of citizen duty. This aura is a product of the state's past, a part of its heritage, and one of the factors which will shape its future.

Qualifications for Membership. Wyoming's "citizen legislature" is bicameral, meaning that it has a senate and house of representatives. Senators must be 25 years old, members of the house must be 21; both must be citizens of the U.S. and Wyoming. Also, senators and representatives must have resided within the county or district that they represent for at least 12 months preceding election. Senators are elected to serve four-year terms; representatives serve for two years.[1] Theoretically, the differences in length of terms and numbers (there are 30 senators and 62 representatives) make the senate better able to take a broader view on issues by being a little less responsive to public "whims."[2] Because there are more representatives and they "answer" to the voters every two years, the theory goes, they will be more responsive to the people. In practice, however, there is probably little difference. Neither the house nor the senate is any more "in touch" with the people. When there are differences between the two branches—and differences do occur—it is usually because the branches have different perspectives about what the public wants and needs.

Apportionment. As was noted in Chapter 1, Wyoming's constitutional convention debated the issue of legislative apportionment. The issue of "apportionment" appears simple at first—what factor should representation be based upon in the house and senate? But the issue is far more complicated than it might seem because everyone wants to draw the districts to his advantage. If the districts are drawn one way, one particular political party may benefit; if legislative districts are drawn up another way, perhaps small counties will get the advantage; or, if representation is done another way, maybe a particular region of the state will get more legislators than other areas. This is how apportionment becomes a political issue.

At the constitutional convention, you will recall, the small counties argued that Wyoming should adopt a system that is similar to the relationship between the national and state governments. This "little Federal Plan" would have given each county equal representation in the state senate (just as each state gets two senators in the U.S. Senate), with representation in the house of representatives based on population. The larger counties convinced the convention to reject this, saying instead that the idea of everyone having the same voice in government (called "one man—one vote") is basic to our system of government; besides, the analogy (or comparison) of counties with states is weak. Counties are not states, the large counties said.

With this issue resolved, the convention passed Section 3 (of Article 3) which based representation in both the house and senate on population, with the counties as legislative districts. Over the years, however, important inequities developed. Particular aspects of the constitution[3] and the state's population patterns resulted in some counties being overrepresented in the legislature. Counties are "overrepresented" when their legislators represent fewer people than other legislators represent. In 1963, for example, some state senators represented 3,000 people while other senators represented 30,000.[4] This means that the 3,000 people had the same representation in the legislature as the 30,000. Remember, everyone is supposed to have the same voice or representation in the legislature. If 3,000 people have one senator, 30,000 people should have 10 senators. But they did not.

In the 1960's the U.S. Supreme Court ruled that apportionment or districting which didn't represent everyone as nearly equal as possible was unconstitutional.[5] To comply with the 1964 ruling, Governor Hansen called a special session of the legislature to reapportion the state legislative districts. Because of extensive infighting, however, it was impossible to work out a compromise. Legislators failed again at the regular legislative session in 1965, for the same reason. During the two legislative sessions there were simply too many partisan overtones for a new plan to be passed. Both parties wanted a plan that would draw the new districts to their advantage. In the end, they were unable to compromise.[6]

After these failures, a federal court reapportioned Wyoming. The federal authorities threw out some of the problem provisions of the Wyoming Constitution, corrected the advantage which some counties had in the house, expanded the number of senators, and paired some of the smaller counties into new senate districts. The state made other relatively minor apportionment changes after the 1970 census.[7]

Since the changes in 1972, the house has had 62 members, divided among the 23 counties. Laramie County (11 representatives) and Natrona County (10 representatives) have the largest representation; Converse, Crook, Hot Springs, Johnson, Niobrara, Platte, Sublette, Teton, Uinta, Washakie, and Weston counties have only one representative in the house. The senate has had 30 members since the federal reapportionment in October, 1965. Again, Laramie (five) and Natrona (four) Counties elect the most senators. Table 4.1 shows the

Table 4.1. Representation in the Wyoming House and Senate, by County

House		Senate	
Albany	5	Albany	2
Big Horn	2	Big Horn	1
Campbell	2	Campbell-Johnson	2
Carbon	3	Carbon	1
Converse	1	Converse-Niobrara	1
Crook	1	Crook-Weston	1
Fremont	5	Fremont	2
Goshen	2	Goshen-Platte	2
Hot Springs	1	Hot Springs-Washakie	1
Johnson	1	Laramie	5
Laramie	11	Natrona	4
Lincoln	2	North Lincoln-Sublette-	
Natrona	10	Teton	1
Niobrara	1	South Lincoln-Uinta	1
Park	3	Park	2
Platte	1	Sheridan	2
Sheridan	3	Sweetwater	2
Sublette	1	TOTAL	30
Sweetwater	3		
Teton	1		
Uinta	1		
Washakie	1		
Weston	1		
TOTAL	62		

present number of senators and representatives that are elected in the various counties.

It is also worth noting that state legislators are elected "at large" in the counties. Candidates for a senate seat in Laramie County, for example, run against everyone else in both parties throughout the county. Both parties nominate five candidates, for a total of 10. On election day voters throughout the county cast their ballots for their favorites. The five people who receive the most votes win the offices. In recent years, a sub-districting movement has received considerable attention. These people believe that it makes more sense to divide the highly populated counties into single districts. Instead of voters in Laramie County considering 10 candidates and electing five, the county might be divided, for example, into five legislative districts. Voters would then select one of two candidates to represent them in the senate. Proponents of sub-districting believe that having fewer candidates to select from would make voting easier and less intimidating for people, that it would make elections more issue-oriented (the idea is that voters can comprehend the arguments of two people better than those of 10), and that it increases legislator accountability to the voters. Proponents also criticize at-large apportionment because it tends not to represent minorities, whether ethnic, rural, or political. In other words, at-large elections make it easier for a large political party, social class, or municipality to win all the seats in a county. Opponents of sub-districting, often legislators themselves who would be "re-districted," say that at-large elections in the counties encourage the "best" people to run for office. They say that sub-districting means that two qualified people who happen to live in the same district could not both be elected as they can under the present at-large system. This, they say, would be a disservice to the people. Of course, the fact that several existing legislators would have to run against each other under sub-districting is on their minds, too. This is always a political problem that arises with reapportionment. Regardless of one's point of view on sub-districting, it is a timely issue and grows more likely as the state's population increases. Sub-districting is normal in states which have a large population.

Length of Sessions. The Wyoming legislature meets for scheduled sessions each year. During odd-numbered years (1981, 1983) the session convenes in early January[8] to consider a wide range of issues. Except for matters that are prohibited by the state constitution or federal law, legislators at these "general sessions" may pass whatever laws they think are necessary. These are often the most exciting sessions, because such a wide range of bills is proposed. During a general session, legislators may consider the state's death penalty, liquor laws, drug laws, motorcycle helmet laws, environmental protection, community aid, or any number of issues that catch the public's attention. But they cannot dilly-dally too much; general sessions must complete their work in 40 days (excluding Sundays).

Since 1974, Wyoming has also had a shorter "budget" session during even-numbered years.[9] These sessions last only 20 workdays and are generally limited to appropriating,

Table 4.2. Special Sessions of the Wyoming Legislature (Selected Examples)

Called By Governor:	When	Issue Considered:
Robert D. Carey	1920	Ratification of 19th Amendment to the U.S. Constitution granting women's suffrage throughout America.
Leslie A. Miller	1933	Depression era measures to economize state government and to take advantage of federal aid to the hard-hit.
Lester C. Hunt	1948	Additional funding for the University of Wyoming, which was flooded with veterans from World War II.
Clifford P. Hansen	1964	Reapportionment of state legislative districts (failed to do so).
Stanley K. Hathaway	1971	Ratification of the 26th Amendment to the U.S. Constitution granting 18 year olds the right to vote.
Ed Herschler	1978	Consider establishment of a college of medicine in conjunction with the University of Wyoming, and additional budgetary and financial matters.

or committing, a large portion of the state's funding for the following two years (called the "biennium"). This "state budget" tells the state agencies and state-supported programs how much money the state is giving them for the next two years. The budget also "outlines" what the money is to be spent for (in the form of various "line items" for personnel, supplies, travel, etc.). This, however, is a tremendous generality because it is relatively easy for an agency to shift appropriated money from one purpose to another. Budget sessions may consider bills that are not related to the state budget if two-thirds of either house passes a resolution agreeing to consider the matter.

Finally, the governor has the power to convene the legislature on "extraordinary occasions." As shown in Table 4.2, special sessions have been rather frequent since statehood. The most recent special session was called in 1978. It was necessary to protect the state's financial reputation after the Wyoming Supreme Court ruled that certain bonds that the state was selling were unconstitutional.

Legislative Duties and Responsibilities

As shown in Table 4.3, the Wyoming legislature is charged with a number of specific and implied powers and duties; some originate

Table 4.3. Major Duties and Responsibilities of the Wyoming Legislature

Responsibility	What It Means	Jurisdiction or Authority Comes From
1. Lawmaking	Authority to pass laws to the public's benefit.	Implied in state sovereignty; 10th Amendment to U.S. Constitution; Art. 3, Sec. 21 Wyoming State Constitution (W.S.C.)
2. Investigation and oversight	Authority to investigate or study potential legislation; authority to review the executive branch to make certain they are within their jurisdiction and the law.	Implied from the above as necessary to provide for public health, morals, safety and welfare.
3. Structure state courts	Authority to draw-up boundaries of district courts and to create subordinate or local courts.	Art. 5, Sections 1, 19, and 20 W.S.C.
4. Impeachment	Authority to try and remove executive and judicial officials.	Art. 3, Secs. 17 and 18 W.S.C.
5. Regulate elections	Authority to guard against election abuses, provide for voter registration, determine certain courts to hear election disputes, schedule special elections, etc.	Art. 6, Secs. 11, 12, 13, 14, 17, 18, and 22 W.S.C.
6. Override veto	Authority to pass bills over the governor's veto, with 2/3's vote of both houses.	Art. 4, Sec. 8 W.S.C.
7. Senate confirmation	Senate confirms various of the governor's appointments to boards and commissions.	Various state statutes.
8. Appropriation of funds	Authority to spend state money.	Art. 3, Secs. 33, 34, and 35 W.S.C.
9. Amend state constitution	Authority to *propose* changes in the Wyoming Constitution.	Art. 20, Secs. 1, 2, 3, and W.S.C.
10. Ratify amendments to U.S. Constitution	Authority to approve or disapprove proposed changes in U.S. Constitution.	Article, 5, U.S. Constitution.

in the state constitution, others originate elsewhere. One of the most important legislative powers, and certainly the most obvious, is the authority to pass or make laws. While this power is not stated literally in the state constitution (not even in Article 2 which covers the separation of powers), it is implied and indirectly stated time and again. Indeed, passing laws is the very definition of the terms "legislate" and "legislature."

In particular, authority to make laws comes from the "police" power, which is the government's general "authority to promote and safeguard the health, morals, safety, and welfare of the people."[10] Because the U.S. Constitution does not delegate the police power to the national government, it is reserved to the states.[11] In other words, when powers are not given to the federal government (nor prohibited to the states) by the U.S. Constitution, they are kept by the state governments. This is true even though the federal government's powers have been expanded in numerous ways. From there on, it is only a matter of logic. Since the state has the police power, laws are necessary to "protect" the people. Laws then, are initiated in the legislature.

In order to make laws, the legislature has the power to investigate or study those matters that are within its jurisdiction. Does this mean that the state legislature can legally study anything? Would legislators be within their rights to open an investigation of your bank account? Clearly not. If you were involved in a crime, the courts might order their own investigation of your account, but it would not be done by the legislature. After all, your bank account has nothing to do with any of the things the state constitution tells the legislature it can do. To put it simply, the legislature has no jurisdiction (or authority) to do such things.[12]

Also, if the legislature is to create state programs to protect the public, its members must also have the authority to review what government agencies are doing. This is the legislative power of "oversight." Thus, the legislature can review or oversee what state agencies are doing, but it cannot order their daily affairs (other than through the passage of statutes). To do so would violate the separation of powers which is preserved in Article 2 of the state constitution, because state agencies are in the executive branch of government. So, the legislature can observe, watch, and recommend actions to state agencies; but legislators cannot order them to take specific actions without passing additional legislation.

Likewise, Wyoming lawmakers have authority to draw the boundaries of the district courts and to create whatever subordinate local courts, such as justice of the peace courts, they think are necessary. While the state constitution created the supreme court as an "equal" of the legislature, it left it to the legislature to determine whether there would be three, four, or five justices on the high bench (supreme court).[13]

The legislature has the power of impeachment. Impeachment is the process of removing certain officials from office. As with impeachment in the federal government, the process in Wyoming has two broad steps. First, the house of representatives must determine that an impeachment is justified by vote of a majority (one more than half) of *all* the members of the house. At present, it would require a vote of 32 representatives to impeach an official. Contrary to what most people believe, passing a resolution of impeachment is not a conviction for misbehavior in office. Rather, impeachment in the house simply means that a majority of its members believe it likely that a crime or inappropriate behavior has occurred. Put differently, the house has *indicted* the public official, saying that he should stand trial before the senate to determine his guilt or innocence. The senate would then hear the trial and act as the jury. A vote of two-thirds of *all* the senators (20 out of 30) would be required to convict an "indicted" official. This trial is the second broad step in the impeachment process. Thus, when the house impeaches a public official, it is charging him with wrongdoing; the senate determines whether the charge is accurate. If the senate finds that the charge is correct, we would say that the official has been "impeached" and "convicted." He would forfeit his office, be unable to ever hold another public office of "honor, trust or profit,"[14] and could then be prosecuted in the state courts for the offense. Notice, impeachment and conviction do not send the defendant to prison nor lay a fine; these things may be imposed in a subsequent trial before the state (or possibly federal) courts.

Two other impeachment questions are answered by the constitution. First, "the governor and other state and judicial officers except justices of the peace" are subject to impeachment. This means that the process covers the governor, top level state officials, and judicial employees such as judges (except justices of the peace.)

The other question that is answered in the constitution is the grounds for impeachment. In other words, what can a governor or judge be impeached for? The answer is that they are "liable to impeachment for high crimes and misdemeanors, or malfeasance in office. . . ." A high crime is a felony, the most serious of offenses. Misdemeanors are less serious crimes and involve fines and/or jail terms in county jail. Malfeasance means "wrongdoing." When the wrongdoing is in office, a public official may be impeached.

There is a significant difference between the state and national impeachment processes. While founding fathers such as Alexander Hamilton[15] talked and wrote about impeachment for malfeasance, misfeasance (doing a job inappropriately), and nonfeasance (not doing a job), no such terms were or are included in the U.S. Constitution. While it is not known for certain, because there is no conclusive precedent or court ruling, the argument that presidents may be impeached for betraying the public trust is strong.[16] In Wyoming there is little confusion on this point; officials may be impeached for crimes or violation of the public trust.[17] While impeachment is important because of its potential to check abuses, no Wyoming official has ever been impeached.

The legislature has a variety of powers over elections. In Wyoming, as elsewhere, the electorate must register in order to vote. People may register at the polls on the day of a primary election or at places designated by the county clerk such as a city hall.[18] This is because the state constitution instructs the lawmakers to provide for voter registration. Also, they are to "secure the purity of elections," establish court procedures for election appeals, and determine certain physical aspects of voting, the ballot, and ballot security.

The legislature may override a veto by the governor. After bills have passed both the house and senate, they are sent to the governor for his signature. The signature is ordinarily the last step in the passage of legislation. However, if the governor objects to a bill (or individual parts of a bill to spend money), he may say "no" to the legislature. This is a "veto" and defeats the bill unless two-thirds of the elected senators and representatives vote to "override" the governor's veto. In the event of an override, the bill becomes a law without the governor's signature. Notice, in Wyoming the governor's veto (even if he objects to only a small part of a bill) "kills" the entire bill. The only exception to this is his line-item veto for appropriations bills, meaning that the governor may veto individual portions of bills to spend state funds. With the exception of Governor Herschler, who has used the veto extensively, vetoes have been used sparingly in Wyoming. Governor Hathaway, for instance, cast only two vetoes in eight years as governor.[19]

As will be seen in Chapter 5, Wyoming's governor appoints numerous people to positions on some 120 state boards, agencies, and commissions. Many of the board members must be confirmed by the state senate. The governor indicates who he wants to appoint to certain boards or commissions and the state senate either agrees or rejects the nominee. If the nominee is rejected, the governor must nominate someone else. Again, not all board and commission members have to be confirmed in the senate. Notice, too, that the house of representatives does not participate in confirmations.

The legislature must also give permission before state money is spent. Permission is given in the form of "appropriations" bills. This does not mean that the legislature must approve every single state purchase. Rather, lawmakers approve broader aspects of spending, while leaving many of the specifics to the agencies themselves. Thus, the legislature gives agencies an appropriation for supplies, but whether an agency buys pens or pencils is essentially left to the agency.

The legislature is likewise involved in attempts to amend the Wyoming or U.S. Constitutions. There are two major phases in amending either constitution. First, amendments must be "proposed" or suggested by the appropriate body. Then they must be "ratified" or accepted by another body. The state legislature proposes amendments to the Wyoming Constitution. These proposals require a two-thirds vote in both the house and senate (two-thirds of the total membership in each chamber). Amendments to the state constitution are ratified by the voters at the next

election. Each proposed amendment is offered as a "yes" or "no" vote; ratification requires a majority of those voting in that election. Notice, ratification requires a majority of the people voting in the election rather than just a majority of those voting on any particular amendment.

Amendments to the U.S. Constitution are proposed by a two-thirds vote of each house of Congress.[20] Normally, amendments are then sent to the states for ratification, which requires a positive vote from three-fourths of the 50 states. The Wyoming legislature, then, is one of 50 states to consider ratification. A proposed amendment must pass each house of the state legislature by a majority vote.[21]

Lawmakers are, of course, given a range of other powers. Generally, other legislative powers are minor. Legislators may, for example, determine whether their members were properly selected; they may hire the employees the legislature needs; they are to keep journals of their proceedings, etc.[22] Still, the foregoing powers are the major legislative powers. These responsibilities take the bulk of the legislature's time and energies.

Finally, notice how many of these powers and duties are "checks" upon the other branches of government. Just as the executive branch (particularly the governor) has several "partial controls" on the legislature (e.g. veto), the lawmakers have investigatory, oversight, impeachment, veto override, confirmation, appropriation, and amending powers. And, again, just as the courts have certain ways to limit the legislature (e.g. interpreting legislation), the lawmakers have structural, impeachment, appropriation, and amending authority over the courts. The existence of these checks and balances between the three "separate" branches of government is one of the major and most unique features of American government.

Legislative Limitations

Just as there are many things that the legislature may do, there are many things that it may not do. Table 4.4 outlines several of these limitations. The most significant limitation is probably the first one, the prohibition against violating federal law. Because the sixth article of the U.S. Constitution says that "the laws of the United States . . . shall be the supreme law of the land. . . ," no state law may conflict with federal law. This means that as long as the federal law is constitutional (passed in accordance with the proper jurisdiction or authority of the federal government, as granted within the U.S. Constitution), the states must comply with it.

Table 4.4. Examples of Legislative Limitations

Limitation	What It Means	Where Limitation Comes From
1. Federal law	May not violate federal law.	Federal constitution, statutes, administratives rules.
2. Bribery	May not sell a vote or accept anything of value in exchange for his vote.	Article 3, Sections 42-44, Wyoming State Constitution (W.S.C.).
3. Conflict of interest	May not vote on, and must disclose, any legislation he has a personal or private interest in.	Article 3, Sections 46 and 31 W.S.C.
4. Length of sessions	May meet for no more than 60 working days every two years, nor more than 40 working days in any one session. Means odd year general sessions last 40 days; even year budget sessions last 20 days. Limitation doesn't include special sessions.	Article 3, Section 6 W.S.C.
5. Disqualified for other office	Legislators may not hold civil offices, such as executive branch administrative positions.	Article 3, Section 8 W.S.C.
6. Salary	May not vote to increase salaries for the session they are in.	Article 3, Sections 6 and 9 W.S.C.
7. Introduction of bills	By the state constitution, no regular appropriation bill may be introduced within 5 days of the close of the session except by unanimous consent of the chamber. By legislative rule no bill, other than general appropriations, may be introduced after the 18th day of a session except by unanimous consent of the chamber.	Article 3, Section 22 W.S.C.; House Rule 8-2; Senate Rule 9-2.
8. Referral to/from committee	All bills must be referred to a committee, reported back by the committee to the floor, and printed for the members to look at.	Article 3, Section 23 W.S.C.
9. One subject per bill	Each bill may have only one subject, appropriation and statute codification bills excepted.	Article 3, Section 24, W.S.C.
10. Special and local laws	May not pass bills to the advantage of one party, city, group of people, etc. only, when general legislation will do.	Article 3, Section 27 W.S.C.

Table 4.4—*Continued*

Limitation	What It Means	Where Limitation Comes From
11. Bidding contracts	Government purchases of certain types are to go to the lowest responsible bidder; no government may house personal interest in the contract.	Article 3, Section 31 W.S.C.
12. Certain state aid prohibited	May not contribute state money to concerns (e.g., charities, etc.) not under state control.	Article 3, Section 36 W.S.C.
13. Municipal government	May not interfere with municipal improvements, money, etc., or to perform municipal functions.	Article 3, Section 37 W.S.C.
14. Aid to railroads	May not make loans for construction of railroads or absorb debt of construction of railroads.	Article 3, Section 39 W.S.C.
15. Municipal debts	Municipal debts shall not be released by the state	Article 3, Section 40 W.S.C.

In most instances, the above "limitations" are qualified, explained or expanded by statutes and precedents.

Like other states, Wyoming is bound by three direct types of federal law. First, Wyoming must comply with the U.S. Constitution. The First Amendment to the Constitution, for example, guarantees relative freedom of speech, press, religion, petition, and assembly. Within reason, then, the state legislature may not interfere with free worship. That guarantee is not absolute, because not all religious activities are protected by the U.S. Constitution. Rather, those activities that the U.S. Supreme Court says are integral to the free expression of religious beliefs, and which do not violate other constitutional principles are protected and are not to be interfered with. So, while the Wyoming legislature may not outlaw the Methodist Church or Buddhist religion, it may outlaw churches from exposing religious converts to poisonous snakes, because other portions of the U.S. Constitution direct government to protect public health, well-being and order (the police power). If this seems terribly complicated, just remember that the principle of religious freedom, like nearly all others in the federal and state constitutions, is a general theme that the courts must interpret.

Second, the legislature may not violate federal statutes.[23] The Congress and President of the United States, for example, decided in 1964, 1972, and other times since, that employers may not discriminate in hiring, promotion, or conditions of employment based on race, color, religion, sex, or national origin.[24] Accordingly, the Wyoming legislature does not have legal authority to establish laws which allow businesses that are engaged in interstate commerce to refuse to hire qualified minorities or women. Yes, these things may happen in the "real world," but they are violations of the law. The woman or Chicano who is not hired or promoted or who is always given the "dirtiest" job could bring suit in court against the offending employer.

Third, the state is not to violate administrative (bureaucratic) rulings by federal departments and agencies. Bureaucrats, as you know, cannot make laws, but they can make *rules* within their areas that have the impact of law. The rules are not law, but they have the same effect. The Congress of the United States, for example, cannot set speed limits on highways in the states. The U.S. Constitution does not give them that authority. But, Congress has constitutional authority to provide for the public in numerous other ways. So, Congress created a national Department of Transportation to administer federal transportation programs. The programs involve federal money. When federal officials initially decided they wanted speed limits reduced to 55 mph, they made it a policy that states would lose their money from the national transportation department unless they complied with the new rule. Thus, there is no national speed limit law, but states set their limits at 55 just the same. Although Congress subsequently passed legislation requiring that states either enforce a 55 mph limit or forfeit federal highway funds, the same policy was already in effect due to executive action. In other words, Congress had the power to either rescind or reinforce the policy through legislation, but until Congress acted (three years for the 55 mph speed limit) the executive branch policy had the effect of law.

Technically, then, the Wyoming legislature does not have to comply with the administrative "quasi-law." But realistically, it does. In fact, the 1979 Wyoming legislature thought about raising the speed limit and telling the bureaucrats to "mind their own business." But when the legislators realized that the state would lose $50 to $60 million per year in federal funds, they changed their minds. We still drive 55. Clearly, federal law is a major limitation on the Wyoming legislature.

Three patterns are found in the other limitations in Table 4.4. One of these themes is personal legislator conduct. They are not to sell their votes or participate in bribery and are not to vote on matters that affect them personally. As the *Casper Star-Tribune*

pointed out in 1979, after a few legislators with liquor interests voted on liquor laws affecting those interests, conflict of interest votes do take place. Likewise, legislators are disqualified from holding administrative jobs with the State of Wyoming. This is to protect the separation of powers concept; the idea is that no one should be employed in the executive and legislative branches at the same time. And legislator behavior is checked by provisions which prohibit them from raising their own salaries. They may raise the benefits for future legislative sessions, but not their own.

Several of the other limitations have to do with procedures in the lawmaking process. Sessions are limited to 40 (general session) and 20 (budget session) working days; bills cannot be introduced at the end of a session unless by unanimous vote in the house where the proposal is made; bills must be sent to committee and reported back out; other than for spending or changing the "structure" or "system" of statutes, each bill may deal with only one subject. While the requirement that all bills be reported out of committee does not always work in practice (e.g., bills can be delayed in committee so long that there is not enough time to consider them on the floor of the house or senate), it does tend to get legislation to the floor for debate. In this respect, Wyoming's lawmaking process is different from that of the federal government. In Congress, it is normal for bills to be defeated in committee. Also, one of the limitations on the state legislature requires that bills deal with one subject only. This is an attempt to keep legislators from adding irrelevant amendments to bills that are sure to pass, sometimes called "riders." Legislators elsewhere (such as the U.S. Senate) have voted for agricultural bills only to find that clauses were added to a bill which legalizes something entirely unrelated to the bill as a whole. This kind of "trickery" generally does not take place in Wyoming.

Other limitations in Table 4.4 deal with state spending. This third area of limitations requires that state contracts for some purchases and services be given to the lowest bidder. This is an attempt to keep government officials from raising the cost of government contracts and giving them to friends. This corrupt practice has been rather common in some other states. In fact, this is what Spiro Agnew allegedly engaged in as governor of Maryland. It led to his resigning as vice president when it was discovered. Other spending limitations prohibit state aid to organizations that are not state controlled, assistance to pay off railroad debts, interference with cities and towns, or releasing a city or town from its debt.

Finally, keep in mind that these are merely examples of the limitations on the legislature. There are many others. Also, remember that these limitations are usually defined, and even expanded, by legislative statutes. The constitution ordinarily establishes principles and themes. The legislature usually fills in many of the specific provisions and guidelines.

A Citizen Legislature

You have already read that Wyoming has a "citizen legislature." But what does that mean and is it true?

Quite simply, it means that Wyoming's legislature is designed to be run by people who understand the public and their desires. If it is truly a citizen legislature, the lawmakers themselves must share those desires. The legislators are citizens who give up part of their time to improve their communities, counties, or state. They make their contribution in Cheyenne and then return home. Unlike professional politicians who legislate and campaign year-round, these citizen legislators do not have full-time political careers, do not receive large financial rewards, and spend only a few weeks each year passing laws. While politicians everywhere might scoff at this description, saying that the motivation of nearly all legislators is a blend of public representation and personal ego/power gratification, people who pride themselves on Wyoming's notion of citizen representation say there are differences in the degree to which this is true. On balance, they say, the majority of Wyoming legislators are more in touch with, and attuned to, "citizen duty" than ego gratifica-

tion. Remember, this concept is idealistic, but it has long been one of the most characteristic aspects of Wyoming politics.

Determining whether or not this "citizen legislature" concept actually exists in Wyoming is difficult. The conclusion in these pages is that the notion is generally an accurate description of this state's legislature. However, while the concept is correct, its romanticism and idealism should be qualified.

To begin with, the legislature fits the concept in a number of important ways. It meets for a short period—40 working days during odd-numbered years and 20 working days during even-numbered years. This means that there are no truly professional politicians in the body. It also means that they must have other interests to which they devote their time, ordinarily another career. These factors emphasize the part-time aspects of the legislature and cause legislators to focus part of their energies on nonpolitical matters. The modest financial benefits that they receive support this; to feed their families and pay their bills, legislators need other interests. Also, the nominal (adequate, but not extravagant) money that they get means that some legislators actually lose money by taking time off from their jobs to go to the legislature. This does not apply to all of them, nor even most, but it does apply to some of them. And it implies that they are particularly oriented toward public service.

This is certainly not to ignore the personal motivations that legislators have. Some like the prestige that being in the legislature gives them, others get a kick out of seeing their name in newspapers. Several have the time on their hands, like retired people and farmers (who can attend because the sessions meet in the winter when they can be away from work). Others get free advertising for their law firms, realty companies, or insurance offices. And

some use the legislature as a stepping-stone to higher office. Governor Herschler, Senator Wallop, and Senator Simpson all served in the state legislature, for example. In fact, some legislators believe that half of their colleagues are running for higher office. Clearly, legislative service is not just a matter of citizen duty, great debates, and an occasional parade. So the first point to be drawn is that while Wyoming fits the "citizen legislature" test in several ways (e.g., part-time service, nonpolitical careers, home town contacts and residences), there are personal reasons for service which temper or qualify the more noble reasons.

Another question that arises in assessing the "citizen legislature" is to what extent the lawmakers are "typical" of their constituencies. After all, the notion of a citizen legislature implies that if the lawmakers share the public's concerns, they probably have the same general backgrounds. So in terms of their backgrounds, how much do Wyoming legislators have in common with the people they represent?

In several important ways, there is less in common than might be assumed. Table 4.5, for example, shows the occupational categories of state legislators since 1965. As indicated, the legislators are heavily from agriculture, business, and the professions. In general, recent legislatures have had about a quarter of their members from each of these three occupations. This, of course, is a generality. The figure changes every two years and several lawmakers earn livings in multiple fields—some wear more than just one hat. The fact that the figures change so often makes the patterns or trends in the data somewhat fickle. Based on figures through 1973, for instance, one author concludes that agriculture's representation has declined.[25] This is not the case through the 1979–80 legislature. The 1977

Table 4.5. Occupations of Wyoming Legislators from 1965 to 1979 (In Percent)*

	1965	1967	1969	1971	1973	1975	1977	1979
				House				
Agriculture	26.2	23.0	21.3	24.6	22.6	21.0	27.4	33.9
Business	27.9	32.9	34.5	24.6	32.3	40.3	29.0	25.8
Professional								
Lawyers	19.7	19.7	18.0	9.8	17.7	11.3	12.9	9.7
Other Professional	19.7	16.4	19.7	24.6	19.4	17.7	24.2	25.8
Total Professional	39.4	36.0	37.7	34.4	37.1	29.0	37.1	35.5
Other Occupations	6.5	8.1	6.5	16.4	8.0	9.7	6.5	4.8
Total	100.0	100.0	100.0	100.0	100.0	100.0	100.0	100.0
	N=61	N=61	N=61	N=61	N=61	N=62	N=62	N=62
	1965	1967	1969	1971	1973	1975	1977	1979
				Senate				
Agriculture	40.0	23.3	23.3	26.7	26.7	23.3	23.3	26.7
Business	28.0	40.0	50.0	36.7	43.3	40.0	46.7	40.0
Professional								
Lawyers	8.0	23.3	20.0	23.3	20.0	13.3	10.0	13.3
Other Professional	20.0	13.4	6.7	13.3	6.7	13.3	6.7	6.7
Total Professional	28.0	36.7	26.7	36.6	26.7	26.7	16.7	20.0
Other Occupations	4.0	0.0	0.0	0.0	3.3	10.0	13.3	13.3
Total	100.0	100.0	100.0	100.0	100.0	100.0	100.0	100.0
	N=25	N=30	N=30	N=30	N=30	N=30	N=30	N=30

*All categories except Business and Other Occupations are U.S. Census categories.

and 1979 elections have actually increased farmer/rancher representation in the house to nearly 34 percent; likewise, agriculture's representation in the senate has been rather constant at between 23 and 26 percent since 1967. Other authors have talked about the large influence of lawyers.[26] True, lawyers are "overrepresented" in the legislature to the extent that there are more there than in the general public, but their numbers have not increased in recent years. Of course, it is natural that lawyers are involved in politics; because they work with law, it is understandable that many would involve themselves in its preparation. Law is also an excellent profession for aspiring politicians, it is a way to gain free publicity and prominence, and lawyers are able to get

time off work without losing money since partners can keep the business going. But the profession that has increased lately in the house of representatives is education (see "other professionals"). While there have nearly always been educators in the legislature, their share of the "other professionals" has increased in recent years. During 1979–80, 16 of the 62 house legislators were active or retired teachers or school administrators. This probably reflects both the increased teacher involvement in politics that the nation witnessed during the 1970s, and added aggressiveness of school administrators in representing school interests where much of the money is controlled. Whether these are new trends which will be long-lasting factors in Wyoming politics remains to be seen.

Lawyers and professionals are not the only overrepresented occupations in the Wyoming legislature. The 1970 census showed that 14.5 percent of the state's population are in professional occupations (with less the one percent lawyers), with 8.6 percent in agriculture, and 16 percent of Wyoming's population in combined business jobs. Compared with the percentages in Table 4.5, the overrepresentation is striking.

Wyoming legislators are also better educated than the people they represent. According to the 1970 census, almost 12 percent of Wyoming residents who are over 25 years old have college degrees. Combining the "college degree" responses with "post graduate" and "professional" degree responses (because a college degree is required before doing graduate and professional work) in Table 4.6 means that 46.7 percent of the senators and 70.9 percent of the representatives to the 1979–80 sessions had degrees. And another quarter of each house had at least attended college. To an extent, of course, these figures reflect their occupations. Most professionals

and businessmen have college educations. Even so, the legislative education levels are very high, much higher than the state's population as a whole.

As with politicians everywhere, Wyoming legislators are joiners. They often join the popular community service, religious, social, fraternal, professional and veteran groups. Some of the widest membership is in local chambers of commerce, Jaycees, American Legion, Wyoming Bar Association, Wyoming Stockgrowers, and the Farm Bureau. Legislators average between four and five memberships in clubs and organizations, not counting their religious affiliations.[27] The fact that legislators are joiners is also understandable. It helps to know a lot of people in order to get elected. Joining groups helps legislators meet people. While the figures are unavailable, it is probably safe to conclude that the legislators join far more of these organizations than their constituents.

Legislators' religious preferences are typical of the state's population. In an earlier study of the religious preferences and affiliations of the state's population, 60 percent said

Table 4.6. Educational Attainment of Wyoming Legislators from 1975 to 1979 (In Percent)

	House			Senate		
	1975	1977	1979	1975	1977	1979
High School	11.3	6.5	3.2	20.0	20.0	23.3
Some College	19.4	12.9	22.6	26.7	36.7	26.7
College Degree	32.3	32.3	40.3	23.3	26.7	26.7
Post Graduate Degree	14.5	21.0	14.5	6.7	3.3	3.3
Professional Degree	19.4	24.2	16.1	20.0	13.3	16.7
Trade or Business School	3.2	3.2	3.2	3.3	0.0	3.3
No answer	0.0	0.0	0.0			
Total	100.1	100.1	99.9	100.0	100.0	100.0
	N=62	N=62	N=62	N=30	N=30	N=30

they were Protestant, 20 percent Catholic, with the remaining percentages scattered among smaller religions such as the Mormons. As Table 4.7 shows, the legislators are rather typical of the whole population. While there are differences over the years and between elections, they are seldom very great. The table shows that the Roman Catholic Church is the best represented church and that Protestant denominations are a clear majority.

So the answer to the question that was asked earlier is that in many respects Wyoming legislators are different than the people they represent. This is not true in all instances, but it is in many. Still, we should not overstate what this means. We live in a representative democracy. If voters select lawmakers who are better educated than the voters themselves, so much the better. And the more groups and organizations that legislators join, the more they increase their contacts with, and presumably knowledge of, the people they represent. And we should not assume that lawyers, Protestants, or Jaycees vote as a bloc on all or even most issues. Some group members do vote alike on some issues. It is not unusual at all that legislators who belong to the Wyoming Stockgrowers tend to vote alike on agricultural issues. But it would be incorrect to think of the legislature as a place where the Catholic bloc votes one way, the Jaycees another, etc. There are simply too many interests, philosophies, and people involved for that description to be accurate.[28]

Table 4.7. Religious Preference of Wyoming Legislators, 1973 to 1979–80 (In Percent)

	House				Senate			
	1973	**1975**	**1977**	**1979**	**1973**	**1975**	**1977**	**1979**
Catholic	22.6	22.6	22.6	24.2	26.6	30.0	30.0	33.3
Episcopal	16.0	22.6	19.4	14.5	16.7	16.7	10.0	3.3
Methodist	14.5	11.3	9.7	12.9	13.3	13.3	23.3	23.3
Congregational	3.2	6.5	6.5	4.8	6.7	6.7	3.3	3.3
Presbyterian	19.4	6.5	8.1	9.7	6.7	6.7	6.7	10.0
Lutheran	6.5	1.6	3.2	1.6	3.3	6.7	3.3	3.3
Baptist	0	1.6	4.8	6.5	6.7	6.7	6.7	3.3
Protestant	8.1	9.7	4.8	6.5	13.3	6.7	6.7	3.3
(no specific denomination mentioned)								
Mormon	3.2	4.8	6.5	6.5	6.7	6.7	6.7	6.7
Unitarian	0	0	1.6	0	0	0	0	3.3
Quaker	0	1.6	1.6	1.6	0	0	0	0
Christian Science	0	0	0	1.6	0	0	0	0
No Answer	6.5	11.3	11.3	9.7	0	0	3.3	6.7
Total	100.0	100.1	100.1	100.1	100.0	100.2	100.0	99.8
	N=62	N=62	N=62	N=62	N=30	N=30	N=30	N=30

Overall, Wyoming lawmakers meet the test of a citizen legislature. The legislature was designed to do so and most of the factors which we have discussed serve to preserve that characteristic of the state. And as long as Wyoming remains a sparsely populated state, this is likely a characteristic which Wyoming politicians will continue to prize.[29]

Structure of the Legislature

Any time that a large group of people get together to work, play, pray, travel, or almost anything else that comes to mind, they organize themselves. This, of course, is true of the Wyoming legislature. The primary structural characteristic of the legislature is its *fragmentation*. The legislature is fragmented or divided in any number of ways. It is divided into political parties, by philosophies, regions, into two houses, and divided further into committees and leadership positions. The discussion which follows is an overview of the major structural groupings in the Wyoming legislature.

Committees. Both the house and senate are divided into a series of committees which deal with specific legislative concerns such as labor, education or tourism. The various committees are very important in the legislative process because bills are sent to them for study and recommendation. Accordingly, committees have great powers over the bills assigned to them. Committee recommendations for passage or defeat of bills, for example, are often accepted when it comes time for a vote of the full legislature on the floor of the house or senate. Notice, too, the Wyoming Constitution says, "No bill shall be considered or become a law unless referred to a committee, returned therefrom and printed for the use of the members" (Article 3, Section 23). This means that

a bill cannot become law in the state without first being considered in committee. But being voted out of committee is no guarantee that a bill will be passed into law. For reasons of procedure and political strategy (e.g., a bill that is popular back home, but which an influential legislator opposes), bills are sometimes released by committees at the last minute, when it is too late to get them through all of the other hurdles before passage. During the 1979 session, for example, the senate Committee on Education, Health and Welfare reported between 25 and 30 bills on the last day, far too late for the bills to be considered on the floor, by the full senate membership.[30] This effectively allows committees to kill bills they oppose while still complying with the state law. Clearly, committees are the site of much of the most important legislative work.[31]

Committee Functions. Can every legislator be an expert on all the issues that will be introduced in any given session? Is it likely that he can talk intelligently about reforming state welfare programs one minute, changes in tax law the next, complicated environmental standards a little later, and then shift to specific questions about the use of water? Generally not. Recognizing that each legislator cannot possibly know everything that will come before the legislature, the house and senate divide themselves into a series of committees. Each committee has the responsibility to specialize in a particular area of legislative business. It is as though the legislature is saying that its members cannot all be experts on everything, but if each legislator narrows his sights a little and concentrates his studies and work in a few specific areas, they can each become knowledgeable about one or two things. And if all 62 representatives do this, the house of representatives will have enough knowledgeable legislators that they will be able to deal with almost anything that comes up.

So the house and senate each break up into the 12 standing or permanent committees shown in Table 4.8. Thus, when a bill which deals with management of wild animals that live on state lands is introduced in either the house or senate, it is referred to the Travel, Recreation, and Wildlife Committee. The

Table 4.8. Standing Committees in the Wyoming Legislature

House of Representatives	Senate
1. Judiciary	1. Judiciary
2. Appropriations	2. Appropriations
3. Revenue	3. Revenue
4. Education	4. Education, Health and Welfare
5. Agriculture, Public Lands and Water Resources	5. Agriculture, Public Lands and Water Resources
6. Travel, Recreation and Wildlife	6. Travel, Recreation and Wildlife
7. Corporations, Elections and Political Subdivisions	7. Corporations, Elections, and Political Subdivisions
8. Transportation and Highways	8. Transportation and Highways
9. Mines, Minerals and Industrial Development	9. Mines, Minerals and Industrial Development
10. Labor, Health and Social Services	10. Labor and Federal Relations
11. Journal	11. Journal
12. Rules and Procedure	12. Rules and Procedure
—Usually 9 representatives per committee	—Usually 5 senators per committee
—Each legislator is normally on 1 or 2 standing committees, 3 in rare instances.	—Each legislator is normally on 1 or 2 standing committees, 3 in rare instances.

committee members have the responsibility to develop expertise in travel, recreation, and wildlife matters. If they are hard-working legislators, they will become quite competent in these matters. In fact, it is common in Wyoming to appoint people to committees that deal with topics that they knew a great deal about before serving in the legislature. While common in this state, it is not always possible to make committee assignments on the basis of previous experience. The point here is that dividing into committees enables the house and senate to have a few "experts" who are able to study and make recommendations on the bills that deal with their area. Once again, this is not to create a false impression that all legislators take their specialization and homework role seriously, because many do not. In fact, in the survey of Wyoming lobbyists which was mentioned in the previous chapter, interest group representatives were very critical that some committee members do not do their homework. Even so, enough members do fulfill this responsibility that it is one of the major purposes and functions of committees.

The second broad function of committees is to oversee the executive branch. The house and senate Travel, Recreation, and Wildlife Committee members, for example, are supposed to pay attention to what the executive branch travel, recreation, and wildlife administrators are doing. This does not mean that the legislative committees have "control" over the daily activities of their executive branch counterparts—they do not. It simply means, for example, that when the administrator for the Industrial Siting Council (an executive branch agency) has trouble interpreting an aspect of the Council's authority because the statute is not clear on the point, and the Council interprets the rule one way or another, certain legislators had better be paying attention in case new or clarifying legislation has to be written. In this instance, legislators on the house Mines, Minerals and Industrial Development Committee and Labor, Health and Social Services Committee, in addition to senate committees on Mines, Minerals and Industrial Development plus Education, Health and Welfare, might all be paying close attention to the policy. In short, the executive branch agency is "watched" or overseen by the legislative committee or committees which have expertise and jurisdiction in the particular area.

Oversight does not receive as much committee attention as one might think, however. This is true for a variety of reasons. One of the most important reasons is that Wyoming has a part-time, citizen legislature. Meeting only a few days a year, being scattered throughout the state, and having other career interests, combine to decrease the energy that legislators can devote to oversight. Another reason that legislators often downplay oversight is that it is the kind of work that seldom helps their political careers. In some parts of the state it might be politically wise to attack certain "meddling" policies of this or that bureaucratic agency, but, overall, oversight is more a matter of quietly doing one's homework than something that gets splashy headlines. Third, legislators often downplay their oversight roles out of friendship with, and faith in, the administrators. If the legislators and administrators share similar philosophies, concerns, and political views, they may work together so much that strong bonds of friendship and trust develop between them. In that case, oversight is downplayed as unnecessary meddling. Finally, some legislators downplay their oversight function because they do not feel qualified to question or keep tabs on the administrators. After all, the legislators are

only part-time employees; the bureaucrats are full-time employees, often with lengthy experience and education in their subject. Legislators who believe that the bureaucrats know more than they do will usually leave the bureaucrats alone. So while oversight is an important committee function, it would generally be wrong to picture committee members at home on a Saturday night reading an agency's annual report.[32]

The third major purpose or function of legislative committees is somewhat philosophical. Committees are "contact points" for the public at large and their lobbyists. In other words, one of the purposes of committees is to help members of the public know who they can approach in the legislature when they want to express their opinions. After all, a teacher who is concerned about a particular education matter might not be willing, or able, to express his opinion to 92 legislators. But a teacher who is knowledgeable of the legislative process will know how to most effectively approach the lawmakers. He would phone, telegram, write or see a member or members of the house Education Committee and senate Education, Health and Welfare Committee. Instead of having to contact all 92 legislators, the committee system lets the teacher, or education lobbyists, concentrate their lobbying efforts on a few people who usually have the greatest influence on the particular issues. This is no small or unimportant function. Anything that makes citizen contact more likely or orderly is of benefit to the legislative process.[33]

Assignment to Committee. Most committees in the house of representatives have nine members; senate committees usually have five members. Each party appoints its own members to the various committees. The leaders of the two parties agree among themselves on how many people each party will appoint to the committees before the beginning of a session. Actually, they divide the spots on the basis of each party's numerical strength after an election. That way, the majority party is in the majority on each committee. Next, the parties meet (called a party caucus) by chamber—senate Republicans meet as a group, house Democrats meet alone, etc. At those party caucuses, the legislators list, in order, the two or three committees that they would like to serve on. The lists are then reviewed by committees of party leaders who make the committee assignments for their party and chamber. Senate Republicans, for example, have a Committee on Committees which is made up of three of the party's senate leaders; the Committee on Committees makes the actual assignments for the party. Senators who are already on a committee are usually reassigned to the committee almost automatically, if they want reassignment. Because the number of vacancies on any committee is limited, not all legislators receive their first preferences. The selection committee tries to give each legislator one of his top two or three preferences. Thus, senate Republicans are appointed to the standing senate committees by senate Republican leaders, house Democrats by Democratic leaders in the house, etc.

While this may seem complicated, it really is not. Legislators caucus with the people in their party who are in the same chamber; they list the committee assignments they would like; the decisions are made by the party leaders, who have agreed among themselves on the number of members that each party gets on each committee.[34]

Committee Chairmen. When the party leaders on the selection committees make their committee assignments, they also pick a chairman for each committee. The leaders pick chairmen who are members of the majority party with long service in the chamber. While this is not the technical definition of the term, committee chairmen in Wyoming are chosen by a form of "seniority."

Committee chairmen are influential legislators. Chairmen have several powers, including: arranging and scheduling committee meetings (ordinarily this is done with the full committee's advice), determining the order that bills will be considered by the committee, appointing subcommittees, arranging for witnesses to testify before the committee, explaining bills during floor debate, planning strategy for passage of major bills during debate on the floor of the chamber, and often representing their chambers on house and senate conference committees (which iron out differences when the house and senate pass the same bill but in different forms).

These powers mean that chairmen are influential, but they are seldom bosses. Most chairmen try to work with the committee members. They do this because they realize that many legislators will balk at a pushy chairman. So the chairmen who ask for advice on matters, who consult with committee members before making major decisions, and who view the other members as partners, will ordinarily be more influential than chairmen who take a hard line. As is generally true of politics at all levels, effective committee leaders rely upon compromise and consultation.

Joint Interim Committees. To this point the discussion has dealt solely with permanent, or standing, committees, the ones that meet during legislative sessions. There is a second type of legislative committee—joint interim committees.

Joint interim committees meet between legislative sessions to study specific issues. They study topics, travel throughout the state to hold public hearings and take public testimony, make recommendations, and prepare legislation. Often the interim committees do all these things themselves, other times their members are organized into smaller subcommittees which focus their work on even more specific topics. The joint interim committee on education, for example, has subcommittees which specialize in higher education, the foundation program, and other educational issues. Subcommittee recommendations, results from studies, and public testimony are then taken to the full committee for their consideration and action.

These committees are ordinarily combinations of standing house and senate committees that have the same jurisdiction. The joint committee on education, for example, is composed of the house Education Committee and the senate Education, Health and Welfare Committee. Both are standing committees which meet during the *interim,* when the standing committees are not in session. These representatives of both chambers join together to form the joint interim committee to study education. This committee—and its subcommittees—are as active or inactive as the members and chairmen desire.

When "new" issues arise that need study, the legislature appoints another type of committee—temporary "select" committees. These committees include members from both the house and senate who are appointed on a broad basis to study the new issue.

Legislative Leadership. The presiding officer in the senate is called the President of the Senate. He is an experienced legislator and is elected by the majority party. The president is assisted by a senate vice president and majority floor leader.

The presiding officer in the other chamber is the Speaker of the House of Representatives. He, too, is chosen by the majority party; the speaker pro tem and majority floor leader assist the speaker.

The president and speaker have a variety of responsibilities. They preside during floor debate, make recommendations on committee assignments of the majority party members, decide to which committee bills are sent, interpret chamber rules, are house and senate spokesmen to the press, and authenticate acts of their chambers with their signatures. Perhaps their most important function is as designers of strategy. The legislation "game" requires careful planning and a bit of calculation. The house speaker and senate president are often at the center of planning strategy. Is the wording of a bill such that it can win enough votes to pass? What is the likelihood of passage in the other chamber? Is the support for a bill changing during floor debate? When would it be wise to report a bill out of committee? All of these are strategic questions that a house speaker or senate president might deal with. This makes sense, because they are both leaders of their chambers and the majority party. As party leaders they are sometimes in a position to influence the stand of the majority party, the form of some legislation, or legislative timing. This is not to leave the impression that a leader is able to order his party to vote as a block on a particular issue. As was mentioned earlier, Wyoming legislators do not vote along straight party lines as much as we might think, and certainly not as often as is the case in some other states. There are simply too many other considerations which determine voting in Wyoming. But party is one of those considerations and the leaders are in a position to have influence. Often the degree of influence varies with the leader's personal skills, such as his persuasiveness, intelligence, and how well he does his homework. Another important factor in the leadership's success is each leader's attitude or philosophy toward his job. Some prefer to be aggressive leaders; others view their role as one of coordination. Leaders who take the more passive role do not exercise a great deal of control or influence over their party because they do not think they should. The view that a leader takes toward his role is truly an important leadership factor.[35]

The senate vice president and house speaker pro tem assist their respective leaders. When the speaker is absent during normal business, for example, the speaker pro tem presides. They, too, are selected by the majority party in their chamber.

Each party also elects a floor leader for each chamber. The majority floor leader works with his party's two presiding officers to plan and coordinate strategy. In addition to consulting with the other leaders on party strategy, majority floor leaders make certain that party members are present for votes, try to hold coalitions together, advise the speaker or president on attitude and vote changes on the floor. In important ways, then, the house and senate majority floor leaders are extensions of the leadership to the floor. The minority party in both chambers elect minority leaders to direct the minority party strategy and coordinate its efforts.

Legislative Staff. It obviously takes a lot of people to make a legislature work. Laws must be researched and stored, papers must be filed, floors cleaned, the chambers secured, and on and on. The legislative staff helps with these and other tasks.[36]

Of the many support personnel, one office plays a particularly important role—the Legislative Service Office (LSO). The LSO was created in 1971 to be a full-time office of legislative researchers. As LSO people are quick to point out, they work for the legislators and will do any job-related task they are asked to do. Before a legislator can introduce a bill, for example, he needs to know what the law in that area is. A legislator would look pretty foolish introducing a motorcycle helmet law, for instance, since Wyoming already has such a law. So, the legislator who is considering the motorcycle helmet issue might contact the

LSO and instruct it to study the question and write an analysis of existing legislation. The legislator will use the LSO study to decide whether the law should be amended or changed, completely thrown out, or left alone. This research function is crucial to an effective legislature. In addition, notice that the office is non-partisan. In other words, the LSO is a staff of professional researchers who avoid partisan issues. It is supervised jointly by representatives of both parties (Legislature Management Council) to assure its neutrality and professionalism.

It might help to think of the Legislative Service Office as functioning or researching in three particular areas. First, much of its time is spent doing work for the various legislative committees. As has already been seen, committees do much of the analysis on complicated questions, both in proposing their own legislation and in going over the proposals of other legislators. It takes a great deal of research to resolve many of the complex issues which arise in committee; the LSO is there to help. Second, the office is involved in the budget process, doing fiscal (i.e. money) research for the Joint Interim Appropriations Committee. The Joint Appropriations Committee works long and hard to make recommendations on state spending. Whenever money—not to mention millions of dollars from the state treasury—is to be spent, questions mount. Recently, for example, the legislature has considered, and even agonized over, whether Wyoming can afford a medical school. Lawmakers considered initial building costs, faculty and administrative salaries, heating costs, the number of students to be graduated, and other issues. These are difficult and somewhat controversial questions that had to be answered before the issue could be resolved. Again, the LSO offered much of the data upon which answers were based.

Third, the office aids the legislature in its oversight of the executive agencies through its audit division. On behalf of the legislature, the LSO audits administrative agencies to make certain that they are complying with state accounting procedures and that state money is not being spent wastefully. When problems are discovered, the information is turned over to the appropriate legislators for their consideration.[37]

This, of course, is not to imply that these are the only functions of the LSO. In fact, they will research any legitimate topic that a legislator assigns. Clearly, the Legislative Service Office is an important component in the legislative process.

Steps in the Passage of Legislation

It is unlikely that anyone has ever devised a way to discuss the steps that a bill goes through that does not bore some students. At the risk of losing a few readers, let's summarize the process.

Figure 4.1 is an excellent illustration of the steps that bills must go through to become laws. In fact, this is the exact flow chart that the legislature has had prepared for new legislators to study.[38] The 25 steps in the figure can be categorized even further into seven broad areas.

First, a bill must be thought up and put into the proper form. Bills are commonly thought up, or proposed, by executive branch administrators, interest groups, and individual legislators. Less legislation originates with "the people" than with these three groups. Suppose, for instance, that a high official in state government proposes that Wyoming change the state symbol from the bucking bronc to a jackalope. Our hypothetical governor agrees and gives the go ahead. The administrator then drafts the bill in very rough form. It is then submitted by a sponsor to the Legislative Service Office. The LSO, after advising the legislator that there are no problems with conflicting legislation, puts the bill in the proper form.

The second major step is in committee. To get to committee the bill is placed on a desk in either the house or senate (or pre-filed weeks ahead of time), given a number, and sent to a standing committee by either the house speaker or senate president. Once in committee, the bill might be left, essentially untouched, until little time remains in the session. In that case, the bill would die. In the case of our example, however, the committee chairman recognizes that the bill is of "great" importance, so he schedules it for committee consideration. The committee studies the question in detail, perhaps assigning the LSO to research the topic. The committee may bring in public or interest group representatives to answer questions and may talk among themselves. Next, the committee either votes to report the bill out with a "Do pass" or "Do not pass" recommendation; or it might send it to the floor with no recommendation. The committee recommendation is very important, because other legislators often accept that recommendation. Also, business is considered on the house and senate floor during general sessions (after the twentieth working day) on the basis of the committee recommendation. In other words, the "Do pass" bills go to the top of the pile for floor consideration and the "Do not pass" bills go to the bottom of the general file. The committee's action and recommendation are crucial steps in the legislative process. Notice, a committee has two alternatives which will usually kill a bill without its going any further—sitting on them until the end of the session and a "Do not pass" recommendation.

The standing committee agrees that the jackalope should truly be the state emblem, so

FLOW CHART OF HOUSE BILL
OR SENATE FILE *

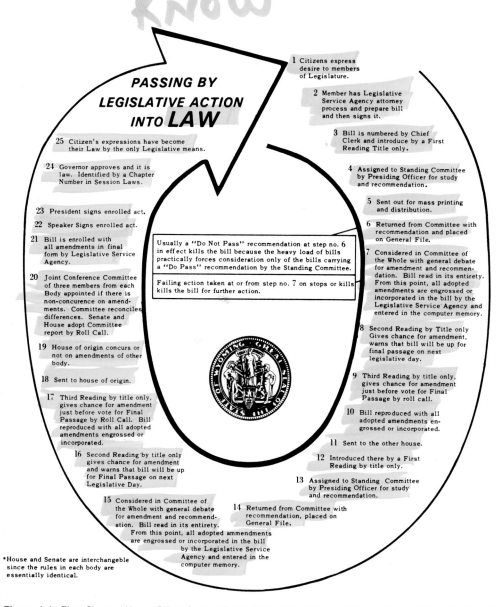

**PASSING BY
LEGISLATIVE ACTION
INTO LAW**

25 Citizen's expressions have become
their Law by the only Legislative means.

24 Governor approves and it is
law. Identified by a Chapter
Number in Session Laws.

23 President signs enrolled act.

22 Speaker Signs enrolled act.

21 Bill is enrolled with
all amendments in final
form by Legislative Service
Agency.

20 Joint Conference Committee
of three members from each
Body appointed if there is
non-concurrence on amend-
ments. Committee reconciles
differences. Senate and
House adopt Committee
report by Roll Call.

19 House of origin concurs or
not on amendments of other
body.

18 Sent to house of origin.

17 Third Reading by title only,
gives chance for amendment
just before vote for Final
Passage by Roll Call. Bill
reproduced with all adopted
amendments engrossed or
incorporated.

16 Second Reading by title only
gives chance for amendment
and warns that bill will be up
for Final Passage on next
Legislative Day.

15 Considered in Committee of
the Whole with general debate
for amendment and recommendation. Bill read in its entirety.
From this point, all adopted ammendments
are engrossed or incorporated in the bill
by the Legislative Service
Agency and entered in the
computer memory.

14 Returned from Committee with
recommendation, placed on
General File.

1 Citizens express
desire to members
of Legislature.

2 Member has Legislative
Service Agency attomey
process and prepare bill
and then signs it.

3 Bill is numbered by Chief
Clerk and introduce by a First
Reading Title only.

4 Assigned to Standing Committee
by Presiding Officer for study
and recommendation.

5 Sent out for mass printing
and distribution.

6 Returned from Committee with
recommendation and placed
on General File.

7 Considered in Committee of
the Whole with general debate
for amendment and recommendation. Bill read in its entirety.
From this point, all adopted
amendments are engrossed or
incorporated in the bill by the
Legislative Service Agency and
entered in the computer memory.

8 Second Reading by Title only
Gives chance for amendment,
warns that bill will be up for
final passage on next
legislative day.

9 Third Reading by title only,
gives chance for amendment
just before vote for Final
Passage by roll call.

10 Bill reproduced with all
adopted amendments en-
grossed or incorporated.

11 Sent to the other house.

12 Introduced there by a First
Reading by title only.

13 Assigned to Standing Committee
by Presiding Officer for study
and recommendation.

> Usually a "Do Not Pass" recommendation at step no. 6
> in effect kills the bill because the heavy load of bills
> practically forces consideration only of the bills carrying
> a "Do Pass" recommendation by the Standing Committee.
>
> Failing action taken at or from step no. 7 on stops or kills
> kills the bill for further action.

*House and Senate are interchangeble
since the rules in each body are
essentially identical.

Figure 4.1. Flow Chart of House Bill or Senate File.* Reprinted with permission of the Legislature Service
Office.

they reported it to the floor of the chamber with a "Do pass" recommendation. The bill is ready for the third major phase in the legislative process—consideration on the floor of the chamber. After the bill's turn comes up on the "general file," the chamber adjourns into a committee of the whole. This is a parliamentary tactic that allows the house or senate to debate and vote on amendments without minutes being taken or votes being recorded. Only the final vote on the bill in the committee of the whole is recorded. Notice, this is the first time that the bill may be amended by the full membership of the chamber. In our example, the committee of the whole votes out the jackalope measure with a recommendation that it be passed without change. After a second and third reading before the chamber in the next few days, the jackalope bill passes the chamber. The second and third readings give additional chances to amend or kill the bill.

After passage in the first chamber (say the house of representatives for our example), the bill goes to the other chamber. The jackalope measure is now ready for consideration in the senate. The fourth and fifth steps in this seven step legislative process are easy. After the second chamber receives the bill, it is sent to committee. Step four repeats step two, but in the other chamber. In the example, the standing committee that receives the bill in the senate agrees that the jackalope should be our state symbol, so they report it to the floor with a "Do pass" recommendation.

The senate floor then considers the bill just as the house of representatives did as a group (step five repeats step three in the other chamber). Once again, when the bill's turn comes up on the general file it is considered in the committee of the whole with the formal rules suspended, and heard a second and third time in the days after the action of the committee of the whole.

The jackalope measure has now passed in both the house and senate. But, there is a problem because the senate changed the house version of the bill. The senate wants the state symbol to be a jackalope with a cowboy riding him; the house left off the cowboy. Because the house and senate versions are different—however slight, even a comma added or taken off in a chamber would make them different—a conference committee meeting is required in order to keep the bill alive. This is step six. The speaker of the house and president of the senate each appoint three people to represent their chamber in conference. Often the presiding officer picks the bill's prime sponsor (the primary author or supporter who introduced the bill) to be on the conference committee. The chairmen of the standing committees that considered the measure are often selected as well. The conference goes over both versions of the bill, line by line, writing a compromised version. Once the compromise version is completed, and this is not always easy, it is returned to the house and senate to be voted on again. In order for the bill to pass, both chambers must accept the conference report as it is. If either house changes the report, the matter goes back to conference in an attempt to try to iron out the new differences. If it is apparent that the two chambers cannot compromise on the bill, it dies even though versions have already passed the two chambers.

Fortunately, for the jackalope supporters, the house and senate resolved their differences. The bill is now ready for the seventh major step, the governor. If the governor signs it, it becomes law. He may, however, veto the bill if he opposes it. A veto kills the bill. But if the governor vetoes the bill, it is sent with a list of his objections to the chamber where it originated. The legislature may vote to override the governor's veto. This means that a bill may become law without the governor's approval, if two-thirds of the legislators in both houses pass it again. The governor's choices are actually somewhat more complicated than that, as you will see in Chapter 5. Even so, his two choices really come down to signing the bill into law or casting his veto. And it is very difficult to raise the two-thirds vote to override.

This summary has obviously left off several points, but the points covered are the highlights of the process and the most important "pressure" points in the passage or defeat of legislation.[39]

Norms of the Legislature

To this point you have read a great deal about the formal aspects of the Wyoming legislature, such as the constitutional provisions, a few statutory directives, and the written rules and procedures of the house and senate. But what about the unwritten rules, the "norms" and values of the chambers? As with so many other things, the unwritten rules—the ones that nearly everyone adheres to, because everyone else does—often say as much about how things work as the formal rules do.

Table 4.9 shows the responses of legislators from the 1975–80 sessions to a question asking them to list the unwritten rules of the Wyoming legislature. As seen, the most frequently cited response was that legislators are not to criticize their colleagues publicly. This is a common legislative norm. In fact, in the survey of legislators from the 1979 session that was discussed in the previous chapter, 65 percent said that they would never personally criticize a fellow legislator on the floor of the legislature (the most public forum available). Clearly, the majority of Wyoming legislators believe that it is appropriate to criticize a colleague's ideas, but not to criticize him personally. There are, of course, exceptions to the rule. Casper's Senator Dick Sadler, for ex-

Table 4.9. Legislators' Perceptions of the Norms or Unwritten Rules of the Legislature

	Number of Responses
Don't Criticize Another Legislator Publicly	11
Respect for Majority Leader's Authority	7
Seniority	7
Floor Debate Concise and on Areas of the Legislators' Expertise	5
Courtesy Toward Other Members	4
Speaker of House Doesn't Seek Another Term in Legislature (if he does, he comes in as freshman)	3
Respect for Speaker of House's Authority	3
Honesty	3
Dress Code	2
Limited Partisanship	2
Attend All Committee Meetings	2
Seldom Override Governor's Veto	2
Chairmen Control Committees	2
No Vote Trading*	1
Vote the Party's Position on Bills	1
Senior Members Sit on Outside Desks	1
Keep Your Word	1
Be Present for Votes	1
Legislators' Independence	1
House Should Prevail in Conference Committee	1
If You Don't Know How to Vote on an Issue, Vote With a Legislator You Respect	1
Inform Party Whip of Vote Changes	1
Don't Try to Force a Bill Out of Committee By Floor Vote	1
Be Well Prepared	1
Bill Is Not Brought Up On Floor When Sponsor Is Absent	1
No Brand Names Used in Debate	1
TOTAL	66

*Also prohibited by statute.

ample, has publicly criticized his opponents a number of times. This norm is perhaps an indicator of another unwritten rule that might be even more common—courtesy among the members. Four of the respondents in Table 4.10 gave that specific response. And the legislators who participated in the 1979 University of Wyoming survey overwhelmingly said that it was very important "to maintain friendly relationships with . . . fellow legislators." Over 78 percent said it was very important, while only 3.6 percent said that friendly relationships are not too important.

Another norm that is indicated in the table is respect for the leadership positions in the legislature, particularly the house and senate majority leaders (seven responses) and the speaker of the house (three responses). Recognition of, and respect for, the leadership's authority is an important factor in keeping party unity during a session. Thus the norm helps the majority party maintain its control.

Seniority (seven responses) means that the senior (most continuous service in the chamber and on the committee) member of a committee who is in the majority party will be considered for the chairmanship. While they often are appointed, the norm may be broken when the senior member does not want the job or when there is some overriding political (e.g. the person notoriously violates political confidences) or personal (e.g. the person is senile) reason why he should not be appointed.

Another important norm is for legislators to keep their remarks short and to the point during floor debate (five responses). Also, they are expected to speak only on issues about

Table 4.10. Factors Which Influence Legislator Voting—Legislator and Lobbyist Views

Voting Influence:	Extremely Important	Quite Important	Slightly Important	No Opinion	Slightly Unimportant	Quite Unimportant	Extremely Unimportant	Total Percentages	Number Surveyed
Party Caucus									
Legislators' View	7.1%	25.7%	32.9%	11.4%	7.1%	11.4%	4.3%	99.9%	70
Lobbyists' View	18.9	40.2	26.6	5.3	3.6	5.3	0.0	99.9	169
Party Platform									
Legislators' View	7.1	17.1	34.3	2.9	11.4	20.0	7.1	99.9	70
Lobbyists' View	7.7	19.6	36.9	14.9	9.5	9.5	1.8	99.9	168
Individual Philosophy or Ideology									
Legislators' View	54.7	26.7	12.0	5.3	0.0	1.3	0.0	100.0	75
Lobbyists' View	29.9	40.9	14.6	9.1	3.7	1.2	.6	100.0	164
Constituency Wishes									
Legislators' View	31.0	42.3	18.3	7.0	0.0	1.4	0.0	100.0	71
Lobbyists' View	8.8	29.4	22.9	11.8	11.8	9.4	5.9	100.0	170
Positions Which Will Help Legislators Advance Politically									
Legislators' View	4.3	30.4	24.6	14.5	7.2	10.1	8.2	99.8	69
Lobbyists' View	19.8	28.7	30.5	12.6	3.6	3.6	1.2	100.0	167

which they are knowledgeable. Considering the short sessions, this makes sense. When legislators have only 20 or 40 days in which to finish their work, there is little time for rambling political discourses.

Several other norms have to do with personal behavior during a legislative session. Legislators said that they are to be honest and aboveboard, are not to trade votes, and are to keep their word, do their homework, attend committee meetings and be present for votes. Actually, there are probably more of these norms than most legislators could recall during the survey.

Again, we should not underplay the importance of these norms. As most people realize, the way we behave is influenced to a degree by what others expect. In the Wyoming legislature this is no unimportant matter. In fact, when the 1979 U.W. legislative survey asked legislators how important these rules are, 77.1 percent said they are very important, 27.7 percent said they are somewhat important, and only 1.2 percent said they are not too important. So, most lawmakers are aware of the significance of the unwritten rules. In some ways, this is another measure of their importance.

Influences on Legislative Voting

Accordingly, norms influence legislative behavior. But what other factors influence lawmakers, particularly their voting? Obviously, a legislator's vote on any individual issue may have been arrived at through a quite complex process, while other votes may have been easy to decide. This section looks at some of the major factors which legislators consider before casting important votes.

Table 4.10 shows legislator and lobbyist assessments of the importance of party caucuses, platform positions, individual philosophies, constituency desires, and political concerns, as determinants of voting. The table indicates that all of these factors are important, but some were cited more often than others. Individual legislator philosophy was scored as the most important consideration, with over 80 percent of the legislators ranking it extremely or quite important and 71 percent of the lobbyists agreeing. It is not unusual for conservatism and liberalism to guide legislator voting, especially since Wyoming is dominated by one particular ideology (conservatism). This voting criterion may be quite in line with the notion of representative democracy, depending upon the legislators themselves. Those legislators who campaign on specific liberal or conservative issue positions, for instance, are merely keeping their "promise" to the voters when they vote according to their philosophies. This is not the case for lawmakers who ignored issues during the campaign, unless they have survey data or an historically intuitive sense (they know it in their bones) that the voters are predominantly of either a conservative or liberal bent. Of course, relying upon their philosophy is another way legislators say, "Trust my judgment," to their constituency. Most legislators want to exercise their own judgment.

The consideration that was mentioned as being least important was the Republican and Democratic party platforms. As was shown in Chapter 2, party platforms are "statements" of what the parties believe and represent. Every two years the parties each hold conventions which, among other things, pass resolutions stating their beliefs. The idea is that the platforms will tell the voters what the two parties represent. But Table 4.10 shows that only 24 percent of the legislators think that their party's platform is extremely or quite important in their voting, 27 percent of the lobbyists thought the platforms were that important. And notice that 27 percent of the legislators think their platform is extremely or quite unimportant when it comes to actual voting. Still, this is not to say that platforms are unimportant in Wyoming, especially considering that a third of both the legislators and lobbyists said their platform was slightly important as a determinant of voting. The safe conclusion then is probably that while party platforms are of substantial importance in determining the votes of some legislators, and are of equal unimportance to others, many legislators view their party platform as merely another "voice" that is often listened to but periodically ignored.

It is difficult to gauge the importance of party caucus positions. In states with strict caucus voting, the majority party in the house and senate meet separately, debate and sometimes compromise issues, vote on the issues among themselves, and then vote as a bloc according to the majority view in the party. If, for example, 10 senators in the majority party caucus are for an issue and 11 are opposed, all 21 will vote "no" on the floor. This way, the majority party remains in complete control as long as the majority party legislators stick to their caucus position.

Clearly, Wyoming caucus positions are not that binding, but to what degree do legislators vote according to their caucus position? Again, it is difficult to tell. In the surveys referred to in Table 4.10, Democratic legislators often said caucus votes were very important. But they are normally the minority party and may say this in part out of frustration. They do lose on many important votes. On the other hand, the lobbyists who were surveyed tended to agree with the Democrats; they also said that caucus positions are very important determinants of voting. Republican legislators, however, tended to take the opposite view. They generally felt that caucus positions are just one of several considerations, and are never binding. Although there is no consensus on the exact role of caucus positions in Wyoming, it is clear that they are not as firm in this state as in others. Caucus positions, while influential, do tend to leave room for maneuvering by individual lawmakers. Table 4.11

Table 4.11. Three Perspectives on the Importance of Party Caucuses as Determinants of Legislator Voting

Lobbyists	Democratic Legislators	Republican Legislators	
26.9%	24.1%	0.0%	Most voting on major issues is done according to party caucus positions. Party is a major determinant in legislative voting.
57.3	58.6	56.1	Some voting is along party caucus positions, but only some. Party position is one of several factors which determines voting.
8.2	17.2	39.0	Little voting is done along party caucus lines. Wyoming's legislators are very independent minded and caucus positions are seldom binding.
0.0	0.0	4.9	Almost no voting is done by party caucus positions. Party caucuses are never binding.
7.6	0.0	0.0	I don't really know.
100.0% (N=171)	99.9% (N=29)	100.0% (N=41)	Totals and Number of Respondents

shows the different perspectives on the importance of caucus positions. The table also shows that caucus positions are important determinants of voting; how important, is debatable.

Finally, notice the differing assessments between the legislators and lobbyists shown in Table 4.10. For example, 73 percent of the legislators said that what the people who elected them want is an extremely or quite important consideration in how they cast their votes; only half (38 percent) as many lobbyists think that is an important concern. Or, look at it in reverse, 27 percent of the lobbyists said that constituency desires are unimportant to legislative voting; only 1.4 percent of the legislators agreed. What does this tell us? It reminds us of something that is very important—neither of these perspectives, legislator nor lobbyist, is "absolutely" accurate. The legislators, after all, are politicians. Most want to be reelected and nearly all are proud of the work they have done. We would expect their assessments to be high. Lobbyists, on the other hand, represent special interests. Some of those interests are unsuccessful during legislative sessions. Some lobbyists are undoubtedly overly cynical and negative about legislators and their motives. Still, both groups have opinions and evaluations that should be listened to in the attempt to understand how the legislature works. But we must recognize that both legislators and lobbyists have their "stake" in the game. It is worth remembering that fact when reviewing their analyses.

Strengths of the Legislature

The legislative survey mentioned above asked state lawmakers what they believe "is the greatest single strength of the Wyoming legislature in either philosophical or practical terms." Table 4.12 shows the most common responses. Nearly half (49.3 percent) of the 67 answers cited the "citizen legislature" as

Table 4.12. Greatest Strengths of the Wyoming Legislature as Legislators See It (N=67)

Citizen Legislature	49.3%
Short Session	10.4
Broad Perspective	9.0
Legislator Independence	7.5
Legislator Integrity	6.0
Legislator Dedication	4.5
Easy to Contact	4.5
Miscellaneous	9.0
Total	100.2%

the greatest strength. In the same vein as the above section on the citizen legislature, lawmakers stressed the positive aspects of Wyoming's part-time, amateur legislature. The lack of full-time, career politicians, they say, keeps legislators in touch with their constituencies; legislators spend most of their time at home; they have a better grasp of the wishes of "the people," so they are more responsive, they say. As has been shown, Wyoming prides itself in its citizen legislature. Notice also that the second most frequent response, short sessions (10.4 percent), is an aspect of the citizen legislature. Meeting for only a few weeks a year increases the contacts that lawmakers have with their constituencies. However, the two strengths are not the same. Some legislators who said the short sessions is the greatest strength, for example, said the time pressure forces legislative action. Since they have only 20 or 40 working days, the lawmakers said, they cannot fool around as if they had six or eight months.

Another popular answer was that our legislators represent a broad social, economic, and political perspective (nine percent). This answer came mostly from Republican legislators. Several other popular responses had to do with the legislators themselves. Legislators said they are independent when it comes to party and pressure group influences (7.5 percent), they believe they are people of integrity (six percent) and dedication (4.5 percent), and they say they are easy to contact (4.5 percent). Thus, nearly one-quarter (22.5 percent) of the legislators surveyed said that the greatest strength of the Wyoming legislature is the high quality of its legislators. While they generally deserve such praise, it is a bit humorous to have people rank themselves as the highmark of what they do.

The "miscellaneous" strengths named included the legislature's size, conservative philosophy, creativity, common sense, majority party power, and the close working relationship among legislators. Each was mentioned only once. Surprisingly, the legislature's size was not mentioned more often. States which have several hundred legislators sometimes complain that they "bump" into one another. Wyoming's legislature, with 92 members, is a manageable size.

For comparison, it is interesting to see what lobbyists say are the greatest strengths of the Wyoming legislature. The 132 interest group representatives who answered this question in the survey mentioned earlier gave a wide variety of answers. As might be expected, they too cited aspects of the citizen legislature (15.9 percent) and the short sessions (10.6 percent) as pluses. They also said that the legislators are easy to contact (nine percent), are conservative in philosophy (8.3 percent), represent a wide array of interests and perspectives (7.6 percent), and that lawmakers are independent in their outlook (six percent). A few of the lobbyists agreed that the greatest single strength is the legislators themselves. A few stressed the honesty (3.8 percent) of lawmakers, that they try hard (3.8 percent), and that they are generally "high quality" people (4.5 percent).

From the lawmaker and lobbyist assessments, two major trends are evident. First, the Wyoming legislature is "in touch" with large segments of the people of the state. Wyoming has a "citizen legislature" that is relatively easy for citizens and diverse interests to contact, whether through lobbyists or by using personal conversations and letters. This is the strength that is mentioned most often by both lobbyists and legislators. The second trend concerns individual legislators. Sure, some are a bit lazy, or slow of mind, or even overly ambitious. But overall, excluding the exceptions just noted, Wyoming legislators are an important strength in the legislative process.

You may see other trends or strengths from what you have read. And perhaps there are many others. But often the others that come to mind depend too much on your individual perspective to qualify for mention here. The two trends just mentioned, however, are two of the distinguishing strengths of the Wyoming legislature.

Weaknesses of the Legislature

While numerous strengths of Wyoming's legislature have been shown, there are shortcomings as well. This, of course, is the case with all large political institutions. Any time one person, group, or philosophy is successful on an issue, the "losers" on the issue will likely find fault with the process. And the winners may themselves think that improvements could be made regarding the way things are done. This is generally true at all political levels and is the case in Wyoming.

The legislators who listed their opinions of the greatest weakness cited a wide range of concerns. There were 74 responses. The weakness mentioned most frequently was that the session is too short (25.7 percent). Several lawmakers said that 40 and 20 day sessions

Sidebar 4–1
Is Wyoming's the Worst Legislature in the Country?

Of course not. A 1971 study of American state legislatures, by the Citizens Conference on State Legislatures, did not rank Wyoming's legislature as the worst in the country. That dubious distinction goes to Alabama; Wyoming ranked 49th. The study looked at five aspects of lawmaking—*functionality* (techniques and facilities for managing time, space, and staff), *accountability* (degree to which the legislature and its procedures are understandable by the public and the degree to which every individual legislator is able to have influence), *informedness* (adequacy of time, committee structure, and staff), *independence* (freedom to establish its own procedures and to operate as an equal of the other branches), and *representativeness* (diverse legislative membership, clear identifica-

tions between legislators and their constituents, and the ability of every legislator to act effectively).

As a result of both legislative self-reflection and the Citizens Conference study, Wyoming embarked upon a number of procedural reforms. Foremost among the reforms was the creation of the Legislative Service Office (LSO) in 1971, to upgrade the legislature's professional staff capabilities.

Although several of the study's criticisms are things that cannot be corrected by procedural reforms (e.g. whether the legislature represents diverse interests among the electorate), it is quite likely that Wyoming's stature has improved in the past decade.

are just too short to get into issues in detail, even with the interim committees. After all, interim committees are sometimes inactive. They also stressed the importance of having a part-time legislature but felt that 40 and 20 days was not enough.

Another legislator criticism is that research and staff facilities are inadequate (9.5 percent) (See Sidebar 4–1). For help with research, lawmakers normally turn to the Legislative Service Office and interest groups. Each house also has a small staff, and some lawmakers have student interns. But several lawmakers report that even these are not enough. This criticism is common in Wyoming and elsewhere. Legal questions are complicated and hundreds of issues face the lawmakers each session. To research these complex issues as thoroughly as everyone would like would take an enormous amount of support. And remember, research people and facilities are expensive.

"Be fair, boys! . . . publish the names of my big political contributors but also expose the cheapskates who only give 5 bucks!"

GRIN AND BEAR IT by George Lichty (c) Field Enterprises, Inc. Courtesy Field Newspaper Syndicate.

A few legislators said that the greatest weakness is the over-influence of interest groups (9.5 percent). In particular, they said that state bureaucrats and agriculture have too large a voice in legislative decisions. While this is a common criticism of interest groups at the outset of the 1980's, the discussion of pluralism in Chapter 3 is well worth remembering. After all, it can be argued that influential interest groups are merely reflections of large segments of the Wyoming people.

A small number of legislators were critical of their colleagues' overall intelligence. The greatest weakness of the legislature, they said, is that many legislators are not very bright (5.4 percent). This is impossible to gauge, because one person's brilliance is another's folly. Still, when all of the criticisms of the legislators themselves are combined—they are not smart enough, are too inexperienced, are too conservative, are self-serving, and have conflicts of interest—16.2 percent of the legislature surveyed said that the greatest weakness of the legislature is the legislators themselves! So just as some lawmakers are quick to praise themselves, others are as quick to criticize the body.

It is also worthwhile to turn the lobbyists loose on the question of weaknesses. Covering the sessions as thoroughly as they do, their observations should be quite informative. Table 4.13 shows the lobbyist perceptions of the greatest legislative weaknesses.

As with the legislators, a large segment of the lobbyists believe that interest groups are overly influential (this was the case with lobbyists for "weaker" interest groups in particular) and that some legislators are narrow and slow in their ability to use their reasoning powers (15.1 percent for each response). Likewise, some were critical of the short sessions as being too brief (12.7 percent) and of the inadequacy of research and staff facilities (11.1

Table 4.13. Greatest Weaknesses of the Wyoming Legislature as Lobbyists See It (N = 126)

Interest Group Overinfluence	15.1%
Lack of Legislator Intellectual Abilities and Broad Perspectives	15.1
Short Sessions	12.7
Lack of Research, Staff, and Information	11.1
Disregard for Wants and Needs of the People	8.7
Leadership Overpowerful	5.6
Personal and Regional Infighting/ Jealousies	4.8
Lack of Social Progressivism	2.4
Legislator Inexperience	2.4
Miscellaneous	22.1
Total	100.0%

percent). On these points, the legislators and lobbyists are in general agreement, although in differing degrees. The lobbyists, however, cited several other major criticisms. Several said that legislators have so many personal reasons for what they do that they generally disregard the needs and wants of the majority of people they represent (8.7 percent). This is a clear challenge to the notion of the citizen legislature that has been discussed somewhat idealistically throughout the chapter. Other lobbyists say that the greatest weakness is that legislative leaders are too strong (5.6 percent). These criticisms were generally geared toward the Speaker of the House of Representatives, some committee chairmen, and party leaders (especially the majority party) in both the house and senate. The bone here is that a very few people have a great deal of say about which bills get to the floor, what compromises are made, and ultimately what passes or fails.

A few lobbyists mention personal and regional infighting as major problems (4.8 percent). To any casual observer of the legislature, this is an obvious fact. While true of personalities here and there, the most noticeable strife is between the north and south, east and west, rural and urban, and individual cities. The Cheyenne-Casper "wars," for example, are known far and wide. These rivalries, of course, are not uncommon in other states. In fact, most states have similar differences.

We see, then, that people who are closely involved with the Wyoming legislature can easily find both strengths and weaknesses in how laws are made in this state. Actually, the strengths and weaknesses are sometimes intertwined. The quality of the legislators themselves is a good example. Some are cited by their colleagues and lobbyists as the greatest legislative asset, but others are thought to be a hindrance. This reminds us that men and women have different abilities and that people do not always see things the same way. In the long run, that is a major point which should not be underestimated. So the legislature is "strong" in many ways and it is "weak" in others. The issue is then one of improving on the weaknesses that can be changed. And remember, not all of them can be changed.

Notes

1. See Wyoming Constitution, art. 3, secs. 1 and 2.
2. Writing about the same concept at the national level, Publius (probably James Madison) said that the senate would be able to provide "defense to the people" by being ever so slightly distant from them. Publius argues for "the necessity of some institution that will blend stability with liberty." See Alexander Hamilton, James Madison and John Jay, *The Federalist Papers,* No. 63. (New York: The New American Library, Inc., 1961), pp. 382–390.
3. Section 3 says that representation "shall be apportioned among the said counties as nearly as may be according to the number of their inhabitants. Each county shall have at least one senator and one representative; but at no time shall the number of members of the house of representatives be less than twice nor greater than three times the number of members of the senate." This section limited changes by saying that all counties were to be represented in both chambers but that there was to be a limit on the size of the house.
4. John B. Richard, *Government and Politics of Wyoming,* 3d ed. (Dubuque, Iowa: Kendall-Hunt, 1974), p. 46.
5. The major cases in the series were: Baker vs. Carr, 1962 (Supreme Court said that apportionment was not a "political" question and could be heard in federal court); Wesberry vs. Sanders, 1964 (dealt with congressional districts of differing population sizes; Supreme Court said that "as nearly as practicable, one man's vote in a congressional election is to be worth as much as another's." This is the famous "one man, one vote" ruling); Reynolds vs. Sims, 1964 (Court ruled that the "equal protection of the laws" clause of the 14th Amendment to the U.S. Constitution requires state legislative districts to be apportioned on the basis of population and to be substantially equal throughout individual states).
6. T. A. Larson *History of Wyoming* (Lincoln: University of Nebraska Press, 1965), p. 573n.
7. Ibid.
8. General sessions convene on the second Tuesday of January in odd-numbered years.
9. Budget sessions convene on the second Tuesday of February in even-numbered years.
10. Jack C. Plano and Milton Greenberg, *The American Political Dictionary,* 4th ed. (Hinsdale, Illinois: Dryden Press, 1976), p. 40.
11. U.S. Constitution, Amendment X.
12. For an excellent discussion of these principles (particularly regarding Congress), see Edward Bennett Williams, *One Man's Freedom* (New York: Atheneum, 1977), pp. 30–87.
13. Wyoming Constitution, art. 5, sec. 4.
14. Ibid., art. 3, sec. 18.
15. See, for example, Hamilton, et al., No. 65, pp. 396–401.
16. Before the tapes were released in the Watergate scandal, for example, impeachment efforts were under way on the basis of malfeasance.
17. Wyoming Constitution, art. 3, secs. 17–19.
18. 1979 Wyoming Election Code, Sections 22–3–101 through 22–3–117 (Chapter 3).
19. Tim R. Miller and John T. Hinckley, "The Office of Governor: Observations of Four Wy-

oming Governors," *Learning Modules of Wyoming Politics,* funded through a grant from the National Science Foundation, Local Course Improvement Program, Grant No. (SER77–03819) (Laramie: Center for Government Research, 1980). This was from one of four interviews with living Wyoming governors by John T. Hinckley. The interviews were conducted in the summer of 1977.

20. The U.S. Constitution also makes provision for the states to call constitutional conventions. While one has been called for to date (and another is close as of this writing), no constitutional convention has been held in this manner.

21. The U.S. Constitution also makes provision for conventions in three-quarters of the states to ratify proposed amendments, rather than state legislatures. Only the 21st Amendment (repeal of prohibition) has been ratified in this way.

22. Wyoming Constitution, art. 3, secs. 10, 13 and 29.

23. The philosophers among us might disagree with this. But unless states wish to either challenge the constitutionality of federal law in court, or consciously decide to ignore the law and take their chances, the states must comply with federal law.

24. See the Civil Rights Act of 1964 as amended by the Equal Employment Opportunity Act of 1972. Notice also that these are statutory acts based upon constitutional jurisdiction. The Congress passed the laws as within the constitutional guarantees of equal protection under the law (14th Amendment), etc.

25. See Richard, p. 49.

26. See B. Oliver Walter and Kendall L. Baker, "The Wyoming Legislature: Lawmakers, the Public, and the Press," (Laramie: Government Research Bureau, 1973), pp. 7–9.

27. Ibid., p. 24. This is also supported in a 1979 survey for this book.

28. Ibid., pp. 30–37.

29. For an article discussing the merits of citizen legislatures see Michael L. Strang, "The Case for the Citizen Legislator," *State Government,* Summer, 1974, pp. 130–136; reprint ed., *Capital, Courthouse, and City Hall,* comp. Robert L. Morlan (Boston: Houghton Mifflin Company, 1977), p. 86.

30. Tim R. Miller, an interview with Senator Don Northrup, former President of the Wyoming Senate, in Powell, Wyoming, June, 1979.

31. In a 1979 survey of Wyoming legislators conducted by political scientists and students at the University of Wyoming, 72.3 percent of the 83 respondents said that more important work takes place in committee than on the floor; 15.7 percent said the floor work is more important.

32. For a more thorough and scholarly discussion of legislative oversight in Congress see Seymour Scher, "Conditions for Legislative Control," *Journal of Politics* 25 (August, 1963): 526–540.

33. For a discussion of the role of committees see William J. Keefe and Morris S. Ogul, *The American Legislative Process: Congress and the States,* 3d ed. (Englewood Cliffs, New Jersey: Prentice-Hall, 1973), pp. 154–158.

34. Miller, interview with Senator Don Northrup.

35. House and Senate Rules as published by Legislative Service Office, 1977: senate rules 6–1 through 6–12, 3–1, 16–1, and 16–2; house rules 4–1, 4–6, 9–2, 12–2, 17–1, 23–2 and 24–4. Interview with Senator Northrup. Also, see Richard, pp. 54–55.

36. These include a chief clerk, legislative attorney, assistant chief clerks, clerical supervisor, journal clerks, bill status clerk, communications clerk, reading clerk, committee secretaries, sergeant-at-arms, doorkeepers, janitors, file clerks, and more. See Herbert D. Pownall (former long-term House Chief Clerk), "Wyoming Manual of Legislative Procedures: Wyoming State Legislature," (Cheyenne: Wyoming Legislature, 1975), pp. 36–88.

37. Tim R. Miller, an interview with Ralph Thomas, Director of the Service Division, Legislative Service Office, in Cheyenne, Wyoming in the summer of 1978. Also, see *A Look at Wyoming Government,* 3d ed. (League of Women Voters, 1975), pp. 23–27.

38. Pownall, p. 2.

39. Each of these steps is discussed in the "Wyoming Manual of Legislative Procedures" and "Rules of the Senate and House of Representatives." Both are publications of the Wyoming Legislature. Also, for an excellent case study

on the legislative process in Wyoming see William O. Guffey, "Distributing New Mineral Royalties in Wyoming: A Case Study of Legislative Determination of Who Gets What, When and How," *Learning Modules on Wyoming Politics,* funded through a grant from the National Science Foundation, Local Course Improvement Program, Grant No. (SER77–03819) (Laramie: Center for Government Research, 1977), pp. 156–201.

CHAPTER

FIVE

The Executive Branch

The previous chapter looked at how laws are made. But, what happens after a law is passed? Granted, to some students this is obvious, but to many others it is not. Are laws just written in a book and then put on a shelf to gather dust? Of course not. Once a law is passed, it must be executed, or enforced. That is the job of the executive branch—to execute, or carry out, the law. So, for example, when the legislature decides that the speed limit on state highways is to be 55 miles per hour, and the governor agrees (signs the act), the executive branch is required to *execute* the law. In the case of a new speed limit, the Highway Patrol is the executor of the law and is instructed to ticket anyone who violates it. Of course, in the real world, the people who have the responsibility to execute the law will also have a certain amount of discretion in how they carry it out. When a Highway Patrolman clocks someone driving 59 miles per hour, for instance, he may decide to forget it. So, there is usually some degree of flexibility in the law. But, that doesn't decrease the responsibility of executive branch officials to carry it out. And, if they decide not to carry out those legal responsibilities, they can be forced to by the courts.[1]

Another example of executive branch functioning occurred when the state legislature decided to build a new athletic complex at the University of Wyoming. The bill was requested by University officials. It was drafted, and lobbied, by and under their guidance. Next, it was passed by the legislature and signed by the governor. At that point, the bill became a law. The university had both the authorization (meaning permission) and appropriation (meaning money) to build the facility. Both the permission and the money were given to the university by the legislature with the approval of the governor.[2] So, who saw to it that the facility was built? The governor, state legislature, or the university? The answer is "no," "no," and "yes." The university had the responsibility to implement the law. University officials took the bids, signed the contracts, and all the rest. The university administered, or executed, the law. Again, the university was the executive branch agency which carried out the "will" of the legislature—to provide higher education to the people of the state, do research, develop a competitive athletic program, and provide adequate facilities.

This means, then, that for the legislature's many programs to be completed, there must be many administrators. Here you see a key to understanding government. Everyone is down on bureaucrats, right? But, who are these bureaucrats? Bureaucracy is "any administrative system, especially of government agencies, that carries out policy on a day-to-day basis, uses standardized procedures, and that is based on a specialization of duties."[3]

123

Reprinted by permission of the Chicago
Tribune-New York News Syndicate, Inc.

So you see, "bureaucracy" and "bureaucrats" are terms that are applied to government administrators. The legislature passes laws which are carried out by executive branch *administrators* or *bureaucrats*. Notice, "bureaucracy" and "bureaucrats" are used in a neutral sense here. When someone in everyday conversation is talking about bureaucrats, it is invariably in a negative sense. But, political scientists normally use the term in a neutral context, without connotations of good or bad. Bureaucracy, then, is simply administrative structure for accomplishing public policy. When bureaucracy is efficient in carrying out the will of the legislature, it is viewed positively. In instances when bureaucrats are wasteful, or overly independent of the legislature (and, indirectly, of the people), it is seen

in a negative light. In these days when disliking government is so common, it is appropriate to remember that as with practically every other occupation or profession, some people and organizations are more efficient than others. The same is true of government.

The sections which follow provide an overview of the executive branch of state government. This is done by briefly discussing the structure of the executive branch and considering the five elected executive branch officials with emphasis upon the office of governor.

Structure of the Executive Branch

The easiest way to describe the executive branch of government is as a flow-chart, with

B.C. by permission of Johnny Hart and Field Enterprises, Inc.

the governor (or President in the case of federal government) at the top, with subordinates who are directly accountable to him listed just below. Below these top subordinates are the people who are directly accountable to them, and so on all the way down to the people who fill completely supportive roles (people who have few discretionary powers or responsibilities). Then, the various "flow charts" can be grouped according to agencies or departments. These, in turn, can be put together into flow charts of the entire executive branch. That

way, when people think of the structure of some state (or federal) executive branches, they can turn to the flow chart and say, "Agency A fits into the structure here. Its director is accountable to 'this or that' function, and it is responsible for 'these or those' agencies that are listed below."

Although this might be the easiest way to describe an executive branch, it would be a simplistic, less than accurate description under the most ideal circumstances. In Wyoming, as elsewhere, this easy description falls far short of the mark.

It is possible, however, to trace Wyoming's executive branch by looking at its two overriding features. These two structural features are 1) a patchwork array of approximately 120 different departments, boards and commissions and 2) management of several important aspects of state government by the five elected executive officers, in a "cabinet-like" fashion. Although somewhat difficult to distinguish from one another (they use similar terms, like "commission"), these two structural concepts are the keys to understanding both Wyoming's administrative branch and the limitations placed upon the governor.

Fragmented Government. Quite simply, only a small part of Wyoming's executive structure is accountable directly to the governor in the chain-of-command fashion described above. Instead, Wyoming's executive branch is a hodgepodge of more than 120 state departments, boards, commissions, councils, and committees. The governor has direct control over 21; the others are only indirectly responsible to him.

Generally, these state agencies were created to administer programs passed by the legislature. As seen above, legislation is enforced in the executive branch. This means that once passed, laws are administered by an agency (or agencies) that handles that kind of function. Political scientists would say that it goes to an agency that has the jurisdiction (or authority) over that kind of law. Consider a recent example.

In 1975, state lawmakers passed legislation in anticipation of dramatic industrial growth in areas of Wyoming. One law, the Industrial Development Information Siting Act, prohibits large energy-related plants from being built in the state unless the builder first assesses the social and environmental consequences of the project upon neighboring communities. If a conversion plant is to be built outside of Kaycee, for example, the potential builder must first study what demands will be placed on the schools, police and recreation facilities when several hundred or thousand people move there to work in the new facility. The 1975 law created an executive branch council, the Industrial Siting Council, to implement the law. The Council consists of seven members. They must be residents of Wyoming and be knowledgeable of (and hopefully interested in) social and industrial impact. They oversee the administration of pertinent laws; they determine whether prospective industrialists have adequately anticipated and provided for the social impacts of their projects. If so, the council issues a license which allows the project to be built.[4] Without that permit, the project cannot be developed.

Members of the Industrial Siting Council serve six-year terms, following appointment by the governor and confirmation by the state senate (meaning the senate must agree before a council appointment is official). No more than four of the seven members may be in the same political party; a governor cannot appoint all Republicans or Democrats. Council members are part-time administrators. This is important for understanding how much of our state administration works. Members of the Siting Council, as with most of the other boards and commissions, have other jobs and

live throughout the state. They meet periodically (often no more than once every few months) to make final decisions. In the meantime, the Siting Council hires a full-time director to head up its full-time staff. These administrators, or bureaucrats, take care of the daily matters. The council meets infrequently to review the actions or policies of the director. Again, the council makes the final decisions.[5]

Although the Industrial Siting Council is but one example, it points out the fragmented nature of most of state government. Two major points are demonstrated in the example. First, the example is typical of the state's administrative approach—creating a series of smaller agencies to manage state programs as they develop. Second, the example shows how these agencies are only indirectly accountable to the state's chief executive. After all, the governor is limited as to who may be appointed to the councils, members may be left over from the previous administration, and directors serve at the pleasure of their council rather than the governor. As a result, then, much of state government appears somewhat disjointed. From the governor's perspective, it clearly is disjointed.

This description of the Siting Council is typical of most of the boards, councils, committees, departments and commissions in the state. Even so, the numerous state agencies often differ from one another in any of several ways. While the Industrial Siting Council has many substantive duties, the Department of Administration and Fiscal Control (DAFC) has relatively few. In other words, while one agency is weighing the merits of an issue and deciding whether the plant is to be built (substantive issues), the other is purchasing equipment, hiring state employees, and providing the money (supportive concerns). Both are state agencies, but they serve different functions.

Another difference between angencies is in the amount of control that the governor has been given (by the legislature) over them. As mentioned above (and developed below), the governor has difficulty getting his way with many boards and commissions, such as the Industrial Siting Council and Highway Commission. In contrast, the governor is clearly in control of DAFC.

A further difference between state agencies has to do with the existence of citizen advisory councils, commissions and committees. Some agencies are run by citizen commissions as outlined above, others have them for cosmetic reasons (to look good), and others do not have advisory councils. There are differences in the length of commission member terms (two, four and six years are common), whether there is a limit to the number of members who are affiliated with one party, and whether state-wide representation is required on councils. Also, some council-board-commissions meet often, others rarely; some are active in making decisions, others come in only after the important decisions are made. Overall, then, citizen advisory councils are quite varied in both their makeup and the degree to which they oversee and direct the state agencies for which they are responsible.

Finally, state agencies vary in their political and administrative influence. Certainly, the Boxing Commission, Pari-Mutuel Commission, and Child Labor Commission serve several important purposes. But the workings and policies of the Game and Fish Commission, Highway Commission, or Department of Health and Social Services, probably have a greater bearing on more citizens of the state.

Wyoming's "Limited Cabinet." Although the governor of Wyoming is provided with numerous sources of authority which he exercises independently of anyone else, such as the constitutional powers cited below, the state's "limited cabinet" system requires the governor to share his authority in six major areas with the four other top executive branch officials.[6] The four other officials are the secretary of state, state auditor, state treasurer, and superintendent of public instruction. Together, these five officials oversee state charitable and correctional institutions such as the State Hospital and Penitentiary (acting as the Board of Charities and Reform); state-owned buildings (Capitol Building Commission); distribution of wholesale liquor (Liquor Commission); rules for employing prisoners (Commission of Prison Labor); state interests in wills (Board of Wills and Trusts); the sale of leases, and certain uses of state land, and a variety of farm loans (Board of Land Commissioners and Farm Loan Board).

These are truly important shared powers. Not only do the officials oversee such important policy areas as state institutions and land use, but they do so *jointly.* Each of the five officials has an equal voice and vote on these boards and commissions, with the governor nominally serving as chairman. On the one hand, then, people often think of the governor as the head of state government, or at least as the head of the executive branch. On the other hand, however, the reality is that in several important areas of state administration (including others discussed below) the governor is not in charge. He or she has a voice and vote, certainly, but only one of several voices and votes. When we consider that a governor may have to share administrative responsibility over a variety of important concerns with other political figures who may be in a different political party—and may even have their eyes on replacing the governor in the next election!—we begin to understand the office and how it differs from popular perceptions.

Four Elected Executive Branch Officers

Each of the five executive branch officials elected in Wyoming supervises a particular area of the executive branch. This section gives an overview of four of these five offices. The governor is discussed shortly, and in more detail.

Notice, the common features shared by these officials are that they are elected statewide, and they supervise or manage a partic-ular "functional" area of state administration (e.g., education). This may seem confusing because Wyoming's United States Senators and Representative are elected statewide as well. But, keep in mind that our senators and congressman represent us in the *federal* government. The five offices that are discussed in the next few pages are the highest ranking *state* administrators. They head the executive branch of Wyoming.

Sidebar 5–1
Duties of the Office of State Auditor

by Jim Griffith
(State Auditor)

In theory and by statute, the Wyoming State Auditor is the general accountant of Wyoming State government. To be certain, he is that for his duties include the design, implementation, and maintaining of the State's accounting system. However, in actuality, as the State's third highest elected official, he is much more.

In addition to the fiscal responsibilities, the Auditor serves on the Board of Charities and Reform; Land Board; Farm Loan Board; Capitol Building Commission; Board of Deposits; Board of Wills and Trusts; Board of Prison Labor; State Canvassing Board; and, he is the Secretary of the Liquor Commission. Inasmuch as students of Wyoming's State government must understand that Wyoming does have a limited cabinet form of government, much of the work of the five elected officials occurs with these various boards and commissions. As examples, the Board of Charities and Reform administers all eleven of the State's penal and charitable institutions; the Land Board administers 3.6 million acres of State owned lands in all 23 of Wyoming's counties; the duties of the Wyoming Farm Loan Board have grown tremendously in recent years, inasmuch as, in addition to making loans to Wyoming's farmers and ranchers, this board now makes loans and outright grants to Wyoming's municipalities, counties, and other sub-divisions of government; the Capitol Building Commission has responsibility for maintaining and constructing all State owned buildings.

The Auditor's Office is divided into two main divisions—the Audit Division and the Accounting Division. The audit division has two distinct, but separate, functions. It pre-audits all claims made against the State to determine their authenticity and accuracy before payment is made. Starting late in 1975, a post-audit program was assumed by the State Auditor's Office. Post-audits of the various State institutions and agencies, as well as the loans and grants made by the Wyoming Farm Loan Board, have, are, and will be conducted.

Activities in the accounting division are primarily involved with the recording of and accounting for revenues and expenditures of the State. For operational purposes, these activities can be categorized as: accounting, financial systems development, and payroll. Each of these functions is essential as a responsibility of the State Auditor's Office. Meeting the State's payroll is an extremely important function of the accounting division. As the State's "bill payer" the Auditor is responsible for writing an average of 2,000 warrants per working day.

To qualify for one of these four offices—secretary of state, state treasurer, auditor, or superintendent of public instruction—a person must be 25 years old, a citizen of the United States, and a legal Wyoming voter. They are elected by popular vote to serve four-year terms. All but the treasurer may be re-elected term after term. The treasurer cannot succeed himself. This means that after serving a four-

Sidebar 5–2
Duties of the Office of the State Treasurer

by Shirley Wittler
(State Treasurer)

When the Wyoming Constitution was adopted in 1889, the restriction was placed on the office of State Treasurer that the Treasurer is ineligible for re-election until four years after the expiration of a term in that office. State funds were in cash and to be guarded zealously.

That constitutional restriction still exists today, although practically all movement of funds is by check or warrant and monitored by computer. State funds, however, are still guarded zealously.

The treasurer is statutorily charged with receiving and holding all monies of the state. Warrants issued by the Auditor to meet state costs are redeemed daily as presented by the bank and funds must be available to make that purchase. Deposits for all state agencies are made by this office and monies not spent that day are invested, until needed, to earn income for the state. Permanent funds are continuously invested and reinvested in fixed income securities as prescribed by law.

Large deposits of state funds are held in Wyoming banks and savings and loan associations. These are secured by pledges of collateral as required by state statute and exacting records are kept on collateral changes. The interest rate on deposits is set semi-annually by the State Board of Deposits.

It is the responsibility of the State Treasurer to make numerous large distributions of various funds, including Government Mineral Royalties, Forest Reserve Funds and Taylor Grazing Fees, which are distributed as prescribed by the legislature. Refunds are made, also by statute, of Car Company taxes and gasoline taxes to agricultural users, municipalities and airports.

Distributions are made from appropriated funds for Homestead Property Tax Exemptions, Veterans' Property Tax Exemptions and payments for Sales Tax and Utility Payment Relief for elderly and disabled citizens. Excheat funds are received and held in trust. If not claimed in five years, they are placed in the general fund. Interest earnings are distributed regularly to state agencies and the general fund.

The Workers' Compensation Department, under the supervision of a director appointed by the State Treasurer, administers the Workers' Compensation Act and the reserve funds held in connection with that office.

The Treasurer serves with the other four elected officials on numerous boards and commissions including: Capitol Building Commission, State Board of Charities and Reform, State Board of Land Commissioners, Wyoming Farm Loan Board, Wyoming Liquor Commission, State Canvassing Board, State Board of Deposits, State Board of Wills and Trusts and the Commission of Prison Labor.

The Treasurer additionally, by virtue of the office, serves on the following boards: Wyoming Community Development Authority, Wyoming Retirement Board, Group Insurance Board, Medical Liability Compensation Fund Board, and is administrator of the Wyoming Public Employees Deferred Compensation Fund.

Monthly and annual reports are rendered, showing the fiscal condition of all state funds and the various investments and investment earnings of each. All records in this office are available for public scrutiny.

year term, the treasurer must wait out a term before being eligible to hold the office again. This has led "to the practice of the incumbent state auditor and the incumbent state treasurer being elected to each other's office every four years."[7] From 1971 to early 1975, for example, Jim (James B.) Griffith was state treasurer with Ed (Edwin J.) Witzenburger

state auditor between 1973 and early 1975 (he was appointed to complete the term of Everett Copenhaver who resigned for health reasons). In 1974, both men sought office for the next four-year term, but Griffith was barred by law from seeking a continuous second term. Thus, Witzenburger ran for treas-

---

Sidebar 5–3
Duties of the Superintendent of Public Instruction

by Lynn Simons
(Superintendent)

As State Superintendent of Public Instruction I am by law responsible for "the general supervision of public schools" and the administration of the State Department of Education. My duties include making necessary rules and regulations for the administration of the schools; maintaining records of the business of the office; enforcing educational law, rules, and regulations; and deciding controversies which arise from the rules and regulations.

In addition I must confer with the Board of Trustees of the University of Wyoming and with the University's College of Education about courses of study, and I must assist the State Board of Education to perform its duties.

My most interesting statutory obligation, in my opinion, is the one requiring me to advise and consult with state and local school boards, administrators, teachers, and citizens about education and "seek in every way to develop public support for a complete and uniform system of education for the citizens of this state."

In carrying out my duties I travel around the state visiting school districts and schools. I call and participate in meetings about education matters. I develop and help others to develop legislation affecting schools and students, and I work with legislators both during the legislative session and after as they work on education matters.

"To develop public support" I communicate to the public through newsletters, newspapers, radio, and television, and I give a great number of speeches throughout the year to groups ranging from college and public school classes, to Kiwanis clubs and PTA's, to high school commencements and clubs.

But my duties are not limited solely to public schools. As one of the state's five elected officials, I serve on such state boards and commissions as the Board of Charities and Reform, the Capitol Building Commission, the Board of Land Commissioners, the Farm Loan Board, and the Liquor Commission. I am an *ex officio* member of the University of Wyoming Board of Trustees and of the Community College Commission.

Because it is important professionally to maintain relationships with people in positions comparable to mine, I am a member of the Council of Chief State School Officers. I serve at the Governor's pleasure as a commissioner of the Education Commission of the States, an interstate organization made up of governors, state legislators, state board members, higher education officials, and chief state school officers. I am also on the governing boards of the National Assessment of Education Progress and the education research laboratory that serves our region, McREL.

I think it is obvious to say that the job is a busy one. What is not so obvious is that it is also interesting, ever-changing, and immensely rewarding.

urer and Griffith ran for auditor, thereby complying with the statute but with both men keeping jobs in state government. Both men won office. This works, of course, only when both men (or women) are in the same political party. After all, a state auditor in one party probably would not want to help a treasurer who is in the other party. Since the Republican candidates win practically every race for these two offices (Democrats have won the auditor position only three times—in 1934, 1938, and 1942—and the treasurer's office only once, in 1934), this situation is unlikely.

Each of these four officials has a wide range of duties and responsiblilties (see Sidebars 5–1 through 5–4). Briefly, the secretary of state is the state's chief keeper of legal documents. Corporations, for example, are certified by his office. The auditor is the state's top accountant; he keeps track of money going into, and out of, the state treasury. The treasurer manages the state's money before it is spent. The superintendent of public instruction directs the administration of Wyoming's public education.

One of the most important responsibilities of these four officials and the governor, as shown above, is their membership on a variety of boards and commissions. Although this cabinet function of these officials may sound dull, it should not. These boards and commissions

Sidebar 5–4
Duties of the Secretary of State

FUNCTIONS:

Acting Governor in the Governor's absence.

Convenes the State House of Representatives.

Custodian of the Great Seal.

Corporations Division—Administers the Wyoming Business Corporation Act, Uniform Commercial Code, as well as laws pertaining to non-profit corporations, trade names, trademarks and limited liability companies.

Elections Division—As Chief Elections Officer is responsible for maintaining uniformity in the application and operation of the election laws. Supervises the operation of the Statewide Computerized Voter Registration System.

Securities Division—Administers the Wyoming Uniform Securities Act and registers broker-dealers, agents and offerings for sale in Wyoming.

Publications Division—Maintains the State Registry of Administrative Rules and Regulations, compiles and publishes the Wyoming Official Directory and distributes the session laws, supplements and statutes.

Serves as Chairman of the Wyoming Collection Agency Board and administers the collection agency laws.

Administers laws pertaining to notaries public.

Maintains records relating to facsimiles of signature, oaths of office, gubernatorial proclamations and executive orders, discharges from the state's correctional institutions, and extraditions and requisitions of fugitives.

Secretary of State serves on the following state boards and commissions:

Canvassing Board
Capitol Building Commission
Board of Charities and Reform
Board of Deposits
Farm Loan Board
Board of Land Commissioners
Liquor Commission
Commission on Prison Labor
Board of Wills and Trusts

control millions of state dollars and determine policies that affect thousands of people. Is the land board's management of state land important, for example? It is if you like to camp on state land, need a loan to keep your farm or ranch in business, want to lease state land, or just value keeping state land in its natural form. Or, consider the late 1970's scandal, sometimes called "prairiegate," that drew national attention to the state. "Sixty Minutes," CBS's television news program, did two segments on Wyoming government and politics in 1978. What started it all? It began with charges of misappropriation of public funds at the Pioneer Home in Thermopolis. Whose responsibility is that? The Board of Charities and Reform.

Certainly, some of these boards and commissions are more important than others. But, considering the broad areas for which they have responsibility—aspects of state money, land, water development, institutions and buildings, liquor, and prison—it is easier to appreciate how important they are.

The Fifth Elected State Official—The Governor

Background. As seen in Chapter 2, the office of governor was created with the formation of Wyoming Territory in 1869. On April 3, 1869, President Grant nominated John A. Campbell as Wyoming's first territorial gov-

Inauguration of Francis E. Warren as Governor of Wyoming at Cheyenne, Capitol Building, April 9, 1889. Wyoming State Archives, Museums and Historical Department, University of Wyoming.

Governor Joseph M. Carey (1911-1915) at his desk. Wyoming State Archives, Museums and Historical Department, University of Wyoming.

ernor. He was confirmed by the U.S. Senate to serve a four-year term. Section Two of the Wyoming Organic Act (the legislation which made Wyoming a territory) gave the territorial governor authority as:

Commander-in-Chief of the militia and superintendent of Indian affairs. The governor was allowed to veto laws but this veto could be overridden by two-thirds of the legislative assembly. He granted pardons for territorial offenses and reprieves for violations of federal laws. The governor commissioned all officers appointed under territorial statutes and was charged with execution of the laws.[8]

Gradually, the powers of the territorial governor grew, much as the territory itself grew. He came to appoint several "important officials including the treasurer, auditor, and superintendent of public instruction,"[9] and occasionally filled other offices created by the territorial legislature. By statehood in 1890, "the governor filled thirty-two offices by appointment." For these responsibilities, Governor Campbell was paid $3,000 per year.[10]

With statehood came a new office of governor. As discussed earlier, Francis E. Warren was elected as the state's first governor in the first state election on September 11, 1890. He served only forty-four days and resigned to accept the legislature's appointment to represent Wyoming in the U.S. Senate. From that beginning, many of the state's most capable political leaders have held the office of governor.

Qualifications For Office. To qualify for governor, a man or woman must "be a citizen of the United States and a qualified elector of the state, who has attained the age of thirty years." Likewise, he must have resided in the state for the five years before the election, and, if elected, he may not hold any other office during the four-year term as governor.[11]

Constitutional Authority. The state constitution specifies several powers and duties of the governor. When the National Guard is called into the service of the state, the governor is the commander-in-chief. And, if Colorado ever invades Wyoming to capture our ski slopes, the governor will call out the state military forces to "execute the laws, suppress insurrection and repel invasion." He may also call the legislature into session on extraordinary occasions. The 1978 budget session of the legislature, for example, became so involved in the question of whether or not to approve the university's request for a college of medicine that it failed to complete all of its work within the 20 day period allowed by law. As a result, Governor Herschler called the lawmakers back for a special session to resolve the medical school question and to finish work on other budgetary matters (approximately 25 percent of the University of Wyoming's budget was bottled up in the legislature).

At the beginning of each legislative session, the governor is required to advise the legislators "of the condition of the state, and recommend such measures as he shall deem expedient." This is the governor's constitutional authority to propose legislation to the state legislature. Further, he is obligated to work with the other executive branch officials to "take care that the laws be faithfully executed." And, the state constitution grants the governor the authority to remit fines, grant reprieves, commutations, and pardons after a conviction. The only exceptions are for treason and impeachment.[12] A pardon is an executive "release from the punishment or legal consequences of a crime." A reprieve "postpone(s)

the execution of a sentence for humanitarian reasons or to await new evidence."[13] While the power to grant pardons and/or reprieves is common to governors and the President in the United States, it is rarely used. President Ford's pardon of former President Nixon's Watergate crimes, however, has drawn attention to the power. Then in early 1979, Tennessee Governor Ray Blanton drew fire when he announced that he would pardon more than 50 convicted criminals in his final days before leaving office. Actually, most governors view their pardoning power with disfavor because the families of convicted felons so often "beg" their governor for a pardon for their loved ones. Accordingly, the trend in many states is to transfer the pardoning power to boards made up of correctional experts.[14] The trend has not yet reached Wyoming.

In addition, the governor has constitutional authority to make certain appointments, fill certain vacancies which arise in government (e.g., appointing someone to fill a vacancy created by the death of a U.S. Senator has been an interesting example in Wyoming history), and to "expedite all such measures as may be resolved upon by the legislature and . . . take care that the laws be faithfully executed."[15]

Finally, the state constitution specifies that the governor may veto legislation to which he objects. As indicated earlier, when legislation has passed both houses of the state legislature, it is sent to the governor to be signed into law. However, if he objects to the legislation, he may send it back to the house that first passed it, with a list of his objections. In this case, the governor has vetoed the bill, or prevented its becoming law by not signing it. But, the issue is not finished. If two-thirds of the members elected in both the house of representatives and the senate vote in favor of the bill after the governor has vetoed it, it becomes law without the governor's signature. In that instance, the governor's veto has been "overridden."[16]

Governor as Leader

In preparation for this text, the author asked the five elected state administrators to write brief essays describing the duties and responsibilities of their office. Sidebar 5–5 is Governor Herschler's essay. The governor, he writes, is the leader or chief of six major roles: chief federal program officer, commander-in-chief of the state military, chief budget officer, chief of state, chief executive, chief legislator, and chief of his political party.

Chief "Federal" Officer. First, Governor Herschler notes that as the federal government grows, its influence in Wyoming and other states increases. Indeed, he says that this state-federal involvement has tripled in the last decade. Consequently, the Governor of Wyoming spends a considerable amount of time dealing with the federal government. This is understandable. Federal "growth" means many things. For one, it means that the state comes to rely increasingly upon federal money to pay for state programs. In a 1977 interview, Herschler put it this way:

. . . a tremendous amount of federal funds come to our state. Many people think those are free dol-

---

Sidebar 5–5
Duties of the Office of Governor

by Ed Herschler
(Governor)

Few positions of leadership in the United States offer the challenges confronted by a state governor, whose position as first citizen of his state places him in the center of American political life.

Limited Powers

Traditionally, the governor is chief of a large and complex organization which in many states, including Wyoming, he has little or no power to change. Our governor may not reorganize, consolidate or reduce the number of governmental agencies and functions without the consent of the legislature. Thus, in the public eye, he is "responsible" for many government services over which he does not have ultimate authority.

There is historical precedent for limiting gubernatorial power. It stems from the harsh experiences of the early American colonists with the royal governors sent by the English crown. One historian has said that our state governor-

ship was conceived, by our early lawmakers, in mistrust, and born in a straight jacket.

A major limitation on a Wyoming governor's prerogatives is the administrative set-up in which each of the five elected officials runs his own department and answers only to the legislative and judicial branches. The governor, unlike the U.S. president, does not have, at the top level of authority, a cabinet or group of administrators appointed by him. All five elected officials, however, serve as the joint overseers of important executive entities such as the Board of Charities and Reform, Capitol Building Commission, and Farm Loan Board.

Among the governor's powers are that of legislative veto with a two-thirds vote required to override. He has limited powers of appointment; he may grant clemency and pardon in criminal cases; he may call special sessions of the legislature. As commander-in-chief he may call the state militia to serve in times of emergency or disaster.

Diverse Roles

The student of the governor's constitutional powers should consider them as the framework for his actual duties and responsibilities, which change with the varying needs of the citizenry. Since territorial days Wyoming governors have adjusted their roles to accommodate population growth, economic and geographic factors and their own personal approach to the job.

The most drastic change has come in the last decade, during which the administrative branch of state government has seen its involvement with the federal government at least triple in volume. Today, I find the area of state-federal relations among my top-priority and most time-consuming responsibilities.

It is relevant to comment here that those who deplore the growth of government at all levels should not ignore the increasing services we require of government in today's world. In Wyoming, for example, the national demand for energy has made protection of our natural resources even more imperative. This is an effort which requires constant coordination among agencies of local, state and federal government as well as a balance with private enterprise and all segments of the economy.

As our communities experience the social consequences of too-rapid growth and industrial impact, we are confronting the need for federal financial assistance at the same time that we are resisting unnecessary or inflexible federal regulation of our resources.

In addition to his roles as Chief Federal Program officer and Commander-in-Chief of the state's armed forces, the governor is also Chief Budget Officer, charged with preparing and submitting a proposed budget to the legislature. This requires detailed study and lengthy hearings, but there is neither a guarantee that the governor's budget will survive the lawmakers' diverse desires to expand and/or cut services, nor assurance that his recommendation of total expenditures will not be drastically altered.

The governor is most visible to the public in his role as chief of state, when he dedicates schools and churches, cuts the ribbon for new hospitals, appears in support of good causes, and fills numerous speaking requests. In my view, he should take every opportunity to report personally to the citizens on the state of their state.

To an amazing degree, the governor of Wyoming is seen by his constituents as the one who can solve both their personal and business problems, and answering letters and phone calls is an important part of every day.

In the role of Chief Executive, the governor is a large employer, but with limited powers of appointment and removal of personnel. He has budgetary and supervisory direction of some, but not all of the state's more than 100 agencies, boards and commissions. As manager of the executive branch, he often finds himself adjudicating differences of viewpoint among interest groups and coalitions of both the public and private sectors.

The Governor may choose to be as active in influencing legislation as he wishes. He must consider both the substance of legislative programs and legislative strategies if he wants to get his favored programs passed and to prevent enactment of measures he opposes.

One of his most demanding obligations is that of a board member of some twenty boards and commissions. Diligent attendance at their meetings keeps him in touch with a large measure of state business, but I am not certain that such adds up to the most efficient use of his time.

The Governor is the titular head and sometimes the active leader of his state political party. As such he is expected to play a role in selecting party leadership, raising funds, formulating issue positions, recruiting candidates and participating in national party affairs.

Tenure

There has been no change in tenure of Wyoming governors—it remains an unrestricted number of four-year terms. No governor has ever been impeached or removed from office.

Opportunity

To this factual and "barebones" account of the Wyoming governorship, let me add the personal comment that I find it a splendid job, a fine opportunity to help people and to get close to the heart of a magnificent state.

lars. They are not. . . . As a result, we sometimes become more or less a federal administrator. . . . We do that because there are many, many programs that we could not complete and could not continue without federal funding. But every time we get federal funds, of course, there are always federal strings attached to them. . . . We don't like it, but if we accept the federal funds, we have to do it . . . although I do feel very strong about maintaining the state's prerogatives.[17]

Another aspect of federal growth deals with compliance with federal legislation which does not directly involve federal money. In 1964 and 1972, for example, the federal government passed legislation protecting equal job opportunities for ethnic minorities and women. This requires adequate record keeping by employers. Because the State of Wyoming is an employer, it too must comply. The records are kept in the executive branch by the state's "Affirmative Action" officer who works for the governor. Again, the governor's involvement with the federal government is increased.

Also, federal growth or expansion often leads to Wyoming governors becoming spokesmen for states' rights. "States' rights" advocates are quick to defend the powers of states, and object to the federal government taking over more and more responsibility for government programs. When federal policies are objectionable to state leaders, the governor typically leads the voices in opposition. Governor Herschler, for example, has been out front in defending Wyoming water interests against what many westerners see as the federal government's unwarranted encroachment (See Chapter 7). He even sued federal officials in defense of Wyoming's water interests.

Once again, this is an important gubernatorial role, particularly at the outset of the 1980's. As is discussed in the final chapter, Wyoming has a long and somewhat contradictory history of viewing the federal government with suspicion. Indeed, this suspicion seems as strong now as at any point in Wyo-

ming history. As national and state opinion polls show, a large segment of the public is disenchanted ("mad" may be more accurate) with government in general and national government specifically. In such times, it is expected that state leaders—particularly the governor—speak out loudly and often in defense of state rights, whether the issue concerns water, land, minerals, or any number of other issues. Just as Governor B. B. Brooks, in 1909, charged the federal government with "meddlesome activity (which) frequently acts as a hindrance to our development, and hence irritates our people," Wyoming governors both before and since have joined other state leaders in criticizing bureaucratic bungling, red tape, centralization of authority, and "silly government orders."[18]

This role has not decreased since Governor Brook's time. Indeed, Governor Cliff Hansen's statement in his 1965 State of the State address to the legislature is as timely today as it was then. He said:

Positive action to strengthen state government is the constructive way to oppose centralization. States' rights are without force unless they are coupled with state responsiblity. We propose to accept every responsibility that we can successfully discharge at the state level.

This, of course, does not mean that all Wyoming governors are strong "states' righters" in the stereotyped sense of southern governors in the 1960's. To say so would be an overstatement. Rather, it is more accurate to say that at various times all Wyoming governors have seen fit to speak out against what they perceive as federal meddling into areas that they believe are state matters.

Commander-in-chief. Herschler also points out that the governor's second role is commander-in-chief of the state's armed forces. As discussed earlier, this grant of power comes from the Wyoming Constitution and makes the governor the head of the National Guard. Wyoming's governors have responded differently to this role, from Governor Hansen and others who never had occasion to call the Guard out, to Governor Hathaway who said, ". . . [I] enjoyed that role. As an old tech sargeant in World War II, I suppose I relished the capacity to tell the generals what to do."

Hathaway tells a humorous story about first encountering the role:

I'll never forget my third or fourth day in office. General Pearson and General Laudson came into my office, pulled up in front of the desk and saluted. This overwhelmed me. I didn't know whether to salute or stand up or sit down or what to do. . . .[19]

Chief Budget Officer. Next, Governor Herschler calls the governor the state's chief budget officer. Every two years the governor, with the assistance of the Department of Administration and Fiscal Control (DAFC), prepares recommendations for how much money he would like to see spent to run state government over the next two years. This is not to say that the governor reviews each budgetary item in detail himself. Community college science departments, for example, receive appropriations (anywhere from several hundred to a few thousand dollars) to buy materials for experiments. Does the governor typically review the number of frogs or cats that students at a community college will dissect? Of course not. He will review the community college requests for state money, including the major costs (or line items) such as faculty salaries, energy costs to heat and light buildings, or amounts to be given to start or support new programs. Because the biannual (state budgeting is done for two-year periods) budget includes hundreds of millions of dollars, it is impossible for the governor to study each item. The governor can and does, however, set spending priorities, limit or even cut spending for some programs, and review overall spending recommendations for state

agencies as prepared by DAFC. These measures form the governor's budget request. The budget is then sent to the state legislature (during even-numbered years), where parts may be accepted, cut, increased, or eliminated altogether. The budget that the legislature passes, when signed by the governor, is the basis for much of state spending during the next two years.[20]

Notice, however, this process applies to "much" of state government, but not all. Some state agencies, such as the Game and Fish Commission and the Highway Department, receive separate "earmarked" funds over which the governor and legislature have less control. When people buy a fishing license or a tank of gas, they pay a tax to the management of fish and operation of highways in Wyoming. Game and Fish and Highway Department officials then spend the money within limits (i.e., "authorizations") established by previous legislatures and governors. This gives these agencies a significant degree of independence from the legislature and governor.

Chief of State. The governor's fourth major leadership role is as chief of state. In this capacity, the governor is Wyoming's symbolic leader. We are told that governors sometimes wonder whether the town celebrations, building dedications and ribbon cuttings, public speeches, parades, balls and banquets ever end. They don't. The governor's mansion in Cheyenne, for example, is the site of several "symbolic" social and political events each month. One day the guests attend a charity luncheon; a few days later the high school delegates to Girls State arrive. Typically, Wyoming's "first lady," the governor's wife, acts as hostess; often the governor at least makes an appearance.

This symbolic role is natural to our democracy. Because America has no royalty as do many European nations, Americans look to their top political leaders to fill symbolic as well as political roles. When the President of the United States enters, everyone rises. Depending upon the circumstances, he may be announced; the band may even strike up a chorus of "Hail to the Chief." While the Wyoming governor clearly has different duties and responsibilities than the President, the offices are similar in this regard.

While the governor's ceremonial role is usually of a "local" nature, this is not always the case. Governor Hathaway, for example, says:

[my] most memorable ceremonial occasion, I think, was entertaining a delegation (of top government and party officials) from the Soviet Union in 1974. This was a return visit. . . . I was among the first American governors group ever to visit the Soviet Union. . . . I entertained the Russian leaders in Wyoming. We floated the Snake River and stayed at Coulter Bay and spent some time in Yellowstone.

Earlier, Hathaway entertained Prince Philip in Sheridan. Are Wyoming governors good hosts? Says Governor Hathaway, "We just try to show them a little western hospitality when we have the opportunity."[21]

Chief Executive. Further, Governor Herschler discusses the governor's responsibilities as chief executive. This is the governor's authority to direct the administration of state government and comes directly from the Wyoming Constitution. The governor's functions here are broad, and include limited powers to manage state resources (e.g., wildlife, water, state buildings) and state personnel (e.g., recruitment and appointments, removal or firings, daily promotion policies). This topic is developed in detail shortly.

Chief Legislator. As mentioned, the governor also has constitutional authority to recommend to the legislature such measures that he believes are important. In the sense that much legislation that passes was originally introduced under the direction of the governor,

he is sometimes called the chief legislator. This makes sense. If something is wrong in the state's programs for support of the poor and disadvantaged, who in government would be more likely to know of the problem than the people who work with those people every day—the Department of Health and Social Services? It is understandable, then, that reform of these programs might come to the attention of the governor through the director of the department involved. If the governor, agency director, field administrators, recipients of the services, and affected lobby groups are able to agree upon a change, it would probably be written as a bill by a department administrator. If the governor approves the bill, it would be given to a legislator who agrees to sponsor the measure in the legislature. The governor would be likely to seek a sponsor in his political party first and a co-sponsor from the other party as well. This support from both parties, when it can be found, makes passage more likely. The governor and his administrators would then lobby for the bill. While this approach would certainly not guarantee that the bill would pass, the governor's support would increase that likelihood. Notice, too, the bill obviously has a better chance of becoming law if the governor is in the party that controls the legislature.

Vigorous legislative programs are common among Wyoming's governors. In his 1977 interviews, NWCC Distinguished Professor John Hinckley asked four Wyoming governors whether they viewed it as part of their job to write broad-based legislative programs and lobby the legislature for their passage. Three of the four said that they had—Milward Simpson, Stan Hathaway, and Ed Herschler; Cliff Hansen said that while he had made legislative proposals "on a number of issues that we thought were important," he did not believe it was his responsibility to propose a broad executive agenda.

Governor Hansen is in the minority in this perspective of the job. In fact, the other three governors felt very strongly that this is an important gubernatorial role. Said Herschler:

I think it's definitely the role of the governor to have a legislative program that . . . is reasonable and that you can present in your State of the State message and at the same time be able to follow the legislation. . . . And, if it seems to be bogged down somewhere, you can go to the committee chairman or someone that you can rely on and say. 'I would sure like to get that out on the floor to be debated.' You have to do lobbying if you're interested in your program. It seems to me that I have a duty to myself and to the state to provide a program which I think . . . beneficial to the state and to do what I can to get it enacted into statute.

Hathaway responded:

I had my ideas, and the ideas of others, of what I thought needed to be done. We prepared legislation to implement these. I found it effective to let legislators come to me. They knew, especially the members of my own party, bills that were forthcoming. And, they wanted to introduce them; they got behind them. In Wyoming . . . the Republicans always invited me to their legislative caucus (a meeting of members of the same party in the house or senate). I found this a good vehicle. I campaigned for legislators. I talked about that in their jurisdiction and they felt some loyalty to me for that . . . the members of the legislature . . . would all, at one time or another during a (legislative) session, come in to see me about getting a particular person an appointment. That gave me an opportunity to say, 'I'd like your support on this partic-

---

Sidebar 5–6
Governor Herschler on the Governor's Use of Party Ties

Question: Is the political party a help or a hindrance in this process?

Governor Herschler: My experience in the legislature is that, and this is just a rough guess, that 90 percent of the legislation is not political. Of course, there are the 10 percent, the 10 percent is political. Most of that is used for window dressing, I think in many instances. The political party doesn't hurt, it helps because your own party that is there with you in the legislature, those members of the legislature generally speaking are very loyal to you for your party, primarily. Secondly, being a member of my party (i.e. Democrat) I believe that I somewhat follow the philosophy of my party. And so, of course, my legislative program is sometimes quite oriented to the philosophy of my party. Sometimes you know that you're not going to get those bills enacted because they are so political, particularly if the other side is controlling both houses (of the legislature). So then you look at areas that perhaps you can compromise a bill and literally get your foot in the door so that a year from now when the

next session comes along, you can get that bill amended more to your liking.

Question: In your situation where you have a divided administration and the legislative control on the other side or party, would there be some hesitancy on your part to make perceptible use of the Democratic party, lest you offend the majority?

Governor Herschler: No, not really. I made use of the people in my party, very much so. I don't say 'made use of them,' I worked very closely with them. And you know every individual who ever comes to the legislature, regardless of their party, always has some legislative program of his own. And you know about that if you're awake, I suppose. There's a lot of horse trading in the legislature. You indicate to a colleague in the other party that, "I know you're very interested in this piece of legislation; I'm also interested in this piece of legislation. The two of us together, we might be able to get this accomplished." And it works.

ular bill.' I had a day-to-day run with what they were doing and I used some leverage in that regard and I don't apologize for it.

Simpson said:

I instructed all of the agents in my administration, like the budget officer, to get up there when a bill was introduced that affected their department and give all the help they could to it and get all the information they could out of it. . . . You're left alone if you don't take the initiative. . . .

Clearly, Wyoming governors are often vigorous "legislators" and "lobbyists."[22] This seems to be true even, as Sidebar 5–6 shows, when the governor is in the minority party.

Party Chief. Governor Herschler then ends his discussion of the governor's office as "chief," calling him the "titular head and sometimes the active leader of his state political party." He is, then, the chief of his political party. While this is true, it is advisable to think of this role as a generality, as Governor Herschler tells us. Clearly, the governor is in a strong position for political leadership; he has a limited power to appoint people to state government jobs (called patronage), the assumption being that those who get jobs will be loyal politically (not always the case); he has the prestige of the office; he is covered almost daily in the media so most people know of him. Even so, it is incorrect to think that he takes control of the party the minute that he is sworn into office. Many other factors influence the degree to which he both heads his party and succeeds with the legislature.

Political parties in Wyoming, as in other areas, sometimes have broad internal differences. One difference that sometimes exists (though not always, by any means) is between regions in the state, such as north and south. While Wyomingites are similar in many respects (See Chapter 7), jealousies exist just the same. Is a governor from Cheyenne the leader of his party in Casper? In Cody? Perhaps, but there are a lot of "ifs." The Chey-

enne-Casper rivalry is almost legendary. Sometimes ideological differences may arise within the parties. Had Dick Jones, a staunch conservative Republican, been elected governor over Ed Herschler, his Democratic opponent in 1974, would moderate Republicans have accepted him as their party leader? Then there are sometimes personality factors. When Governor Herschler was first elected in 1974, he found a party with a flashy U.S. Senator (Gale McGee) who had been in office since 1959, and a congressman (Teno Roncalio) who had been involved in Democratic politics for decades and was idolized by the party faithful. Who was the party leader? There probably wasn't one. Other events had to happen to establish Governor Herschler as the party leader. The point, then, is that while a governor has a number of advantages which can be used to establish control over his political party, there are other factors besides holding office which also determine party leadership. In each of these instances, then, the governor was or would have been *a* leader of his party. But, whether or not he would have been *the* party chief is much more complicated.

The Governor's Office—Tieing It All Together

Thus far we have looked at the governor's powers in a very traditional way, and should by now have a feel for both his constitutional powers and the various policy areas where he is active. But, what does it all mean?

It means that the governor is the head of Wyoming's state government. He is not a political "boss," but he is the state's "leader." Technically, he is only the leader of one of the three branches of government, the executive. He is not a legislator in the legal sense, nor does he have direct control over the state judges. This is not to say that the governor has no "checks" on the other two branches. He does; he may veto legislation and makes the final selection of state judges, for two examples. Even so, technically and legally the governor is in charge of only one branch of state government, not all three.

Rather, the governor is the head of the government because he has wider-ranging political and symbolic activities and impacts than other political figures. The generality that governors are "more active" than other political figures is difficult, but true. Governors are ordinarily more active that other political leaders in taking wide-ranging ideas and transforming them into legislation. Most governors lobby vigorously for their programs, twisting a few arms under the right circumstances. They have influence over their political party and may even be its most forceful voice. The governor can gather a crowd of newsmen in minutes and the public sees him in the newspaper several times each week. In addition, the governor is our symbolic leader. More than any other state official, people look to the governor for creativity and action, and generally with a degree of admiration.

The governor has a variety of tools at hand. Some are constitutional, such as his ability to call special legislative sessions and to veto bills. Others are statutory, or come from legislation passed by the legislature, like various appointment powers. Other gubernatorial powers are political. At times, for example, the governor may determine or frame the major issue of a legislative session or campaign. As another aspect of their political tools, governors are sometimes able to influence or even shape public opinions or attitudes. Accordingly, the governor may be able to force concessions from political opponents who are pressured by public opinion. Other tools are

ceremonial, traditional, and cultural. Put simply, most people look to the office for direction.

Notice, while the governor has all these tools and many others to work with, his success seems to depend more on personal skill, approach and integrity than anything else. A student of American governors writes:

> The chief resource of the modern governor is that of persuasion—the use of charm, reason, solid arguments and the status of his office to make it difficult for those he must deal with to say no.[23]

This is a fair assessment of effective use of gubernatorial power in Wyoming. Certainly, a governor's influence varies according to various political considerations such as his, and the legislature's, party labels (if they are both controlled by one party, usually the Republicans, the balance is easier for both), his political philosophy, and the demands of history. But even recognizing the importance of these differences, the key to a governor's influence is normally his persuasive skills. Two terms are particularly important here—persuasion and influence. The observer who realizes that effective governors use *persuasion* to gain *influence,* has an initial understanding of the office of governor in Wyoming and politics in general.

The Governor's Office—A View of Weakness?

Being governor of Wyoming is to hold a prestigious, important position. As has been seen, successful governors are adept at persuasion and influence. But, what is the picture or impression that most people have of the governor's office and its powers? In the movies, he is always someone of power, someone to be reckoned with. People who meet a governor or visit his office are usually impressed. "This," they typically think, "is someone who is important." So he is.

There are many reasons that the office of governor is important and prestigious. For one thing, governors often go on to hold higher public office. This is common both in Wyoming and the nation at large. The office tends to take on an added importance because of the potential it carries for whoever holds the position. Eight Wyoming governors, for example, have gone on to serve in the United States Senate. In fact, the eight include some of the state's most historically noteworthy political leaders: Francis E. Warren, John B. Kendrick, Robert D. Carey, Lester C. Hunt, Frank A. Barrett, J. J. Hickey, Milward L. Simpson, and Clifford P. Hansen. And although Wyoming is not included in the list, several states have produced governors who went on to occupy the White House. The 1980 presidential race, for example, was between two former governors.

Another reason that most people look upon their governor with respect may have something to do with the language that candidates for the office use. Campaign rhetoric so often implies that if the right candidate is not elected, the state is going to go straight "down the tube." So, campaign advertisements dramatize the importance of the office even further. Theme, image, and style become important aspects of candidates' "messages" to the voters. But, these media themes also define our expectations of the governor and in the long run transform our attitudes toward the office. The media conveys the impression that the candidates are "larger than life." This reaffirms our impression that the office which they are seeking must be important; it, too, must be "larger than life."

Also, there are several cultural and social factors which probably add to the prestige of the office. As was discussed earlier regarding the governor's role as chief of state, Americans often expect their public servants to fill roles as both political and ceremonial leaders. To put it simply, many people expect their high government officials to symbolically "represent" their state and nation. This combination of symbolism, patriotism, and hero identification certainly does not lessen the public's perception of the importance of the office of governor.

The impression that is sometimes given of the governor being an all-powerful wheeler and dealer—through movies, television, campaign rhetoric, or teachers—is overdone. Certainly, there is likelihood that the picture drawn above is changing. In the post-Viet Nam and post-Watergate era, the polls tell us that Americans are rapidly growing cynical toward their government. In fact, in a statewide poll taken in 1978, 35 percent of the Wyoming people surveyed said that they "don't have *any* say in what the government does." If this frustration with government continues, people will increasingly discard the notion outlined above that the governor, no matter who holds the office, is to be respected. If this happens, more and more people may come to view top government positions such as governor as weak and ineffective. Indeed, evidence strongly suggests that this is happening to the presidency at the outset of the 1980's.[24]

However, even considering these possible changes in public attitudes, American governors are often less powerful than their constituents realize. This is particularly true of the office in Wyoming. Don't misunderstand. In Wyoming, the governor is obviously important. As seen throughout much of this chapter, the office is one of influence, leadership, opportunity, and authority. Wyoming's governor, however, is seldom as powerful as people tend to think. At best, our governor is a persuasive, influential "leader." In modern Wyoming, the governor is not a political boss. Yes, Governor Warren was called a political "boss" by his opponents in the early part of this century and yes, the governor is the head of state government. But a "boss," in the sense of "a political leader who dominates a highly disciplined state . . . party organization that tends to monopolize power . . . through . . . control over nominations, use of . . . graft, and manipulation of voting and elections"? Clearly not. Again, the office is one of influence and persuasion rather than monopoly and manipulation.

What is a Strong Governor? During the colonial period of American history, governors were given vast powers by the British Crown. Typically, governors had authority to suspend legislatures at will and appoint whomever they liked to fill government jobs. This eventually led to opposition among colonial revolutionaries. After the revolution, state constitutions usually made legislatures the dominant branch of government. In the early states (except New York and Massachusetts), the governor was actually elected by the legislature instead of the people. That way legislators could select a governor who would accept the legislature's dominance. Likewise, legislatures could rotate governors, keeping the office weak. Gradually, however, the picture changed. Because legislatures are generally ineffective administrators, people made increasing demands upon state executives. As a result, all governors were popularly elected by 1830 and usually had expanded veto powers. Since then, states have tended to give increasing authority to governors, particularly since the beginning of the twentieth century. In varying degree, states have often shifted to the view that governors should have vigorous, "independent" powers in leading state government. States that have followed this pattern are said to have "strong" governors.

There is no magic formula which determines whether states have strong or weak governors. After all, the states have different political, social, and cultural settings. The type of office that is appropriate for New York or California may not be appropriate for Wyoming. Still, the strong governor concept has several features. But notice, the discussion that follows deals with a concept. In practice, the concept varies from state to state. In other words, states can have different variations of the following and still have strong governors.

There are no limitations to the number of terms a strong governor may serve, other than the will of the voters. Ordinarily, terms are for four years rather than two. Advocates of unlimited tenure argue that placing a limit on the number of terms a governor may serve tends to make the state bureaucracy too independent. If they know the governor won't be around very long, proponents say, bureaucrats won't do what he wants. And if he has to face voters every two years, the governor will be too busy campaigning to pay attention to his office. Opponents believe that turnover brings new ideas to office, cuts corruption, and helps prevent political bosses from springing up.

Secondly, strong governors do not have dominating legislatures. In weaker systems, "the legislature in many ways ties up the governor's hands and is unresponsive to his programs."[25] Proponents of the strong governor allege that this makes it difficult for the governor to show creative leadership and that legislatures are slow to act, dominated by special interests, and narrow in their thinking. Opponents say that legislatures are more in touch with the people, better reflect the will of the people, and are less likely to react too quickly to rash political whims.

Strong governors operate in states with relatively few earmarked funds. When states "earmark" funds they say, either by statute or constitution, that portions of various tax revenues must be spent on particular government programs. When commerical operators register their vehicles in Wyoming, for instance, they pay a tax that goes directly to support Wyoming roads (through the state Highway Fund, with shares to the counties). Opponents of earmarking funds say that the governor is unable to propose a broad based program to solve problems because funding is not available; rather, earmarking locks money into vested interests. Proponents of earmarking say that it eliminates tax policy from political finagling and inconsistencies.

States with strong governors often cut the number of executive branch officials that are elected, believing that "separately elected officials tie the hands of the governor."[26] Why, they say, would a lieutenant governor who is elected pay any attention to the governor? A lieutenant governor may even view the governor as a rival, and may even intend to run against him in a future election. Proponents say that electing more officials is democratic. Besides, they continue, some areas need to be out of the governor's control, like management of state funds (ordinarily managed by a treasurer).

Next, strong governors are granted broad powers to appoint other administrators. This, proponents say, is the only way to assure that the governor is in control of state agencies. Otherwise, officials who were appointed by a previous governor are likely to be unresponsive. Opponents of a broad appointment power say that it is asking for appointments to be based on political considerations rather than ability.[27]

Wyoming Considered. How does Wyoming's governor stand? Is he a strong or weak governor? This section considers both the criteria outlined above and looks at what state governors have to say.

First, Wyoming governors may serve an unlimited number of four-year terms. There are neither statutory nor constitutional limits. There is, however, another type of limit—tradition or precedent. No Wyoming governor has served beyond two terms. In fact, few have even sought a second term. The 1978 gubernatorial election was Wyoming's 28th election for governor; 19 men and one woman have been elected to the office; eight people have briefly held office as acting governor upon death or resignation of an elected governor. Of the 20 people elected to the office, only seven have been elected to two terms.[28] But, of the seven who have been elected to serve two terms, only one has completed two full terms to date. Governor Hathaway served two terms, from 1967 to 1975; and Governor Herschler is scheduled to hold office through early 1983. The other five served one full term and, for reasons of death or retirement (either their own or their predecessors') a portion of another full term.

On this issue, Wyoming generally meets the strong governor test. Still, the two-term precedent should not be ignored, it is important in the state. Near the end of Governor Hathaway's second term, there was considerable discussion throughout the state about whether he would break tradition by seeking a third term. And some people wondered whether the voters would elect a governor to a third term. Hathaway was quite popular and may have been successful had he tried for another term. But he did not. This same debate will probably be heard again at the end of Governor Herschler's second term.

Generally, it is incorrect to say that Wyoming's governor is "dominated" by the legislature. The legislature obviously has strengths of its own; just as it has weaknesses. To take examples, it is a full partner in the budget process. This is a legislative strength. At the same time, however, it meets for such a short period each year that legislators are sometimes faulted for having to take a "patchwork" approach to their assignments. While some people view the part-time aspect of the legislature as an overall benefit to the state, it clearly weakens the body vis-à-vis the governor. To determine whether the legislature or governor has an upper hand, we have to look at specific issues and the circumstances surrounding them. Such factors as statutory or constitutional requirements, lobby group pressures, political considerations (like party identification or ideologies), or public opinion may make the legislature dominant on any particular issue. But the situation which may give the legislature the upper hand on one issue may shift to the governor's advantage on the next issue! On balance, then, Wyoming's gubernatorial-legislative balance tends to yield two branches that are equal overall. While political "skirmishes" are relatively common between them, the balance generally prevents the legislature from handcuffing the governor.

This is not to downplay the importance of these skirmishes. Governors are normally jealous of their prerogatives and somewhat watchful for any legislative attempt to alter the balance. Sidebar 5–7 shows two recent examples of legislative actions which alarmed the governor. Responding to public concern that state bureaucrats are too powerful—that they make unreasonable rules and implement or interpret laws differently than the legislature intended—the 1977 legislature began adding footnotes to legislation. The footnotes would have required administrators to take cues or directions fron legislative committees. Also, the session passed a law requiring state agencies to get legislative approval for all proposed rules (administrative rules have the effect of laws). The governor was alarmed by these legislative acts. This is an important issue, because it goes to the heart of the separation of powers.

Sidebar 5–7
Governor Herschler on Legislative Incursion into Gubernatorial Powers

Question: I wonder if sometimes the legislature doesn't think it should be the executive as well. Has that been your experience?

Governor Herschler: Yes, I think that did occur on many occasions. Some . . . would try to do that. And I see that happening more and more as we go along every year. A typical example, of course, is in your appropriation bill where the legislature has now adopted the philosophy that they should add footnotes to various appropriations as to how I can spend that money or have a program done. And I might add that I have vetoed a number of those footnotes where they have in effect said, "You will do a program, but at the same time, you must consult with the legislature or with a committee that is established by the legislature, to do these things." I thought these things were taking away some of my prerogatives. . . . There also was a drive in the legislature, particularly in the (1977) session, to require that the executive branch submit all proposed rules for review by the Management Council of the legislature. We got some amendments in it; I think we can live with it. But I'm watching it, because I would say that if we get to the point where the Legislative Service Office and the Management Council want to take over that particular arena, then I'm going to test them in court, because I don't think they have constitutional authority to do that. I think that's something that is reserved to the executive branch.

Article Two of the state constitution specifies clearly that our state government is to have three separate branches. Each branch, and no other, is to perform its own duties, as outlined in the constitution. Put simply, the legislature is to make the laws, the executive is to enforce them, and the judiciary is to interpret the law. In passing the two laws mentioned in the sidebar, legislators were responding to their belief that bureaucrats have too much power. After all, when a law is passed, the bureaucrats must interpret what the legislators meant by the words they used before they can enforce it. Sometimes bureaucrats have to establish their own rules if the law is fuzzy or does not cover a particular circumstance. This, some legislators object, violates the separation of powers concept because executive branch bureaucrats actually become legislators and judges with these rule-making powers. So the legislators, their argument goes, passed laws explaining in detail how certain laws were to be implemented (in the form of legislative footnotes) and to "check" bureaucratic rule-making authority.

The governor disagreed. He must; as chief executive he is obligated to defend executive branch prerogatives in order to keep the executive-legislative balance in proportion. From the governor's perspective, the 1977 legislature was trying to make itself the legislature *and* the executive. This view says that legislators are at fault when they pass confusing legislation and that the constitution (and American history) clearly specifies that legislatures are ineffective when they get into executive branch functions. Defenders of executive branch independence contend that the legislature has a remedy to correct bad bureaucratic rules. The remedy is specific legislation, not the creation of small committees to handcuff their constitutional equal. Clearly, these are classic issues of the balance of power

and show how the two branches in Wyoming (and elsewhere) jealously protect their interests.

The rap against excessive earmarking of state revenues, as mentioned, is that it ties the governor's hands, making it difficult or even impossible for him to respond to new problems. This is particularly the case in states which have earmarked funds in their state constitutions. While a significant portion of Wyoming tax revenues are earmarked to various state funds, this doesn't seem to be a major burden on Wyoming's governor. This, of course, is a generality. There are areas of state government in which the governor and legislature have relatively little control. In terms of its budget or money for operation, for example, the Game and Fish Commission and Highway Commission are relatively free of the governor's direct control. While recognizing exceptions such as this, the conclusion that earmarking is not a major challenge to the governor's authority in Wyoming is true, nevertheless.

There are at least four reasons for this. First, earmarking in this state is essentially done by statute (meaning laws passed by the legislature). This means that problems which might arise due to excessive earmarking could be corrected by the legislature alone, without having to go through the more cumbersome and difficult steps of amending the constitution. Second, over half of state revenues go into the general fund.[29] Money from this fund may rather easily be shifted by the legislature to problem areas as they arise. Third, Wyoming is one of those states in the envious position of raising more revenues than is normally spent. Unlike some of the larger states, then, this means that money is available to address problems in all areas that the legislature thinks appropriate. In other words, enough money is available in the state that different state funds and concerns are not under as much pressure to fight each other for tax dollars. This is not the case in some states, where tax dollars are fought for tooth-and-claw. If the legislature and governor agree that something needs to be done, the money is usually available. The intensity in Wyoming's "dollar politics" often shifts from whether we can afford to do something to whether it is wise to do it. No one doubted in 1977–78 that Wyoming could pay for a medical school. Rather, the issue was whether there were more economical ways to train Wyoming doctors. In fact, Governor Hathaway "predict(s) that by 1985, we'll have difficulty in spending the (tax) money legitimately. It's going to flow quite rapidly. . . ."[30] Again, the point is that because Wyoming is in an enviable tax position, money is available to address many problems regardless of earmarking. Finally, one could argue that state history supports this conclusion. Wyoming has to date addressed its most pressing problems, and money, whether state or federal, has been available. And governors, in fact, have often been leaders in both "finding" money and addressing problems.

This brings us to the next two characteristics of a strong governor—the short ballot and the power of appointment. Strong governors, as mentioned above, do not have a lengthy list of other elected executives to share power with. Instead, strong governors are in charge of the executive branch themselves, with no executive branch rivals, and are able to appoint their subordinates. On this measure, Wyoming fails the strong governor criterion.

Scholars of organizations have long contended that authority should go to the highest officer in an organization. Classical scholars of management have been nearly unanimous in accepting the idea that "the boss" should have the necessary power and authority to supervise the people under him. Otherwise, he is not really the boss. And, they say, it should

be clear to subordinates who their boss is; ideally, any subordinate should have only one boss. This is not as obvious as it may seem. In many organizations, it is difficult to tell who really runs the show. And employees are sometimes responsible to several bosses.[31] In many instances, this is the case in Wyoming, as the governors themselves explain.

The Views of Recent Governors. As has already been mentioned, the temptation is to view Wyoming's governor as heading an organization that is not unlike a military commander, sitting at the top of a pyramid-like chain-of-command in which all the decisions are either made by the commander or by people who are directly accountable to him. This ideal—called a "unified hierarchy"—is not present in Wyoming. Instead, you will remember, the state treasurer, auditor, secretary of state, and superintendent of public instruction each direct their own jurisdictions within the executive branch with relative independence from the governor. Even worse from a governor's standpoint, the vast majority of state programs in Wyoming are administered by a fragmented, disjointed array of approximately 120 boards, commissions, councils and departments. While the heads of 21 state agencies are directly accountable to the governor and can be removed at his pleasure, the other 100 generally are not.[32] Often, these boards and commissions are appointed for set terms, some of which run longer than the governor's own term. Also, state law requires that various commissions and boards have balanced memberships in terms of political party affiliation, professional or occupational experience, and region of the state. The major commissions, in turn, hire full-time directors to manage affairs within their jurisdictions. These directors are accountable to their commission rather than the governor. For these reasons and others, then, numerous state agencies and their

Sidebar 5-8
Governor Herschler on Whether the Old Adage "the Buck Stops Here" Is an Accurate Description of the Governor's Authority over the Executive Branch

No, it really isn't, because there are a number of areas where I am unable to make appointments. There are a number of commissions that I appoint, but they in turn are then authorized to make the appointment of the director for that position—For example, I am able to appoint the members to the . . . Game and Fish Commission and the Highway Department. I appoint the commissioners; they in turn appoint the superintendent or the Game and Fish Director. Then, of course, if he does things well, the Game and Fish Commission gets the credit. If he has everyone in the state upset with him, I get the 'credit.' It sometimes isn't fair.

. . . I find that in some instances I can't work with that individual either by virtue of the fact that there's a personality clash or there's a difference in political philosophy or things of this kind. I do not even have the power of removal which makes it difficult. In some cases, it creates some very definite problems. For example, which

way is this department going to go? Whether they are going to try to follow my philosophy or whether they are going to be "anti-administration?" We're not able to work closely together; we're not able to get our budget put together in such a way. And there is sometimes a lack of communication that creates some very severe problems. And as a result, I think the state suffers.

. . . I also find that in many cases, some of my commission and board appointments are politically motivated because the person comes in and says, 'Well, I've been a member of your party for years and I work for you, and I want you to know that I will work closely with you.' He comes in as a politician; when he's on board he immediately becomes a statesman, and pays no more attention to me, and tells me to go fly a kite.

directors show an independence from the governor; they are sometimes unwilling to follow the governor's lead. This disjointed structure of state administration destroys the notion of unified hierarchy and undermines the governor's ability to manage other executive branch administrators. The four governors who were interviewed agree that this fragmentation is a drag on the governor's ability to function effectively, as illustrated in Sidebar 5–8.[33] From the standpoint of governors and organization theorists alike, these are significant problems for a strong executive.

On the rationale for the fragmentation, Governor Hansen speculates that it goes back to the thinking and intentions of the Consti-

tutional Convention. Governor Hathaway is less philosophical, however:

I'd have to say as a Republican that this is mainly a product of Republican thinking, in that in the earlier days they felt that in the years that they didn't control the governorship, they could still pretty much run the government with boards and commissions and the lapover of appointments.

The governors are unanimous in their opinion that Wyoming has too many boards and commissions. This parceling out of administrative authority only decreases the governor's accountability. Could one man possible stay on top of 120 agencies, boards and commissions? Probably not. As a result, state agencies, indeed bureaucracy, often become more unwieldy and less responsible to the elected leader. Although the governors do not agree

Sidebar 5–9
Governor Hathaway on the Need for Reorganization of the Executive Branch

We consolidated Health and Welfare and brought vocational rehabilitation into it. That became the Department of Health and Social Services . . . That was a good move; we felt it was necessary. They were spending so much money . . . with so little control, they had to be brought together. They wouldn't even walk across the hall to talk to each other. The welfare people and the health people; we tried to bring them together.

on the best method of accomplishing it, they believe a reorganization of state government is necessary (See Sidebar 5–9).

Further, no consensus was found in opposition to the present cabinet system of sharing important responsibilities among top elected officials. Opinions range from Governor Simpson, who likes and defends the present system, to Governors Hathaway and Herschler who are more apprehensive. In particular, however, the governors agree that the cabinet system has the benefit of increasing the sharing of ideas, perspectives, and backgrounds by the members. But this system, which in many respects makes the governor merely one of several "chief" executives, clearly leaves the office of governor in a weaker administrative position than does a unified hierarchy with the governor at the top. Governor Herschler would prefer to eliminate two offices from the present cabinet, secretary of state and superintendent of public instruction. Governor Simpson agrees concerning the superintendent. In some degree, these actions would increase the influence of the governor by decreasing the number of voices (and sometimes competitors) on the boards and commissions; also, his appointment power (and perhaps his accountability or control) would be increased.

Putting the Pieces Together. We find from all of this that the governor of Wyoming, regardless of the individual person who holds the office, does not come to a position made uniquely "strong" by our constitution or statutes. Nor is it a weak office overall. Several characteristics of the office offer increased authority. He may seek two or more terms, is active in the budget process, and may veto individual appropriations without killing whole bills (called the line-item veto). On the other hand, the governor suffers severe limitations in the extent to which he is able to direct policy among executive officers. The conclusion reached earlier seems all the more correct. The effectiveness of the governor of Wyoming depends in large part upon his or her individual leadership skills, party support in and out of the legislature, public support, and issue popularity.

Finally, don't be misled by what you have just read. Some readers may have a tendency to think that the "strong" model is the "good" model. This may be the case if you are a governor, but may not be the case if you aren't. The intent here is not to convince anyone that one system is better than another. Rather, the intent is to show the merits of each. Regarding the weaker aspects of the Wyoming governor, remember three things. First, in those areas where the governor lacks certain prerogatives, the legislature usually has them or has intentionally kept them from the governor. Whether statutory or constitutional, the gubernatorial limits were seldom, if ever, accidental. Second, the governors interviewed are generally satisfied with the powers of the office. Unanimous objections are present in only one area, the appointment powers. Overall, the governors find that they are able to move or work with the office. Third, the system works. Don't underestimate this. Wyoming has a unique political system. The state has a part-time legislature which is made up of citizen politicians, and a governor with enough room to be creative and show leadership, depending upon his individual skills and political good fortune. There is much to be said for this balance.

We see, then, that the office of governor has both constitutional, statutory, and personal strengths and weaknesses. Asked for his overall assessment of the position and whether the office truly has the wherewithal to fit its popular image, Governor Hansen was particularly articulate. Better than any other comment during the hours of conversation, Hansen's comment captures both the effectiveness and limitations of the office. He concludes:

Well, I'm sure there are times when one is frustrated, that it would be nice to have the power to do a little bit more than presently is constitutionally possible. But, I think it is not badly organized, not badly set up. I have this feeling, that few people have gone into the office any more naive than was I, but I think that a strong executive can make his convictions felt. And, really, to make the office stronger constitutionally doesn't necessarily assure the success of every incumbent in the office by any means.

Notes

1. In this instance, a citizen could seek a writ of mandamus by the state supreme court, thereby ordering the police to enforce the law.
2. In this instance, this is an accurate summary of the events. But, remember, there are ways that laws can pass without the governor's signature. See Chapter 5 for an explanation.

3. Jack C. Plano and Milton Greenberg, *The American Political Dictionary,* 4th ed. (Hinsdale, Illinois: Dryden Press, 1976), p. 220.
4. Tim R. Miller, an interview of Dr. Blaine Dinger, former Director of the Industrial Siting Administration, Summer, 1978.
5. Ibid.; see the *1979 Wyoming Official Directory,* comp. Secretary of State Thyra Thomson, pp. 43–44.
6. For the most part, these six boards and commissions trace their origin to the Wyoming Constitution and a variety of statutes which strengthen and interpret them. For example, see the Wyoming Constitution, art. 4, secs. 13, 18 and 22; art. 18, sec. 3; and art. 19, sec. 10.
7. *A Look at Wyoming Government,* 3d ed. (League of Women Voters, 1975), p. 33.
8. Maris H. Erwin, *Wyoming Historical Blue Book: A Legal and Political History of Wyoming, 1868–1943* (Denver: Bradford-Robinson Printing Co., 1946), p. 151.
9. Howard Baldwin Bouton, "The Office of the Governor of Wyoming" (Masters thesis, University of Wyoming, 1950), p. 6 quoting *General Laws, Memorials, and Resolutions of the Territory of Wyoming, 1869,* chaps 7 and 23.
10. Ibid.; also, see Erwin, pp. 544–545 .
11. Wyoming State Constitution, art. 4, secs. 2 and 3.
12. Wyoming State Constitution, art. 4, secs. 4 and 5. Also, the constitution specifies that "the legislature may by law regulate the manner in which the remission of fines, pardons, commutations and reprieves may be applied for."
13. Plano and Greenberg, p. 205.
14. Ibid.
15. Wyoming State Constitution, art. 4, secs. 4 and 7.
16. Actually, it is even more complicated than that. The governor has three days after receiving a bill to sign it or veto it. If he does not sign and return it in three days (not counting Sunday), it is law without his signature, if the legislature is still in session. If the legislature has adjourned during the three-day interval, the governor may veto the bill within 15 days by filing his objections with the secretary of state; otherwise, it is law even without the governor's signature.
17. Tim R. Miller and John T. Hinckley, "The Office of Governor: Observations of Four Wyoming Governors," *Learning Modules of Wyoming Politics,* funded through a grant from

the National Science Foundation, Local Course Improvement Program, Grant No. (SER77–03819) (Laramie: Center for Government Research, 1980). This was from one of four interviews with living Wyoming governors by John T. Hinckley. The interviews were conducted in the summer of 1977.

18. For a few examples, see T. A. Larson, *History of Wyoming* (Lincoln: University of Nebraska Press, 1973), pp. 357–358, 429, 468, 486, 498, 528, 535, 538–540. Also, see Chapter 7.

19. Miller and Hinckley, Hathaway interview.

20. State money is allocated from, or given out of, a variety of state "funds." The bulk of the operating expenses of state government comes from the "general fund." A portion of most Wyoming taxes go to this fund, with other amounts earmarked for other more specific funds.

21. Miller and Hinckley, Hathaway interview.

22. Ibid., interviews with Simpson, Hansen, Hathaway and Herschler.

23. David R. Berman, State and Local Politics (Boston: Holbrook Press, 1975), p. 104.

24. For a brief analysis of this trend in the presidency, see "The Incumbency Factor: History is Working in Carter's Favor," *Congressional Quarterly Weekly Report* 37 (May 5, 1979):825.

25. Samuel K. Gove, "Why Strong Governors?," *National Civic Review,* March, 1964, pp. 131–136; reprinted in *Capitol, Courthouse, and City Hall,* comp. Robert L. Morlan, 5th ed. (Boston: Houghton Mifflin, 1977), pp. 107–109.

26. Ibid.

27. Ibid.

28. The seven men were DeForest Richards (1899–1903), Bryant B. Brooks (1905–1911), Frank C. Emerson (1927–1931), Leslie A. Miller (1933–1939), Lester C. Hunt (1943–1949), Stanley K. Hathaway (1967–1975) and Ed Herschler (1975–present).

29. See "More Than You Want to Know About Wyoming Taxes" (League of Women Voters of Wyoming, Dec. 1976), p. 12. Also, see Chapter 7.

30. Miller and Hinckley, Hathaway interview.

31. The characteristics of bureaucratic organizations were first discussed systematically by Max Weber. Numerous other articles have also been written. For more on the subject, see James G. March and Herbert Simon, *Organi-zations* (New York: John Wiley and Sons, 1958); Peter M. Blau and W. Richard Scott, *Formal Organizations* (San Francisco: Chandler Publishing Co., 1962); Theodore Caplow, *Principles of Organization* (New York: Harcourt, Brace and World, Inc., 1964); *Handbook of Organizations,* edited by James G. March (Chicago: Rand McNally and Co., 1965); and Anthony Downs, *Inside Bureaucracy* (Boston: Little, Brown and Co., 1967).

32. A few important examples of officials who are directly accountable to the governor are the attorney general, state engineer, director of the Department of Administration and Fiscal Control, director of the Department of Health and Social Services, etc.

33. Governor Hathaway:

He'd (i.e. governor) appoint the commissioners but that would be the end of it. They selected the head of the department—the director or superintendent, whatever he may be. I found some of those departments to be very unresponsive to what I thought was the public will. We enacted some legislation during my term that gave the governor some authority with respect to those boards and commissions—at least gave him a vote on many of them.

Governor Simpson's response (Question—Do you feel that the appointive power of the office was sufficiently broad?):

Well, John, it used to be more so. But they've watered it down now so that, for instance, the law tells you who you appoint. It may eliminate some awfully good men and women. For instance, if you have a Democratic governor and he wants to get a Livestock Commission with a Democratic preponderance you're confined to one to make a majority, like four to three. And that's not particularly good. . . . I called Scotty Jack to my office because I think he was one of the best students of government in the State of Wyoming. And I had a chance to put him in the Board of Equalization after our election (Wm. "Scotty" Jack was Simpson's Democratic opponent for Governor in 1954. Simpson won in a very close race, 56, 275 to 55,163. . . . He was delighted to get the job but we had an awful time trying to get it for him because of that maladjustment of the Board. . . .)

CHAPTER

SIX

The Courts

Civil and Criminal Law

There are two broad bodies of American law—civil and criminal. Civil law involves actions between private persons, including individuals, organizations, or corporations, and increasingly common suits against the government. Under civil law, "the government provides the forum for the settlement of disputes between private parties in such matters as contracts, domestic relations, business relations, and auto accidents."[1] Civil suits, then, result from a variety of circumstances in which one party believes that it has been injured by another party, as in the case of divorce, nonpayment of debts, or tort claims (i.e. "a wrongful act involving injury to persons, property or reputation, but excluding breach of contract . . ."[2]). Suppose, for example, that someone's car is struck by a car that runs a stop sign. Maybe someone else buys a piece of land in Louisiana with the realtor's assurance that it is part of a developed community, but it turns out to be swamp. Or, perhaps someone incorrectly tells a roommate that his government professor is incompetent at his job. In each of these instances, the victim (a "plaintiff") has the right to bring a civil action against the person or persons having committed the wrong (a "defendant"). After all, each of us has the right to be secure against damage to our property (e.g. car) or reputation, or being taken advantage of through deceptive, fraudulent business practices.

The amount of damages that these plaintiffs might win would vary according to the degree of their suffering (See Sidebar 6–1).

Sidebar 6–1
Plaintiff Negligence

by Justice of the Peace Hunter Patrick

It is correct that the amount of damages a plaintiff receives varies according to the degree the individual has suffered. It is also true that the amount of damages may vary according to the degree that the plaintiff was negligent himself where a tort claim is involved. Many states still follow the traditional common law doctrine under which if the plaintiff is negligent even in the most minute amount, he is completely barred from recovering any damages whatso-ever. Other states, including Wyoming, have abrogated the common law and adopted a comparative negligence doctrine, under which, if it is determined that the plaintiff was negligent as well as the defendant, the amount that he is able to recover is reduced by the extent of his negligence, and, under most such statutes, if the plaintiff's fault exceeds 49 percent, he cannot recover anything at all.

They must, of course, first prove that they were actually harmed by the defendant. If so, the plaintiffs have a clear right to damages. Notice, civil damages, called "judgments," are ordinarily awarded in money. In the United States, people are never jailed for civil offenses.

Criminal law involves actions "against the public order." Criminal offenses are actions against the people of the particular political unit. The people's representatives—acting through the state constitution and legislatures—have said that certain actions are against the best interests of the people of Wyoming. When someone sticks a gun in somebody else's face and takes his money, commits rape, or deals in heroin, he has broken the law, committing an act against the people of this state. For these acts, the offender would be arrested by the state (police), prosecuted by the state (county attorney), tried by the state (district court), and perhaps even "housed" by the state (state prison).

By statute, there are two types of criminal offenses in Wyoming. Misdemeanors are less serious criminal acts. In Wyoming, misdemeanors include crimes with maximum fines of $750 and/or sentences of up to six months in city or county jails. These offenses may be disposed of by a justice of the peace. Thus, most traffic violations, underage possession of alcoholic beverages, "insufficient funds" checks for $50 or less, and shoplifting small items are misdemeanors. The more serious crimes are felonies; felonies are crimes that are punishable with a term in the state prison. Violent crimes such as murder, rape, burglary, and armed robbery are felonies, as are embezzlement and theft.[3]

Although the statute draws the distinction between felonies and misdemeanors as outlined here, distinctions can also be drawn between high and low misdemeanors. While the "use" of marijuana is an ordinary misdemeanor as defined above, "possession" of marijuana—a legal distinction—is punishable by a possible fine of $1000 and six months imprisonment. Because the penalty exceeds the $750 and/or six months (in county jail) maximum, it is a "high" misdemeanor. Accordingly, high misdemeanors are heard in district court.

These two bodies of American jurisprudence, or law, exist within a foundation of "democratic constitutionalism." However, this tells only part of the story. To fully appreciate America's legal system, it is crucial to consider the law within the context of the overall framework—the "rule of law." So, America has both criminal and civil laws. In so many nations of the world, however, the law means relatively little. This is not the case in Wyoming or the United States because of the rule of law. This simply means that we are a state and nation "of laws, not of men." The law is supreme; no men are above it. The rule of law:

requires that each individual accused of crime be treated equally under the law, receive a fair trial with established procedures, and be accorded due process (meaning procedural safeguards which must be followed when determining guilt and innocence, or validity of government actions) in all official actions undertaken against him.[4]

Although this is not to imply that every person who is convicted of a particular crime will receive the same exact sentence (after all, judges must consider unique aspects of every case), it is to say that all people enjoy the same rights and privileges under the law. Thus, the bodies of civil and criminal law in Wyoming, and the United States, exist within the framework of the "rule of law" and "due process." These are major tenets, or principles, of our constitutional system of government.

Structure of Wyoming Courts

Article Five of the Wyoming Constitution begins by saying, "The judicial power of the state shall be vested . . . in a supreme court, district courts, and such subordinate courts as the legislature may, by general law, establish and ordain from time to time." The first section of Article Five establishes a three-tier court system, as is common throughout the United States. The constitution creates the supreme court as the highest court in Wyoming and district courts to handle the bulk of cases, and instructs the legislature to create local courts to resolve less serious issues. Courts in each of these three levels hear both civil and criminal cases.

Also, the "jurisdiction" of the supreme and district courts are established in Article Five.[5] Jurisdiction means, "authority vested in a court to hear and decide a case."[6] There are several types of jurisdiction (See Sidebar 6–2).

"Geographic" jurisdiction means that courts have authority to hear cases stemming from events which occurred within a particular geographic area only. The Wyoming Supreme Court, for example, hears cases which stem from events occurring only in Wyoming; Casper Municipal Court hears cases which occurred in Casper.

Courts also have "subject matter" jurisdiction or authority. The subject matter of some events, for example, means that local courts have authority to hear cases, rather than the higher courts. A person who pleads innocent to violating a city ordinance against letting dogs run loose would have his case heard before a municipal court in his city. The municipal court has jurisdiction, or authority, to hear cases involving these kinds of subject matter disputes. At the other extreme, Squeaky Fromm, who tried to assassinate President Ford, was tried in federal court; the federal courts have jurisdiction over such sub-

---

Sidebar 6–2
Jurisdiction over the Parties and Subject Matter

by Justice of the Peace Hunter Patrick

Easily we speak in terms of jurisdiction over the subject matter and personal jurisdiction over the parties. Personal jurisdiction over the parties may or may not depend upon their residing within the geographical boundaries of the area in which the court presides. Personal jurisdiction over the parties may be based upon their presence in the area of the Court, or upon the occurrence of an incident within the area over which the Court presides, the conducting of business within that area, the making of a contract within that area, and so forth. Ordinarily defendants are sued in a place where they can be served with process, unless personal jurisdiction over them has been bestowed upon a court in some other area. For example, Wyoming has a long-armed statute giving Wyoming district courts the authority to hear and try cases regarding automobile accidents which occur within their geographic boundaries, although the defendants who are being sued live outside of the state. Criminal cases ordinarily must be prosecuted in the county in which the criminal act took place. In civil cases, there is also the concept of jurisdiction by reason of the fact that property involved in the case is within the territorial jurisdiction of the court—for example, Quiet Title actions to determine the title to real property, are filed in the district court which presides over the territory in which the real property is located.

ject matter (i.e. federal crimes, like attempts to kill a federal official).

Whereas cases involving national law, civil suits between citizens of different states involving more than $10,000 (federal and state courts share this jurisdiction, called "concurrent jurisdiction"), and disputes between states are heard in the federal courts,[7] state courts have jurisdiction over violations of state law, civil suits between citizens of the same state, civil suits between citizens of different states involving less than $10,000, and civil suits against state government. The discussion which follows considers the specific jurisdiction and structure of the three levels of Wyoming courts.

Local Courts.[8] The legislature has created three local level courts in Wyoming to handle the least serious cases. Municipal courts, also called police courts, are at the lowest level in Wyoming's court system. There are about 70 municipal courts throughout the state. Judges are appointed by their city or town mayors and councils. Municipal judges hold court once or twice a week, depending upon the case load. Obviously, being a municipal judge is a part-time job. In fact, only half of them are lawyers. When the city council cannot find an attorney who is willing to accept the appointment (because many attorneys can make more money by concentrating on their private practices), they appoint laymen (non-lawyers). All of these judges (whether attorneys or not) are then trained to preside over misdemeanors, the lowest level criminal cases. Municipal courts hear violations of city ordinances, such as municipal traffic offenses.[9] A city ordinance is a low level "law" passed by a city council. These ordinances regulate behavior in the particular community. Typically, towns and cities pass ordinances against people letting their dog run loose, failure to properly provide for trash, having open liquor containers in public, being

out after curfew and watering lawns at improper times.

Sidebar 6–3, from the *Powell Tribune,* shows a 1979 instance of someone being arrested for violation of a Powell city ordinance against public obscenity. The youth who violated the ordinance was fined $200 in Powell's municipal court. Like anyone else charged with disobeying a city ordinance, he was instructed (through issuance of a complaint and warrant) to appear before the municipal court. When a defendant (any person charged with a crime or against whom a civil action is brought) appears before a judge, he is advised of the charge against him and his rights to have an attorney, to appeal to district court if convicted in the municipal court, etc. Also, the defendant enters a plea. If, as in the Powell obscenity case, the defendant pleads guilty, the judge will set the fine. If the defendant pleads innocent, a trial date is set and the issue is heard before the municipal court. Failure to appear on the scheduled trial date is treated as a guilty plea.

Notice that in this discussion of municipal courts no reference has been made to civil suits. Municipal courts have no civil jurisdiction; they do not hear civil cases.

The second local court, one which is widely known, is the justice of the peace (called JP) court. There are some 50 JP courts in communities across Wyoming. Like municipal courts, they are part-time courts directed by judges who may or may not be attorneys. About half of the state's justices of the peace are lawyers, half are laymen. The JP's, whether laymen or trained in the law, also undergo training under direction of the state supreme court. JP's are elected in non-partisan elections (they run as independents rather than Republicans or Democrats) to four-year terms.

Sidebar 6–3
A Case before Police Court

(From an article appearing in the Powell Tribune)

'Public Acceptance' is general criteria for obscenity violations

Powell's obscenity ordinance was recently put to a test when Powell police charged a young T-shirt wearer with a violation of that city law because of a certain four letter word stenciled on his shirt and displayed in a public place.

The case, and the subsequent decision of city police judge John Lake upholding the charge with a $200 fine, raised a question as to what standards of obscenity exist in the Powell community, how these standards are set, and who in the community determines what constitutes an obscenity.

Powell police chief Bob Coorough explained his views on the interpretation of the local obscenity ordinance, which reads: "It shall be unlawful for any person to sell, or offer to sell, or display, show, or exhibit any indecent, lewd, or obscene book, picture, drawing, or other thing, or exhibit or perform any indecent, immoral, lewd or obscene play, film, or other presentation."

How is this ordinance interpreted? "With great difficulty," Coorough asserted. "And the U.S. Supreme Court hasn't helped a whole lot. They say that each community must set its own standards."

Coorough pointed out that if the police feel there has been a violation of the ordinance, they make a charge, but the court system itself ultimately determines what constitutes a violation. Decisions may be appealed all the way up to the U.S. Supreme Court, which is wrestling with numerous such cases.

"Ours is not the final say," he stressed. "There's got to be a line drawn somewhere. I know the lines are changing and there is now public acceptance of things that would not have been acceptable ten years ago. Personally, I'd like to do more than we are doing and get rid of some of these magazines on the stands. I think we're far too permissive."

Coorough noted, however, that public acceptance is the general criteria used by law authorities when making a decision to press charges for obscenity violations. They recognize this acceptance, he went on, "by a feeling that we have."

Coorough noted that people have asked him why wearing the T-shirt in the bowling alley was a violation, but an "R" rated movie at the local theater would not be considered an obscenity violation. Choice in viewing material that is offensive to some but not to others seemed to be the guideline.

"People that would be offended by what is being shown at the theater at a given time do not have to buy a ticket to go in and see it," he elaborated. "But when you are in a general public place you are more restricted than you would be in a place reserved for a specific audience, for example."

The T-shirt in question was worn in a general public place where everyone would have to view it, Coorough continued, and "the only way you could miss seeing it would have been to shut your eyes."

"A lot of people are offended by that word," he declared. "I know you can see the same word over and over again in certain magazines, but the words there are under wraps."

People who do not want to read that word do not have to buy the magazines that contain them, he reflected.

The shirt itself was not a violation, Coorough added. The violation arose from where the shirt was worn. It would also not be a violation to make such a shirt, he said, unless the shirt were being lettered where the general public could view the process.

Justice of the peace courts have wider jurisdiction than municipal courts. They are empowered to decide civil suits involving up to $1,000 (e.g. through no fault of your own, someone runs into your car. You sue for the $600 damage done to your car, plus $200 for your inconvenience); they hear criminal cases with a maximum penalty of six months in jail and/or a fine of $750 (traffic violations, a minor in possession of alcohol, petty larceny, and game and fish violations are common). JP courts also act as small claims courts for issues involving $200 or less. Small claims suits allow individuals to sue others when they have been wronged, *without* having to hire an attorney. When a person thinks that a merchant has taken advantage of him, for example, he can bring suit against him in a small claims court. The plaintiff (the person who brought suit) and the merchant (the defendant) then appear before the judge and explain what happened in their own words. Although either party could hire an attorney, they are neither required nor expected to do so (See Sidebar 6–4).

Justice of the peace courts also perform several procedural duties, such as conducting marriages, administering oaths and supervising intial appearance, arraignments and preliminary hearings. The "initial appearance"[10] takes place the first time that a person appears before a justice of the peace. At that time, the judge explains the nature of the charges and the maximum possible penalty for the charges and explains the defendant's constitutional rights to him, sets bail[11] and determines whether a court appointed attorney is necessary. No plea is entered on a felony charge until the defendant appears before the district court.

The next hearing before the justice of the peace on a felony charge is a preliminary hearing, which determines whether there is a prob-able cause to believe that the offense was committed and committed by the defendant. "Probable cause" may sound so obvious that it seems unnecessary in the law. But, how many times have stories been heard, particularly abroad, but at times in American history as well, of unpopular figures being imprisoned while the authorities look for trumped up charges? Because of the probable cause standard, such outlandish abuses, with notable exceptions, are uncommon in American jurisprudence. Since the state must show probable cause, prosecutors are likely to pursue only legitimate matters. Clearly, this is not the case throughout the world.

Probable cause is ordinarily found, because the standard of proof is mere "probability." Probable cause exists if a reasonable man, after looking at the facts, would conclude that a crime had probably been committed and that the defendant had probably been involved. Notice, the standard of proof for probable cause is considerably less than the "beyond a reasonable doubt" standard in determining guilt. If probable cause is not found, the case is dismissed.

If the case is a misdemeanor, however, the first appearance is called an arraignment, because the judge explains the nature of the charge, the maximum possible penalty, pertinent constitutional rights, and accepts a plea. The case is ordinarily disposed of (sentence given on the spot) at the time, in the event that the defendant pleads guilty. If the defendant pleads not guilty, the case is set for trial at a later date. In the event that the defendant wants a jury trial on a misdemeanor, he must make it known at the time of the arraignment. The right to a jury trial, in contrast, is automatic in felony cases.

In 1971, the Wyoming legislature authorized the creation of a new local court, with

Sidebar 6–4
Small Claims in Wyoming

(Excerpts of an interview of J. P. Hunter Patrick, from the June, 1979 issue of Wyoming News, *by Tim Miller)*

Question: How does the small claims court work? Suppose that somebody believes he got a bum deal from a merchant or whatever. What can he do?

Answer: He can go to his friendly JP and say, "I have this problem and am interested in filing a small claims case." Most people who come in don't know how the court works and are really in to find out. The maximum that a person can sue for in small claims court is $200. . . . There's a $5 filing fee (plus $1 or $2 for the sheriff to serve the papers). . . . We make out the papers . . . and the sheriff serves them on the person being sued. . . . You can only sue someone who's in the county where you're filing suit. Otherwise, you have to sue them in a county where they can be served.

Question: Does the plaintiff have to hire a lawyer?

Answer: Both parties may bring lawyers if they want. . . . They usually don't. The idea of the small claims court is that it's a layman's court, and rules of evidence are not followed. So, you don't have to be familiar with the formalities. . . . The person who files the suit states his case first (in plain English). Usually the judge will have a few questions to ask. . . . Then the other party has the right to question him or cross-examine him.

Question: They are merely to ask questions?

Answer: Right. . . . And if the plaintiff has other witnesses he can use them too. . . . After the plaintiff gets through it's the defendant's turn. He goes through about the same procedure. Then the plaintiff gets the last word. . . . Then the judge, if he feels that he knows what his decision is at that point, will go ahead and announce his decision. If he thinks he needs to listen to the testimony again (a tape recording) and study it a little . . . he can take it under advisement and give his decision after he has a chance to do that.

Question: If it comes down to who you believe, do you ever compromise? Say, give the plaintiff $50 when he's asking for $100?

Answer: No, I can't say I've ever compromised one like that. . . . Sometimes I will allow a claim, but less than requested because I don't think the amount that's requested is legitimate.

Question: Suppose I have a claim for $100, but have suffered some inconvenience too. Can I sue for more than the $100?

Answer: Incidental damages may be what you're looking for. You can sue for incidental damages, (like) . . . the inconvenience of not having your car, for example, and for any extra expense that you were put to. . . .

Question: Who uses this court?

Answer: They're rarely used by citizens. They're used more by collection agencies than anyone else. . . . I think for disputes between private citizens, and disputes between private citizens and businesses other than collection agencies . . . maybe small claims court should be used more.

Question: Can you give me an example of a case you've heard?

Answer: I had one suit over $20. The plaintiff sold an old hay rake to the defendant for $20. The way the plaintiff told it he told the defendant nothing about how well it worked or anything. . . . The defendant took it home. . . . Then the defendant called the plaintiff and said, 'It's nothing but junk!' . . . the defendant said that the plaintiff guaranteed him that it would work . . . so there you are. There were only two witnesses and their testimony was exactly opposite. So, I had to weight the credibility of it and decide who was telling the truth. And I don't know what the probabilities are of my being right in a given case.

authority to hear both civil and criminal disputes, called county courts. County courts are an attempt to "professionalize" or upgrade municipal and justice of the peace courts, by having full-time county judges, who are to be attorneys selected in the same manner as district and supreme court judges. The law requires counties which had a population of 30,000 in the 1970 census to establish the new court (as of this writing, there are rumblings of lowering the population figure to 20,000). However, only two counties—Natrona and Laramie—fell under the mandatory requirement of the statute. The 1971 act has been so riddled with amendments and delays, that the first two courts were not created until 1979. While the act allows smaller counties to voluntarily create county courts, none of the smaller counties has done so as of 1979. The 1971 legislation has been amended and delayed so often that there is considerable confusion regarding this new level of local courts. Even so, the "reform" is an attempt at correcting some of the procedural, caseload, and professional shortcomings of the other local courts.

Local courts—whether municipal, justice of the peace, or county—have authority to try cases for the first time. Hearing cases the first time they are tried is called "original" jurisdiction. They have no "appellate" jurisdiction, meaning that local courts do not hear cases which have been tried in another court and are being appealed.

District Court. Wyoming is divided into nine judicial districts. Fifteen judges hold court in the nine districts. The courts have original jurisdiction for criminal cases with penalties greater than six months in jail and/ or a $750 fine, and for civil suits where more than $1,000 are sought in damages. Actually, a civil suit seeking between $500 and $1,000 can be started in either district or justice of the peace court ("concurrent" jurisdiction). Thus, civil cases involving more than $1,000 must be tried in district court; cases involving less than $500 must be heard in JP court; civil

A district court in session. Photo by K. T. Roes.

suits which ask damages of between $500 and $1,000 may be brought in either court. Serious criminal cases, then, are tried for the first (and often last) time in a district court.

Also, district courts have appellate jurisdiction. Cases which have been adjudicated (or decided) in a local court can be appealed to this, the next higher level. People often misunderstand the grounds for making an appeal. In the movies, it appears as if a defendant who has been convicted of a crime (or a party who has lost a civil action) can appeal on the basis that he is really innocent. In reality, this is not the case. An appeal must be based on a contention that the lower court made an error of law which was prejudicial to the defendant in the trial. The person who brings the appeal claims that because the judge who first heard the case made an error of law (the judge incorrectly instructed the jury about the law, was prejudiced against the defendant, erred by not admitting relevant evidence, etc.), the original verdict must be either reversed or thrown out and the case retried in the lower court. Again, the key is the allegation that an error of law has been made. An error of fact does not justify an appeal. It is not enough, for example, to appeal on the basis that the witness who said she saw the defendant shoot the victim was mistaken. The defendant might, however, appeal on the grounds that the judge who tried the case made an error of law when he refused to admit testimony that the witness was blind.

When the district court tries a case for the first time, it operates as we usually think of courts operating. In criminal cases, juries are normally called; in civil suits, juries are seldom called. Attorneys for both sides present evidence, call witnesses, and cross-examine witnesses for the other side. When district court is considering an appeal from one of the local courts (or an administrative agency's ruling), the procedure is different. The district court reads written arguments, called "briefs," prepared by the attorneys involved in the suit. The appellant's brief argues that errors were made; the other party argues that significant errors were not made. After reviewing the briefs and the tape recording of the lower court's deliberations, the district court rules on appeals.

Some 10,000 cases are filed annually in district courts throughout the state. In 1977, the most recent year for which figures were available at the time of this writing, 10,333 cases were filed across Wyoming. Of these, 87.5 percent (9,049) were civil cases. As Table 6.1 indicates, the vast majority of issues taken to district court are civil disputes. Also, the figures reveal that the district court caseload is growing.

Although the figures are not given for the lower courts, it is interesting to note that the number of cases filed annually in local courts exceeds the district court rate several times over. Thus, the only experience that most people have with the court system is an appearance before one of the minor courts. This is a persuasive argument for having strong minor courts, since that is where most impressions are formed.

Table 6.1. District Court Caseload Totals 1975–1978

| Year | Number of Cases Filed | | |
	Civil	Criminal	Total
1975	7,987	1,629	9,616
1976	7,981	1,329	9,310
1977	9,049	1,284	10,333
1978 (estimate)	9,700	1,430	11,130

Supreme Court. The highest court in Wyoming is the supreme court. It is composed of five justices, who serve eight-year terms. The court has both original and appellate jurisdiction.[12] However, except for a few court orders (called writs), the supreme court nearly always acts just on appeals from the district courts. This makes sense; it is a procedural safeguard. When the supreme court exercises its original jurisdiction, no appeal can be made (unless a federal issue is involved), because there are no higher courts. But by hearing cases on appeal, the safeguard is built in. The matter will have been tried in one court and the decision reviewed in at least one other (See Sidebar 6–5).

The justices elect one of their members to serve as chief justice. In the past, the justices rotated the chief justiceship among themselves, depending upon who was about to stand for re-election (the election process is explained later). In recent years, however, the chief justices have served longer terms. The chief justice, in many ways, is the chief administrator for the court. He is a leader, but not a boss. His duties are to preside (or direct events) over the court when it is in session and hearing arguments and over conference meetings when judges get together to discuss cases. Another responsibility of the chief justice is to assign a justice to write the majority opinion on a particular case. After the judges complete their deliberations (the lengthy process of considering the arguments of a particular case) and arrive at their decision, one of the justices who voted in the majority writes down the reasoning behind the ruling. The chief justice also coordinates dissent among the judges, trying to shape common opinions based on compromise. Also, the chief justice handles the daily administrative responsibilities of the court, approving and signing a large number of procedural and administrative matters. Ac-

cording to the court's coordinator, former Judge Reuel Armstrong, there are "a jillion of them."

The Courts in Action—Three Hypothetical Cases

The section that you have just read is brief. It is meant to be an outline, or summary, of the court system in Wyoming. The question which comes to mind now is "how does it all work?" The examples which follow are typical of the many cases which are considered yearly in the state's courts.

Justice of the Peace—Criminal Case. Section 31–5–229 of the Wyoming Statutes (1977) reads, "Any person who drives any vehicle in willful or wanton disregard for the safety of persons or property is guilty of reckless driving." The maximum state penalty (some municipal ordinances are higher) is a $100 fine, plus $10 court costs, and/or 10 days in county jail if it is the first traffic offense within the previous year (20 days for the second offense and six months for the third). Driving privileges are also suspended for 90 days.[13]

Consider this hypothetical case study. Johnny Yellowstone, a Wyoming college student, was observed by a city police officer, Patrolman Law N. Order, in the school parking lot cutting figure-eights in his car, throwing rocks with his tires. Three other people saw Johnny, a friend who was with him in the car and two high school students who were in the parking lot. Johnny was arrested and ordered to appear before the local justice of the peace for arraignment the next week.

At the outset of this example, the police may have already been faced with a choice. Reckless driving is a violation of state law; however, several municipalities have copied

Sidebar 6–5
Former Chief Justice Rodney M. Guthrie on the Philosophical Perspective of the Wyoming Supreme Court

Question: How would you describe the political philosophy of the Wyoming Supreme Court, either over the last few years or throughout state history? I assume that you don't like the characterizations "liberal" and "conservative," but use them as a starting point.

Answer: I don't think the words liberal and conservative fit the courts. I don't think it fits anything much. I've always taken hombrage at the description of the court in that manner. I might say the word "activist" may be what you're talking about. . . . An activist court can either be what you apparently conceive as being very conservative or they can be very liberal. By activist I mean a court that tends to impress their own philosophy upon the law. The people talk about the Warren court (Earl Warren was Chief Justice of the U.S. Supreme Court from 1953–69) being very activist or being very, very liberal. They were very much activists imposing their own personal philosophy. However, they were no more activists than the court (U.S. Supreme Court) from 1910–20 when they reached a high—they were described as very conservative. They were still very much activists. Their decisions really were just implementations of their own philosophy. . . . I don't think the Wyoming courts through the years have been particularly activist, except the fact that a lot of people don't realize it. In the seminars that I have attended, the Wyoming view of the law was what . . . might be called liberal. . . . You know the Supreme Court in this state, for over 50 years recognized the exclusionary rule and enforced the rule that the U.S. Supreme Court says it "discovered" in Mapp v. Ohio (a 1961 ruling that a state may not use illegally seized evidence in criminal trials). We also had very strict construction [in other ways] . . . long before Miranda. As I've said and still believe, neither Escobedo nor Miranda would have ever gotten out of Wyoming district court and I'm not describing the Wyoming court as liberal. I'm describing them as

at least being activists in their inclination to be left alone—don't interfere. They weren't encouraging official action that would impinge on your activities, is maybe what I should have said . . . . The courts that the average person describes as liberal, are activists usually trying to embody the law in their own personal philosophy. Understand that . . . a man can be so strong for the so-called phrase "law and order" that he wouldn't believe in the exclusionary rule which a lot of states didn't and, of course, which we have for years. To me it's just a choice of term. I think that presently the court that we have attempts to apply the law as precedence seems to establish, rather than being too strong for implementation of their own personal philosophies. They follow what they believe the body of the law is rather than . . . the way they believe is socially desirable. You sometimes have the feeling reading opinions of some judges that they decided the way they believe is socially desirable. Then they look back, find the authority to justify what they've done or what they choose to do. This court generally follows precedent. There are some areas that our court hasn't been operating long enough . . . to have enough cases. There are some cases that arise—several a year—that we don't have a rule for . . . we pick the rule we believe is better. . . . It's pretty hard not, in some manner, to have your thinking influenced by your background, your experience, your environment, a great many elements which may make you believe that a certain thing is more reasonable. . . . Of course, there isn't any question that the courts respond to changing social conditions. That's the beauty of common law—law by decision—it adapts itself to conditions as they change.

Question: Should courts pioneer those social or sociological needs?

Answer: No. I'd say they should adapt, but be careful not to attempt to be legislators. There's a happy medium.

various state offenses—such as reckless driving—in their municipal ordinances. If so, police in this illustration have the choice of filing the case in either JP court (state jurisdiction) or municipal court (city or town jurisdiction), because Johnny was in both the municipality and the state at the time of his offense. The major difference between the courts is often the severity of the penalty. The maximum JP fine for reckless driving, as mentioned above, is $110; municipalities with a reckless driving ordinance often raise the maximum fine to $210. Thus, in this example, the city either lacks the ordinance or the police opted for JP court for some other reason.[14]

Johnny, however, does not agree with Officer Order's version of the events. Sure, Johnny says, he threw a few rocks by accidentally spinning his tires. When he put his car in gear, he argues, his pedal stuck. He made a loop in the parking lot to avoid entering the road with the pedal stuck. While making the single loop, he reached down and pulled the pedal loose. So, while Officer Order thinks he acted irresponsibly, Johnny says he actually acted maturely and avoided a serious accident. Anyway, Johnny contends, Officer Order has never liked the town's young people. Realizing that his insurance rates will rise if convicted, and believing that he is really innocent of the charge, Johnny hires an attorney. Together, they plan Johnny's defense.

Next, Johnny appears before the court, with counsel, to be arraigned. Because this is a misdemeanor, he enters his plea—"not guilty"—after listening to the judge's explanation of the charge and pertinent issues. Because there is an outside possibility that he might be sentenced to jail for reckless driving, Johnny makes it known (as he must if he wants to be tried by his peers) that he wants to exercise his right to a jury trial.[15] The judge then schedules the case for trial at a later date.

At the outset of the trial, the jury is empaneled. Actually, the process of jury selection begins weeks, sometimes months, before any given trial. Initial lists of qualified voters are prepared by the county clerks, who take the names of qualified jurors from the list of registered voters in the county. These lists are then given to the appropriate clerk of the district court, who prepares small ballots, each containing the name of one of the persons on the list of qualified jurors. The ballots are then placed in the jury box. The names of the people who will serve on jury call for the next term are then drawn from the jury box. All of these people whose names are drawn (with the exceptions for people with valid reasons to be excused) are required to appear for each trial during the term. Before each trials begins, an initial 12 names are drawn. As seen below, however, being among the initial dozen names is no guarantee of being selected. A challenge process follows.

For JP courts, the clerk of district court has a special box containing only the names of qualified jurors who live within five miles of the municipality in which the JP serves. As outlined above, 12 names are drawn on the day of the trial from the box containing the names of the people on jury call.

The attorneys then proceed to examine the jurors. The purpose of this "cause" is to determine whether any bias or prejudice on the part of the jurors can be detected. If actual bias or other disqualifications are found, another juror is drawn and questioned by the attorneys. This procedure continues until a panel of 12 jurors remains. These jurors have been "accepted for cause" by the attorney for both sides.

At that point, the "nailing down" process begins. Remaining panel members are probed further for bias. This may even mean that particular jurors do not "sit right" with one of the attorneys. Admittedly, this is at times a guessing game. Typical questions are whether potential jurors can presume the defendant's innocence until (and unless) guilt is established beyond a reasonable doubt, or whether they know or have had dealings with any of the parties (including the attorneys). Gradually, the attorneys indicate which people are to be "excused," until the panel is whittled to six. Potential jurors may be excused for any reason; they are not told why they were excused or by which attorney. When the panel has been narrowed to six, the other people on jury call are dismissed. The trial is ready to begin.

With the panel at six, the judge advises the jurors of the law and gives them initial instructions. Next, the attorneys make their opening statements, followed by the testimony and cross-examination of witnesses.

Returning to the Johnny Yellowstone illustration, the county attorney (or an assistant) calls Officer Order, who tells the jurors what he saw by answering the prosecutor's questions. In this instance, the county attorney shows the jury a chalkboard and asks Officer Order to diagram the parking lot, his vantage point, where the figure eights were made and the location of parked cars. The defense attorney cross-examines by asking Officer Order any questions that might tend to discredit his testimony. He might ask the patrolman (particularly if he thought that the answer is yes), for example, whether it is true that 30 minutes before he saw Johnny in the parking lot he had been to an optometrist and had his eyes dilated (eye drops which blur vision). Next, the prosecutor calls his two other witnesses (the two students), who testify one at a time. They testify for the prosecution. The defense attorney cross-examines each of them. Again, he tries to poke holes in their testimony by showing contradictions or bias. After the prosecution is finished, the defense attorney calls Johnny to explain his version of what happened. Johnny disagrees with Officer Order's version of things, right down to the chalkboard drawing of how many times he drove the figure eight. This time, the prosecutor cross-examines. Next, the defense attorney calls Johnny's passenger, who supports the defendant's version; again, the prosecutor cross-examines. Notice, when there is conflicting testimony the jurors must decide which witnesses were the most believable. This, of course, is an extremely subjective matter. A witness's testimony may be accepted or rejected in the minds of the jurors because of his appearance, demeanor, or reputation. As a result, cases sometimes turn on a witness's race, sex, smile or voice intonation (See Sidebar 6–6).

Following the examination of witnesses, the judge repeats his instructions to the jury. He reminds them of the law and their responsibilities. Jurors are to determine whether the facts, as they interpret them (weighing the credibility of witnesses, etc.), warrant the conclusion "beyond a reasonable doubt" that the law was violated by the defendant.

Before the jurors begin their deliberations, however, the attorneys get a final chance to state their cases. An attorney for each side makes a final argument, tieing the judge's instructions to the case his side presented. Whether through an informative address or teary emotionalism, or both, each attorney "proves" to the jury that his is the only case that they can accept.

Next, the judge will repeat his instructions to the jurors. He again tells them what issues they are to determine, reads the appropriate law to them, and may even provide a copy of the law.

The jury then goes directly to its chamber room. They elect a foreman, review the evidence and law, discuss the issues, and vote.

Sidebar 6–6
A Personal Experience on a Jury

by Tim Miller

Several years ago, I served on a jury in a reckless driving case heard in JP court. During the empaneling process, we were repeatedly asked whether we could presume the defendant's innocence, unless shown otherwise beyond a reasonable doubt—the judge asked, both attorneys asked, and we swore an oath to that effect.

After the testimony, we retreated into the jury chambers to review the evidence and make a determination, according to the judge's instructions. When we sat down at the table, the first person to speak was a man in his late 50's or early 60's. He spoke before we had considered any of the things that we were instructed to discuss. The first thing he said was, "I think I know what happened here. This kid (he may have said 'punk,' but I can't swear to it) was showing off and hot rodding around, maybe showing off for a girl friend." His remarks showed that he had his mind made up before we reviewed the evidence (after all, there was evidence on both sides). And as I saw it—and this

is only my interpretation of what took place—his attitude (and other things he said) showed that the overriding factor in the case, for him, was that the defendant was only 19 years old. I also sensed that the defendant's Chicano ethnicity worked to his disadvantage with this juror. It seemed to me, then, that this particular juror voted "guilty" more on the basis of who the defendant was, than the evidence (which I agreed supported our "guilty" verdict).

There is nothing new or startling in this, of course, even if my "reading" of the situation is correct. It simply points out that, as with everything else people do, juries are subject to human frailties.

"Yes, Your Honor, I have an open mind." "Yes, counselor, I have an open mind." But let me find out that the defendant is a New York Yankee fan—where my prejudices take over—and I think I know what happened. "This young 'punk' is guilty. Now, Your Honor, bring on the evidence."

When the vote is unanimous (all six must agree), they return to the courtroom, where the judge reconvenes the proceedings and the foreman reads the verdict. If the jury is unable to arrive at a unanimous verdict, it is a "hung jury" and the state must schedule a new trial at a later date or drop the charges. The state (i.e., prosecutors) would, for instance, withdraw their case if they decided that it was a weak legal argument, or that it cost the taxpayers too much to pursue the matter.

In this case, it is bad news for Johnny. The jury has concluded that he is guilty beyond a reasonable doubt. The presiding justice of the peace sets the fine at $100 plus $10 court costs. Johnny may be bitter; he may not be willing to accept his guilt. But he shouldn't be. He

had his day in court, before his peers and with counsel to represent him. All things considered, justice was served. Besides, he has the right to appeal to the district court.

The trial outlined here is a brief one, as JP criminal trials usually are. This whole process would probably be completed in three to five hours.

District Court—Criminal Case. Trying not to lose sight of the lessons in this hypothetical case study, let's take it a step further. When Johnny left the Justice of the Peace Court, he was feeling low. He had just lost $110 and was convinced of his innocence. He went back to his college, where his government teacher returned tests taken a few days earlier. Johnny

got a "C−." He pulled out his 44-magnum and "wasted" his instructor (after all, he was in a bad mood). Johnny, of course, was arrested and charged with homicide—murder in the first degree.

Shortly thereafter, Johnny's latest series of legal battles opens with an initial appearance before a justice of the peace. The judge will explain his constitutional rights. He has the right to be represented by a lawyer, and to have one appointed by the state (called a "public defender") if he cannot afford one; he has the right to remain silent, and to know that statements he makes may be used against him; and he has the right to a trial by jury.[16] The judge will also set bail (releasing the prisoner after an amount of money is posted, to insure against the defendant's fleeing), using his judgment as a guide to the amount.[17] Although bail may be refused in a death penalty case, it is unlikely that the prosecutor would be asking for the death penalty in this case.

Following further preparation by Johnny and his attorney, he reappears before the Justice of the Peace Court for a preliminary hearing. The major determination at this proceeding is to determine whether *probable cause* exists. When deciding whether there is probable cause, the judge considers two major questions: Could a reasonable man conclude from the evidence that a crime has been committed? Could a reasonable man conclude that the defendant committed the crime? In this case, there is no doubt that a reasonable man could conclude that a crime has been committed, and committed by Johnny—the professor's body was easily located, the other students are witnesses, Johnny's fingerprints are on the gun, the gun is registered in his name, and he had a motive.

With probable cause established, necessary legal documents are forwarded to the District Court for arraignment. At the arraignment, the judge reviews the charge(s) against Johnny and the amount of bail set by the justice of the peace (to assure that it is not unreasonable). Also, Johnny enters his plea ("Not guilty," he tells the judge), and the trial date is set. Had the defendant pleaded "guilty," the judge would ordinarily have scheduled the sentencing date for a later time, following a pre-sentence investigation by a probation officer (if requested by the judge). The defendant's attorney would also submit a few pre-trial motions. He might, for instance, ask that the trial be moved to a different location in the state (called a change of venue) because of prejudicial publicity against his client. The judge considers and rules on these motions, although he does not have to give his decision immediately. A few months later, following a defense motion to delay the trial to allow Johnny and his lawyers time to adequately prepare their case, the trial begins.

District court procedure is essentially the same as that outlined in the JP trial above. As mentioned, jurors are selected from voter registration lists to serve on call for six months. Some 50 to 100 names are drawn from the box to appear for a particular case. Twelve of these names are then drawn in the district court, and examined for bias or prejudice by the attorneys. If a juror is successfully challenged for bias or prejudice, he is excused "for cause" and another juror is drawn and questioned by the attorneys. That way, as in JP court, a panel of 12 jurors who have been passed for cause by the attorneys is established. Then the attorneys proceed with "peremptory challenges." The difference between these (dismissals "for cause" or "peremptory challenge") is that "an unlimited number of challenges may be made for cause with approval of the presiding judge. Peremptory challenges, for which no reason need be given, are limited to a specific number. . . ."[18] The actual number of peremptory challenges available to each attorney varies according to the state and type of offense. As jurors are dismissed, others are drawn and examined until 12 are agreed upon. In the case of prolonged trials, one or two alternatives are also selected. The process of introducing evidence, calling and cross-examining witnesses, and jury deliberation in district court is the same as JP court. Continuing with Johnny's murder trial, his defense, based on an incompetent mental capacity, fails—the jury returns a guilty verdict.

Johnny, of course, will want to appeal the ruling to the Wyoming Supreme Court. As mentioned earlier, Johnny cannot appeal solely for the sake of appealing (unless his is a death penalty case; they are appealed automatically). Instead, his appeal must show that errors were made at the district court level which were prejudicial, or prevented him from receiving a fair trial. It is not enough that errors were made—they must have been prejudicial errors.

In order to initiate the appeal, the losing party in the district court (whether in a criminal or civil case) must file a "notice of appeal" with the clerk of the district court in which the decision was rendered. The appeal must be filed within 15 days from entry of the judgment. Likewise, the losing attorney must file the district court transcript (the portions upon which the appeal is based) and a "docketing statement" on his client's behalf. The docketing statement is a summary of the earlier proceedings, facts of the issue or issues being appealed, the questions presented by the appeal, a list of cases and authorities which the appellant believes support his client's contentions, and a copy of the judgment or order which is to be reviewed.[19] Once the appeal has been filed and docketed, the parties may file various motions pertaining to procedural defects in the appeal, failure to meet deadlines for filing the various instruments involved in the appeal, and the like. Note again, the appeal is automatic in death penalty cases (which Johnny's case is not). This appeal process may take months. Johnny remains out on bail during the appeal.

Next, the appellant's attorney (Johnny has filed the appeal, thereby becoming the "appellant") files a "brief" with the supreme court on Johnny's behalf. The brief is crucial to the case. It is a well-organized summary of his client's case. Johnny's brief includes a referenced table of contents; "a statement of the issues presented for review"; and a "statement of the case," which outlines the nature of the case, proceedings, and the disposition in the lower court. An "argument" is also included which contains "the contentions of the appellant with respect to the issues presented, and the reasons therefore, with citations to the authorities, statutes and parts of the record relied on"; a short conclusion states the precise relief or outcome that is being sought. The appellee (in this case, the prosecutor) then files his brief. Each side files a "reply brief" in response to the opponent's brief. The briefs are not to exceed 70 pages in length, the reply briefs 35. Johnny's brief is to be filed with the supreme court within 30 days of the time that the record on appeal was filed with the court. Johnny and his attorney have 10 more days to respond (submit a reply brief) to the state's brief. And, if either party needs more time to prepare a brief, the court may grant an extension.[20]

At this point, Johnny's case has probably been underway for nearly a year (maybe more). In fact, the appeal has taken several months itself. But now that the supreme court justices have the briefs, their work can begin. When the case comes up (criminal cases take precedence in the agenda over civil cases), the justices read the briefs. Then they schedule the matter for oral arguments. Ordinarily, the attorneys appear before the court. If either party needs more time, it is usually granted.

In Johnny's case, both attorneys are ready. Johnny's lawyer gets to make both the opening and closing arguments because his client brought the appeal. Both attorneys raise all the points and arguments that they believe prove their cases. They argue their respective cases by talking to the justices, often answering questions from them. If the questions are lengthy, they may be given additional time for their arguments. And, notice, neither attorney is able to call witnesses, introduce evidence, or question anyone. That simply is not done on appeal to the supreme court. Rather, the attorneys each use their allotted time to discuss, or argue, their positions to the judges.[21]

After the lawyers have finished, the justices meet in a conference room to discuss the case among themselves. These discussions are gen-

B.C. by permission of Johnny Hart and Field Enterprises, Inc.

erally based on the briefs and oral arguments rather than the trial court's (meaning the district court) record. After this conference, the chief justice assigns one of the justices who agrees with the majority position on the case to do a thorough review of the case. The assigned justice, with his staff attorney, reviews the material in the case file—motions, rulings, evidence, briefs, court transcripts and the judgment. The justice who reviews the case then writes a tentative draft of an opinion for the case which is circulated among the other members of the court. The other justices review the tentative opinion, suggesting additions, deletions, or other changes. If any justice disagrees with the tentative majority opinion, he may write an opinion on behalf of the minority (or even his personal) point of view. The majority opinion is then rewritten to accommodate agreed upon changes, and the ruling announced. As Woodward and Armstrong's book, *The Brethren,* shows of the U.S. Supreme Court, the process of arriving at a final opinion is truly a matter of compromise and negotiation.

In the Johnny Yellowstone case, the ruling is unanimous. His conviction is affirmed; the court has ruled that the district court made no reversible errors. If the ruling had been that prejudicial errors were made, the Supreme Court might have reversed the lower court's ruling. More likely, however, they would have sent the case back to the district court for retrial. This depends upon the circumstances of the error and the particular law involved.

Finally, Johnny's attorney will file an application for rehearing with the justices. The application, which is to be filed within 15 days of the court's ruling, lists ways that the attorney believes the supreme court itself made errors. If the justices agree that they erred, they "set the case for hearing and oral argument as permitted in other cases." Ordinarily, however, the application is a formality which is denied.[22]

At its completion, the appeals process has taken a full year. This is the normal time for appeals in Wyoming. In fact, because of the seriousness of the issue, this appeal would probably take longer than a year (See Sidebar 6–7).

District Court—Civil Suit. Distraught over her son Johnny's conviction, Joanie Yellowstone stopped for a few drinks while on her way home from court. Once back on the road, she drove her car through a neighbor's fence, yard, porch and front room. The neighbor filed a civil suit against Joanie in district court, seeking $5,000 in damages for negligence.

Essentially, the process facing Joanie is the same as a criminal trial. In this civil suit, the opponents are both private citizens. The government is not involved as in a criminal case (unless, of course, the government is suing or being sued). And, nobody goes to jail in a civil case; it is just a matter of money. Also, there are a few procedural differences. In a civil suit, for example, the jury is ordinarily composed of six people rather than 12 (unless one of the parties to the civil suit requests the larger jury). Even so, the process is generally the same.

At first, Joanie considered settling the issue out of court. Her neighbor offered to accept $2,000 and drop the complaint. Out-of-court settlements are common. When insurance companies are involved, they typically try to settle outside of court. That way, the plaintiff (person who brought the suit) gets something for certain, the defendent (person being sued) is protected against losing a larger amount (especially if the jury feels sorry for the plaintiff), the issue is resolved quickly and without as much publicity, and both parties are likely to save legal fees. Joanie, convinced that she had done nothing wrong, refuses to settle out of court.

At this point, the defendent has several choices. She could ignore the complaint against her. But, if she does, the court will enter a judgment against her and seize her property and/or money if she refuses to pay the judgment. Next, Joanie might "file a counter-claim (suing the plaintiff in return). She may file a cross-claim (alleging the responsibility for the matter is someone else's), or she may outline [her] defense."[23] Or, the defendant might do each of these things at the same time. In fact, if she has a counter-claim, it must be filed in connection with the same suit or it can never be filed.

Upholding her family tradition, Joanie decided to see the matter through. As with the criminal case discussed earlier, a civil suit is a slow process. After several months of preparation and the trial, Joanie lost and paid the $5,000 judgment handed down by the court. She would, of course, have the right to file an appeal. The supreme court would consider her petition, but as with nearly all criminal cases could decide not to hear the case (if they decide that prejudicial errors were not made).

Background on the Supreme Court

During the territorial period, Wyoming was divided into three district courts. Each district had a judge who was appointed by the President. The supreme court was composed of the three district judges meeting to hear appeals. But, since appeals are based on the losing party's contention that the lower court made errors, this system had obvious weaknesses. After all, the court hearing an appeal included the judge who made the initial ruling, and most appeals alleged that the judge himself had made prejudicial errors. So, judges were often in the awkward position of having to decide whether they themselves had made mistakes. The risk of bias is obvious. To correct this difficulty, the constitutional convention voted in 1889 to create a separate supreme court, one whose membership would be independent of the district courts. Creation of the separate supreme court was not as easy as one might think, though. Several convention delegates thought it would be too expensive to have a separate supreme court, especially since it would have a relatively small workload. And, remember, concern for economy was an important issue during the convention. Even so, the key vote to eliminate the separate supreme court from the constitution failed by a narrow 21–17 vote.[24]

The constitution, then, created a supreme court made up of three justices, a chief justice and two associate justices. The justices were to be elected by the voters of the state for eight-year terms, although the first three justices drew lots to see who would run for re-election after serving four-, six-, or eight-year first terms. That way, all three justices would not stand for election at the same time, except for the first election. In the early years, the member with the shortest term remaining was elected chief justice by the three-member

Willis VanDevanter, first Chief Justice of the Wyoming Supreme Court (photographed about 1895-1897). Wyoming State Archives, Museums and Historical Department, University of Wyoming.

court, giving him added prestige to aid his re-election bid. As mentioned earlier, this is no longer the case. Today, the chief justice serves at the pleasure of the other justices, and is appointed for reasons other than his chances of re-election.[25]

Among the early figures in Wyoming jurisprudence, Willis Van Devanter is probably the most noteworthy. Born (April 17, 1859) and raised in Indiana, Van Devanter studied at Asbury (now De Pauw) University and in the law school at Cincinnati College (LL.B. 1881).

After a short period practicing law in Marion, Indiana (1881–1884), he travelled west,

opening a law office in Cheyenne. He served as city attorney from 1887–88 and in the Wyoming Territorial Legislative Assembly in 1888. In 1889, President Benjamin Harrison appointed him chief justice of the Supreme Court of Wyoming (territorial status). He was subsequently elected chief justice of the Supreme Court of Wyoming at the first state election. After four days in office (October 11, 1890–October 15, 1890) he resigned to resume his private practice.

Van Devanter's stature in Republican party politics led to his prominence in the federal government. A high ranking member of the F. E. Warren-ranching interest political stronghold (he is sometimes called "Warren's man in Wyoming"), Van Devanter served as chairman of the Republican State Committee (1892–94), as a member of the Republican National Committee (1896–1900), and as a delegate to the Republican National Convention (1896). He was appointed Assistant Attorney General of the United States (1897–1903), from which he resigned upon his appointment as U.S. circuit judge for the Eighth Judicial Circuit (1903–10). From December 16, 1910 to June 2, 1937 he served as Associate Justice of the Supreme Court of the United States. Thus, Wyoming's first chief justice following statehood (and last chief justice as a territory) served on the U.S. Supreme Court for approximately 27 years. Clearly, Van Devanter's judicial and political accomplishments were extraordinary. He died in Washington, D.C. on February 8, 1941.[26]

A 1971 study of the supreme court's history shows that the early justices were born, raised, and educated outside of Wyoming. In fact, no member of the supreme court had been born in the state until Justice Rodney Guthrie was appointed by Governor Hathaway in 1971. Likewise, no justice had been educated in

Wyoming prior to Justice Glenn Parker, who joined the court in 1955. Until the 1970's, most of the judges had been educated in the East or Midwest (70 percent between 1890 and 1963).[27] But these trends have changed in the 1970's. At the outset of the 1980's, this pattern of the Wyoming courts relying upon other states for leadership has been reversed.

Modern Selection of District and Supreme Court Judges

At the outset of the state's history, "judges ran for election with political party designations, just as candidates for the legislature do today." But, in 1915 the state legislature changed the law, disallowing judges to run for election using party labels. Since then, judges have been required to run as "nonpartisan" candidates. In 1959, the legislature strengthened the nonpartisan provisions "by making it illegal for judicial candidates to advertise publicly their party memberships or whom they support for partisan public office." Likewise, judges are barred from "knowingly accepting money from any 'political committee or organization' for campaign purposes," although contributions from individuals may be accepted.[28]

Now you know something about how judges are *not* selected. But, how *are* they selected? First, a potential judge must meet the qualifications listed in the constitution. District court judges must be 28 years old, a United States citizen, be "learned in the law," and have resided in the state for at least two years.[29] To be eligible for the supreme court, a person must also be a citizen of the U.S., learned in the law, have practiced law (or been a judge of a lower court) for nine years, be 35 years old, and have resided in Wyoming for at least three years.[30] To be eligible for either the supreme court or a district court bench,

the nominee " . . . must have practiced law in the state of Wyoming at least one year immediately preceding his election or appointment."[31]

Next, there must be a vacancy, whether by resignation, retirement, or death. When a vacancy occurs, the Judicial Nominating Commission meets and submits a list of three nominees to the governor within 60 days of the vacancy. The Judicial Nominating Commission, modeled after the Missouri Plan, was created in an attempt to eliminate partisan politics from the process of selecting judges. Thus, in 1972, the voters ratified an amendment to the state constitution which authorized the creation of a commission to nominate people to fill future judgeship vacancies. The commission is composed of seven people—the Chief Justice of the state supreme court (serves as chairman), three members selected by the Wyoming Bar Association, and three non-lawyer members appointed by the governor. No more than two Judicial Nominating Commission members may be from the same judicial district. But notice, the commission does not select new judges. Rather, the commission nominates three people who they believe would make excellent judges. And, keep in mind, nominees are chosen on the basis of their abilities rather than political party affiliation. Commission members are prohibited from holding any office in a political party, may not serve more than one four-year term on the commission, are themselves ineligible for appointment to a judgeship during membership on the commission and for one year thereafter, and receive no salary (they do receive travel mileage and accommodation expenses).

After the list is submitted, the governor has 30 days to fill the vacancy by appointing one of the three people from the commission's list.

If the governor fails to make the appointment, the chief justice makes the selection from the list within 15 days.

The new judge then serves a full year in office. If the judge wants to keep the office at the end of the year, he must file a "declaration of intent to stand for election for a succeeding term" between three and six months before the next general election (they are held every two years). If the judge files for the position, he is listed on the ballot with the question of whether he shall be retained. If a majority of the people voting on that question vote "yes," the judge serves a full term (six years for district and county courts, eight years on the supreme court). If the majority votes "no," or if the judge does not file the declaration within the alloted time, a vacancy exists and the nominating process begins again. Judges who win full terms—and those who seek office typically do win—serve their terms and must follow the same steps in order to win successive, or future, terms. Thus, district judges must be re-elected every six years, supreme court justices every eight years. The judges are bound by the campaign provisions outlined above—they may not accept contributions, endorse candidates, or publicize their party affiliation.[32]

As the above discussion shows, it is difficult to become a judge. A person must meet the age, education, citizenship, residency and legal practice qualifications; he or she must be selected by the Judicial Nominating Commission; likewise, by the governor; and the judge must be re-elected by the voters of his (or her) court's jurisdiction. District court judges stand for election within the district. Supreme court justices are elected statewide.

Also, notice how a person is *not* selected for the judgeship. A person does not seek office like a candidate for an executive or legislative branch position. He does not run against anyone. Rather, ours is designed to be "a plan which replaces the popular election system with a means by which intelligent selection and popular will are blended together to take judges 'out of politics.' "[33] While this is an ideal, it is neither without merit nor significant impact.

Removal of Judges

Judges may be removed in several ways in Wyoming. Some of the ways are obvious, such as voluntary retirement, death, or defeat by the voters. In addition, there is a mandatory retirement age of 70 for judges. They are, however, allowed to complete unfinished terms of office. And, most people know that federal judges can be and have been impeached. Likewise, judges in this state (including justices of the peace) may be impeached "for high crimes and misdemeanors, or malfeasance (meaning improper performance of duties)." The house of representatives has the power to impeach. They do so by passing a resolution containing articles of impeachment, which alleges specific high crimes, misdemeanors, or instances of malfeasance. The impeachment, then, is really an indictment by the house. If the house passes an impeachment resolution, the senate tries the articles, meeting like a jury. The chief justice (assuming that he is not the judge who was impeached) of the supreme court presides over the senate trial. As with other trials, evidence is given, testimony is made by witnesses, and senators vote to determine whether the impeached (or indicted) party is convicted. A two-thirds vote of all the senators is necessary in order to convict.[34] This impeachment process is the same as the federal process of impeaching a president or federal judge. No Wyoming judge has ever been impeached.

In addition, Wyoming law provides for a "quality control" commission, called the Judicial Supervisory Commission. This commission also consists of seven members—two district judges (selected by all the district judges), two members of the Wyoming Bar Association (with ten years of experience or more), and three non-attorneys appointed by the governor.

The Judicial Supervisory Commission may remove judges from office or force them into retirement, when the state supreme court agrees. Removal action will be taken (either removal or censure, proposed by the commission and approved by the supreme court) when there is found to have been "willful misconduct in office, willful and persistent failure to perform . . . duties, habitual intemperance, or conduct prejudicial to the administration of justice that brings the judicial office into disrepute." Likewise, state judges will be removed for conviction of a felony or "moral turpitude." Notice, this method of removing a judge is initiated by the commission and ultimately determined by the supreme court.[35]

People's Perceptions of the Courts

The 1978 statewide survey asked Wyomingites whether they think the courts in their area of Wyoming deal too harshly, not harshly enough, or about right with criminals. Two percent of the more than 1000 people surveyed said the courts deal too harshly with criminals. Twenty-four percent said the courts were about right, 63 percent said that the courts were not harsh enough in their treatment of criminals, and 11 percent were undecided. These figures were approximately the same among the various residents living in different regions in the state, the different age groups, the two major political parties, the level of education, and between men and women.

The trend here is unmistakable. The residents of Wyoming are clearly disenchanted with their courts' treatment of criminals. Two possible explanations for the negative assessment of the courts come to mind almost immediately. First, this is a conservative state and law and order have long been one of the major tenets of convervatism. And, secondly, the survey also showed that a seemingly high percentage of the state's residents have themselves (including their property) been victims of "violent" crimes in the 12 month period prior to the survey—11 percent said that they had suffered a burglary, 18 percent larceny, 15 percent vandalism, two percent robbery, and three percent assault. Considered in light of these figures, frustration with the courts is more understandable.

In short, conservative people often believe that severe penalties are a deterrent to crime (See Sidebar 6–8). When so many people have recently been victimized by violent crimes to themselves or their property, it is understandable that they might believe that the courts had failed to provide the deterrent. Put simply, they would think that the courts are "soft" on criminals (See Sidebar 6–9). One might question, of course, whether there is any rational way that the courts can be connected with the crime rate.

The above conclusions about the cause of the disenchantment with the courts, of course, is speculation. But, the point of these figures stands out. Something is wrong. And the political candidate or party which taps this issue will undoubtedly improve its position with voters as a whole. Beyond that, we might ask ourselves this, "Is it healthy in a democracy for so many people to believe that their court system is weak?" If not, what are the implications?

Sidebar 6–8
Former Chief Justice Rodney M. Guthrie on the Leniency of Courts

Question: The charge is often made that the courts in general are too lenient or "soft." How do you respond?

Answer It's a misstatement. Here we go—What is too lenient? I read the papers and wonder why judges do things. I was a trial judge for a great many years and maybe people wondered why I did things sometimes when I gave probation. It's usually an attempt by a judge to apply the law to an individual in a way that is proper, better for him, the individual. He may not have thought much of the right of society. Of course, now I'm right back to an area of controversy—God only knows what is right for society. What is the purpose of criminal punishment, anyway? Is it as a deterrent? Is it to rehabilitate? What is it? Some people believe it's vengeance and deterrence. If you don't give a man the limit they say, "Oh, too easy." But if you give him a pretty substantial sentence, the people who believe in rehabilitation and attempting to "rescue" the individual, feel you're barbaric. It's just another example of a clash of philosophies.

Sidebar 6–9
Former Chief Justice Rodney M. Guthrie on Legal Technicalities

Question: What about the charge that courts let criminals go on technicalities?

Answer: That, of course, is the thing that outrages me. . . I'm thinking of confessions and searches and seizures where you hear that criticism most often—I've never been able to equate the protection of a constitutional right with a "technicality." Most people have such a hard time conceptualizing the fact, but a judge who may be holding out a confession or . . . who may suppress a search and seizure may be sitting up there saying in the back of his mind, "Look, you lucky 'so and so,' I'm sorry I have to do this, [but I have to]". If he doesn't do it for the defendant . . . down there at the bar, he doesn't have to do it for you or me either. And the people who sound off the loudest sometimes don't realize that, but for the grace of God, . . . when a court asserts one of those so-called technicalities . . . they're striking a blow for the man that's complaining, not particularly for that defendant. As I say, I was a trial judge and I know trial judges feel that way. You say to yourself, "Well, this 'so and so,' nothing too bad could happen to him. But if I let this search and seizure stand, what will they do next?" Or, "If I let this confession stand, will they hit the next fellow over the head with a 2 × 4 to get a confession?" So many laymen are unable to apply that kind of thinking—that this defendant makes not a damn bit of difference—which gives the man in the street the right to do what he chooses without being pushed around . . . . The actions of judges are pretty much responsible for the form of government we have today and the liberties we have.

Notes

1. Jack C. Plano and Milton Greenberg, *The American Political Dictionary,* 4th ed. (Hinsdale, Illinois: Dryden Press, 1976), pp. 241–242.
2. Ibid., p. 264.
3. See Wyoming Statutes, 1977, 6–1–102. The statute reads, "Offenses which may be punished by death, or by imprisonment in the penitentiary, are felonies: all other offenses are misdemeanors."
4. Plano and Greenberg, p. 17.
5. See Wyoming Constitution, art. 5, secs. 2, 3 and 10.
6. Plano and Greenberg, p. 253.
7. See U.S. Constitution, Art, III, sec. 2.
8. Much of the material in the following section is from an interview with former Judge Reuel Armstrong, Coordinator for the Wyoming Supreme Court, conducted in Cheyenne, Wyoming, Summer, 1978.
9. Most municipalities have adopted the same traffic code that the State of Wyoming has adopted. Thus, many offenses which are violations of state law also violate municipal law if they occur within the corporate limits of a municipality.
10. At times, this is mistakenly referred to as the arraignment. It is incorrect to call it "arraignment" because arraignment contemplates taking a plea, and a JP does not take a plea in a felony case at any time.
11. Bail is an amount of money (determined by the court) which is posted with the court, so that an accused person may be released prior to trial. If the accused person "skips out" or flees, the bail is forfeited. Bail, then, is a "guarantee" that a defendant will appear at his trial.
12. The supreme court has original jurisdiction in writs of quo warranto, mandamus, and habeas corpus. See Wyoming Constitution, art. 5, sec. 3.
13. The suspension can be modified to allow the defendant to go to and from work, however.
14. Another difference is that fines that are collected in municipal court go into the municipality's general fund. Fines collected in the justice of the peace court go to the schools; court costs go to the county.
15. Under the "Wyoming Rules of Criminal Procedure for Justice of the Peace Courts and Municipal Courts" there is no right to a jury trial unless a "jail sentence is to be imposed." As a result, many municipalities have deleted jail terms from their ordinances as sentencing alternatives. Accordingly, these municipalities avoid the expense, red tape, and delay resulting from the requirement of having jury trials in misdemeanor cases. The question of the constitutionality of this rule was taken to the supreme court in a recent case from the town of Jackson. The majority of the court resolved the case on a procedural basis without getting to the constitutionality question on the jury trial issue. However, there was a strong dissent in that case indicating that the dissenting justices would be inclined to rule that there is a constitutional right to have a jury trial in municipal court on the issue of driving while under the influence regardless whether a jail sentence is to be imposed. On the other hand, it is argued that the Wyoming Constitution, Article 1, Section 9, provides that "the right of trial by jury shall remain inviolate in criminal cases . . ." The word preserved, usually has been construed to mean "as it was under the common law." Under the common law, in the traditional sense of that term, there was no jury trial for petty offenses, and, of course, reckless driving, driving while under the influence, and the like were not offenses. Therefore, jury trials are generally denied in municipal courts under the specific ability of Rule 5(d) and will continue to be denied, at least until the Wyoming Supreme Court rules that there is a constitutional right to have a jury trial in such cases. This would apply equally to driving while under the influence and to reckless driving, although the test case mentioned above was a DWUI case. Notice, however, for *state* misdemeanors the rule is still valid.
16. These rights were established in the famous Supreme Court cases Gideon v. Wainwright, 372 U.S. 335 (1963), Escobedo v. Illinois, 378 U.S. 478 (1964) and Miranda v. Arizona, 384 U.S. 436 (1966). The right to trial by jury is provided for in Article III, Section 2, and by the Sixth and Seventh Amendments of the U.S. Constitution. The right to jury trial has also been extended through various court rulings, such as Duncan v. Louisiana, 391 U.S. 145 (1968).

17. The determination of the amount of bail is governed by Rule 8 of the Wyoming Rules of Criminal Procedure: in determining which condition of release will reasonably assure appearance the judicial officer shall on the basis of available information, take into account the nature and circumstances of the offense charged, the weight of the evidence against the accused, the accused's family ties, employment, financial resources, character and mental condition, the length of his residence in the community, his record of convictions and his record of appearance in court proceedings or of flight to avoid prosecution or failure to appear at court proceedings.

18. Plano and Greenberg, p. 240. For crimes punishable by death, as many as 40 peremptory challenges may be allowed; as few as five may be permitted for minor offenses.

19. The appellant has 40 days from the filing of the appeal to file the record on appeal with the supreme court and have it docketed within the specified period. In the first 10 days, the appellant must give the appellee "a description of the parts of the transcript which he intends to include in the record." See the *Wyoming Rules of Appellate Procedure,* adopted April 12, 1978; effective August 1, 1978, Rule 2, pp. 8–13.

20. *Wyoming Rules of Appellate Procedure,* Rules 2–4, pp. 14–22.

21. Ibid., Rules 5–6, pp. 19–23.

22. Ibid., Rules 7–10, pp. 23–26.

23. K. T. Roes, "The Court System and You," *Powell Tribune,* a four-part series, 4–23 August 1977.

24. T. A. Larson, *History of Wyoming* (Lincoln: University of Nebraska Press, 1965), pp. 247–248.

25. *Wyoming Blue Book,* gen. ed. Virginia Trenholm, 3 vols. (Cheyenne: Wyoming State Archives and Historical Department, 1974), 3:29–30.

26. *Wyoming Blue Book,* 1:121.

27. Philip P. Whynott, "The Wyoming Supreme Court and Municipal Corporations: A Study in Judicial Policy-Making" (Masters thesis, University of Wyoming, 1971), pp. 25–54.

28. Michael J. Horan, "Choosing Judges in Wyoming: Popular Election or 'Merit Selection'?" (Laramie, Wyo.: Center for Government Research, 1972) pp. 1–5.

29. Wyoming Constitution, art. 5, sec. 12.

30. Ibid., art. 5, sec. 8.

31. Wyoming Statutes, 1977, 5–1–101.

32. Wyoming Constitution, art. 5, sec. 4.

33. Horan, p. 9.

34. Wyoming Constitution, art. 4, secs. 17–19 and art. 5, sec. 1.

35. Ibid., art. 5, sec. 6.

CHAPTER
SEVEN

The Years Ahead
Policy Issues of the Present and Future

Wyoming's Political Heritage

Behavioral scientists have long understood that people living under different circumstances often behave differently. This is understandable considering that people living in the *same* circumstances often behave differently. But in a broader context, appreciating this simple fact helps us better understand ourselves and the setting in which we live.

The point here is relatively simple: much of what people "are"—how they act, what they believe, and even daily routines—is influenced and shaped by their cultural heritage. This has nothing to do with how often a person goes to the opera. "Culture" means something quite different; it is actually basic to our daily lives. A few terms and illustrations will make the point.

Whether through logic, superstition, coincidence or whatever, it is likely that all groups of people throughout history have formed beliefs of "right" and "wrong." If a beautiful maiden dies in a primitive society and needed rain appears the next day, for example, the leaders of the tribe may "logically" conclude that the gods were pleased. The next year, the tribal leaders might offer the gods another maiden. Soon, such sacrifices may be ritualized and ultimately become integral parts of the society's traditions, the sort of thing that is done unquestionably because it is accepted as right or proper.

Sociologists and anthropologists explain that this dynamic is behind a great deal that is both common and foreign to us. The scenario explains events that are as dramatic as human sacrifices, and as common as shaking hands, the place settings at the dinner table, and the latest in popular language and fashion. When such behavior is repeated, whether a handshake or human sacrifice, it may become so common to a group of people that it becomes a folkway. In other words, the behavior may become a "customary, normal, habitual way a group does things."[1] From this, it is a short step to doing things not because they are customary, but because they are the "right" thing to do. Folkways, then, may be reinforced to such a degree that a society accepts or rejects certain behavior as proper or improper. The folkway has become a social "more" (social pressure the society "values" as right or wrong).

In turn, mores collect around, and are reinforced by, various social institutions (and vice versa) such as the family, church, state, school, and economic system. A young boy, for example, is no longer supposed to see his older sister in the nude, because she has reached puberty. Mother explains that it's "just not right." The school board dismisses a homosexual teacher because his behavior "just isn't right." Accordingly:

mores . . . become transformed into absolutes—into things which are right because they are right, and wrong because they are wrong. In other words, mores become self-validating and self-perpetuating. They become sacred. To question them is indecent, and to violate them is intolerable. Every society punishes those who violate its mores.[2]

As a result, norms are often written into law. Lawmakers enter the complex area of regulating morality, in the name of prohibiting those activities that society, the majority, or an influential minority believe are wrong.

These mores are passed from generation to generation. Quite often, there is a tendency over time to accept such mores without serious questioning. These values become an important aspect of the social heritage of the new generation. In this manner, the present influences the future, just as the present is shaped by the past. The sum of these dynamics is "culture." A society's culture, then, is a composite of its mores, values, and beliefs; it is the sum of who and what those people are, what they value, how they behave, and what they believe.

At first glance, this may seem irrelevant. It is not. Without a doubt, America has its own, unique culture, as anyone who has travelled abroad, or had close friendships with foreigners, can attest. In fact, American culture is a composite of numerous regional subcultures. As most people realize, the lifestyle in New Orleans is quite different from that of New York. Although Mobile, Alabama and Cheyenne, Wyoming are similar in so many ways (for example, citizens in both communities cherish the right to own private property),

they are quite different in many others. These communities, as is true of other cities and regions across the nation, were typically settled by people from different parts of Europe, who had different traditions and often faced different geographic, social, religious and economic hurdles. Thus, a locale's unique cultural history is an important piece—perhaps the key—in the puzzle of its understanding.

Further, political events (e.g., legislature, elections) take place in settings that reflect the dominant culture. When a noted political scientist studied th American South, for example, he found a region steeped in elitist, nondemocratic traditions.[3] When he looked specifically at political operations within the Southern culture, he found that they, too, were elitist and had strongly nondemocratic overtones. Clearly, a state's values, mores and traditions are reflected in its politics. This section outlines several of the major tenets of Wyoming's culture which have political implications.

The value of this section is twofold. To begin with, it would be naive to think that the institutions and events discussed in the previous chapters exist in an antiseptic vacuum. In large measure, for example, the sharp contrasts between the Illinois and Wyoming legislatures are due to their different cultural settings. Secondly, and perhaps more importantly, it is worthwhile to keep an eye on the state's unique heritage as the drama surrounding development unfolds in the years ahead. Indeed, aspects of the state's culture will in large measure influence the outcome of various policy issues discussed in this chapter. But the reverse is also true—these public policies and pertinent issues will determine the way of life in the Wyoming of the future.

Individualism. As the first chapter shows, Wyoming's early settlers were a hardy lot who braved many formidable obstacles. Consider the challenges they faced: sparse vegetation and little water, threat of Indian attack, extreme weather conditions, and prolonged isolation. The geographic conditions meant that agriculture, particularly cattle ranching, was a risky proposition. The 1870's and 1880's, for example, were a roller-coaster of boom and bust in the cattle industry. Years of growth were frequently followed by periods of misfortune. All too often, freezing winters, drought, overgrazing, and shortsighted government policies reappeared in a Jekyll and Hyde fashion. Following one such boom, the winter of 1886–1887 hit; "the repeated hurricane blizzards, the heavy falls of snow, and the blood-chilling rains . . . combined to kill off about one-third of all the northern range cattle."[4]

Likewise, fear of the "hostiles," as Indians were often called, was understandable. Wyoming's early history is filled with examples of white men abusing red men, and the reverse, which periodically resulted in violence and death on both sides. Prior to the resolution of the famous Indian Wars of 1875–1876 (in which the Sioux, led by Sitting Bull and Crazy Horse, wiped out Lt. Col. George Custer's Seventh Cavalry at the Little Big Horn River in Montana), which forced "hostiles" out of Wyoming by the spring of 1877, Indian attacks against isolated settlers were relatively common.

Also, the isolation which early pioneers faced was a problem. Unlike modern television and movie portrayals, many settlers seldom saw neighbors, visitors, or women, particularly during the long winters. Thus, loneliness and depression were common among many settlers. Accounts say that the resulting loneliness and depression were particularly troublesome for the relatively few women who came west, only to be isolated at home.

As a result of these hardships, many adventurers failed in Wyoming and were either buried or moved on. But those who stayed laid the groundwork of a unique western culture. Natives of the West, in general, and Wyoming, in particular, pride themselves on their heritage of individualism, as embodied in the cultural values of strength, masculinity, independence, democratic equality, and the cowboy ethic. While this is not to say that people in Wyoming are any more "individuals" than people living anywhere else, it is to say that the legacy of the early pioneers—coupled with the unique cowboy trappings of strength and masculine superiority (as glamorized in books, movies, and television)—have left their own imprint on the western and Wyoming "ways of life." Indeed, individualism is probably the basis of the western culture.[5]

The political impacts of the individualistic ethic are numerous. Professor Daniel Elazar's classic study on American political culture is insightful. When he turns his attention to Wyoming and the West, he finds an individualistic culture which views society as a marketplace. Individuals are seen as capitalists competing in the marketplace. Individuals with abilities prosper; those without abilities fail. According to the dominant values of this culture, each person should succeed or fail on his own abilities, without government help or interference. Government is not to interfere in the lives of citizens or the operations of businesses. Politics is viewed as another way for people to advance themselves socially or economically. While politics is viewed as a somewhat dirty business best left to professionals, public officials are expected to provide high quality services in return for the status and economic rewards they receive. Even so, corruption is neither uncommon nor unexpected in the public's opinion. People do not get excited about this type of soiled business (government corruption), unless an exceptional reformer catches the public's fancy or unless the corruption goes beyond "normal" or "acceptable" limits.

Political life in an individualistic political culture is "rooted in personal relationships" much as they are in the business community. Political parties are viewed as instruments for harnessing or managing these relationships. Thus, people in the political arena tend to know and deal with one another more in personal than in formal ways. Also, Dr. Elazar concludes that while two parties ordinarily operate in an individualistic culture, one party is usually dominant. Finally, because politicians are geared toward giving the public what it wants, they are not highly innovative or creative. Government responds to public desires in individualistic cultures; it does not set up massive new programs in anticipation of new problems. Also, the individualistic culture is skeptical of bureaucracy, because bureaucratic rules and regulations interfere with personal dealings, particularly by and between politicians.[6]

It sounds as though Elazar is talking about Wyoming, doesn't it? Indeed, he is. Although he isolates pockets of the individualistic subculture in Pennsylvania, Ohio, Indiana, Illinois, Kansas, Oklahoma, Texas, Colorado, Nebraska, South Dakota, Montana, Nevada, and California, he concludes that it is the dominant cultural element in Wyoming.

Conservative, Anti-Federal Government Philosophy. The terms "conservative," "moderate," and "liberal" are often misunderstood and frequently misused. Putting aside older historical definitions, people who are called liberals today generally view government as a tool or vehicle to solve domestic problems (such as health, education, civil rights, labor and unemployment problems). They often support the creation of large federal programs to address domestic problems. Until recently,

deficit federal spending did not bother liberals. In addition, liberals have often favored cuts in defense spending as a very moral way of financing domestic programs. Conservatives, on the other hand, tend to oppose the creation of large federal programs, relying instead upon individual initiative and state programs to solve social problems. Conservatives say the large federal programs are wasteful and do not work; liberals counter that the conservative position favors corporate interests while ignoring the poor and needy. Conservatives have always sought a balanced federal budget (except during major wars) and would usually spend more on defense than their liberal counterparts. Political scientists Erickson and Luttbeg summarize both the philosophical and more practical issue-oriented differences. They explain:

At the philosophical level, political thinkers who have reputations as liberals and conservatives depart from each other in several, somewhat overlapping ways. Conservatives view society as a control for man's intrinsically based impulses; liberals view man's condition as relative to the quality of his society. Conservatives consider men to be inherently unequal and due unequal rewards; liberals are equalitarian. Conservatives venerate tradition and—most of all—order and authority; liberals believe planned change brings the possibility of improvement. Of course, people who are liberal or conservative in their practical politics need not be strict adherents to the "philosophy about man" that is associated with their particular ideological label. Nevertheless, we can see the implications of these philosophical distinctions at work in the common application of the ideological labels to particular political points of view. Conservatives are more afraid than liberals of "big government," except on matters of law and order; in foreign policy, conservatives are more aggressive than liberals in their Cold War posture and are more fearful of Communism. Conservatives are more likely to see harmful consequences of government attempts to help the disadvantaged, while liberals see the advantages.[7]

GOV'T. SPENDING

TIMBERRR!

Reprinted by permission of the Chicago
Tribune-New York News Syndicate, Inc.

Moderates are ordinarily thought of as taking the middle ground between liberals and conservatives. They are less certain than liberals and conservatives of the philosophical nature of man and society. On some specific issues they agree with the liberals; on others they side with conservatives; moderates often want to compromise the more extreme or hardened liberal and conservative positions.[8]

As befits a state with individualistic roots, Wyoming is rich both in conservative traditions and sentiments. The statewide survey mentioned earlier asked people where they fit on a liberal-moderate-conservative scale. In Wyoming, self-identified conservatives outnumber liberals two-to-one (40 percent to 21.5 percent), with 35.3 percent saying they were moderate or middle of the road. However, if the people who said they were "slightly" lib-

eral or conservative are removed, and only those who were stronger in their identification are considered, the ratio is three-to-one (21.9 percent conservative to 6.8 percent liberal). In terms of political clout, these percentages translate into a political setting dominated by conservatives and conservatism. This, of course, is common throughout much of the Rocky Mountain region. Considering the national shift toward conservatism that has taken place in recent years, it is likely that the actual figures lean even more to the conservative end than the survey indicates. In fact, since survey respondents sometimes think they are more moderate than they actually are, it is quite likely that the 40 percent figure is "conservative" by itself.

DOONESBURY   **by Garry Trudeau**

One way to probe the depth of Wyoming's conservatism is to look at public attitudes on a variety of liberal/conservative issues. Although it is wise to look at numbers such as those which follow with caution (after all, attitudes change over time, and the figures do not measure the "degrees" of strength with which the attitudes are held), they do make the point; 64 percent of the 1,068 people surveyed agree with the conservative belief that the courts "do not deal harshly enough with criminals"; only 15 percent are liberal on the legalization of marijuana; a mere 18 percent oppose Wyoming's conservative right-to-work law; 76 percent favor "forcing the federal government to balance the national budget each year except in time of war," a conservative position (See Sidebar 7–1). Although figures could undoubtedly be found to show different trends, it is probably not an exaggeration to look at these figures as a measure of the conservatism in Wyoming.

Perhaps the best way to consider Wyoming's conservative bent is to discard the polls and look directly at state history. Again, the theme stands out. Although Wyoming history has witnessed progressive leaders and periods, it is debatable whether Wyoming has ever produced a full-blown liberal, in the modern sense, who was able to champion liberalism

while maintaining an ability to win elections. Professor Larson raises the question of whether former Senator Gale McGee was a liberal. He wrote, in 1965, "Until McGee came along, Wyoming had never had a talented, articulate, consistent defender of the federal government."[9] Although McGee had various liberal beliefs, he was hardly foremost among liberal champions. In fact, many liberals still remember his conservative stance on the Vietnam War. So, while McGee and other Wyoming leaders (Governor Joseph M. Carey and Congressman Teno Roncalio) have had progressive veins in their thinking, and have appeared liberal by Wyoming standards, it is probably more accurate to think of them as moderates. In another sense, it is a measure of the state's conservatism that McGee was finally defeated by the conservative Malcolm Wallop, who convinced voters that McGee was too liberal to represent them. Roncalio, to take another example, was continually hounded by conservatives. From early Senator Francis E. Warren to Malcolm Wallop, former Senator John B. Hendrick to Ed Herschler, and from long-time Senator Joseph O'Mahoney to Clifford Hansen, the conservative theme reappears. Indeed, considering public sentiment at the outset of the 1980s, it

Sidebar 7–1
Tolerance of Communists and Homosexuals in Wyoming

by Douglas Parrott
(Professor of Political Science, Sheridan College)

Tolerance for nonconformity has long been a subject of concern to social scientists. Samuel Stouffer completed his now-classic study of political tolerance in 1954 during the turbulent and intolerant McCarthy era, and other similar studies have been conducted. Generally, such research has indicated that while many Americans are willing and eager to profess a dedication to the ideal of political and social tolerance, they are, nevertheless, often reluctant to apply this principle to real-life situations. The 1978 Wyoming Election Survey included several items that addressed this concern.

These items were designed to determine the level of tolerance for "communists," a group that has long been a source of concern in American politics, and for "homosexuals," who, as a group, are becoming more visible and are establishing homosexuality as a major social issue. The question was asked, "Should a communist be allowed to make a speech in your community?" The same question was asked substituting "homosexual" for "communist." Both questions are related to a basic liberty guaranteed by the First Amendment, the right to speak freely.

One might expect that "conservative" Wyoming, populated by the stereotypical "redneck," would show rather high levels of intolerance. The survey results indicate that this is not so. In fact, they indicate that Wyoming residents are more tolerant than the national average. Specifically, 71 percent of those interviewed in Wyoming responded that they would allow a homosexual to speak in their community, whereas only 62 percent nationwide agreed to allow such speech. Concerning communists, 66 percent statewide would permit such individuals to speak, but only 55 percent would do so according to the national average.

However, "enlightened" Wyomingites should not be too quick to congratulate themselves considering that one quarter of those surveyed statewide still would not allow a homosexual to speak and nearly one third would not extend this right to a communist. These figures do reflect a less than complete commitment to the basic ideal of free speech.

These survey data also illustrate another interesting point—that people are slightly more likely to tolerate the exercise of a homosexual's freedom of speech than that of a communist. This is true at both the state and national levels. Wyomingites and Americans generally seem to take their politics seriously. It appears that we perceive less threat from some types of social nonconformity than we do from political nonconformity.

The survey results also reveal relationships that are perhaps considered common knowledge between tolerance and such factors as age and amount of education. As age increases, so too does the level of intolerance. Seventy-seven percent of the "under 30" age group would allow a communist to speak in their community, 69 percent of the "30–49" age group would do so, and finally, only 54 percent of the "50 and over" category would tolerate such speech. (The respective percentages for homosexuals are 81, 75, and 55). Younger people display more tolerance in these situations.

Tolerance also increases with the increasing educational achievement. Only 63 percent of those with a high school education or less would permit a homosexual to speak in their community, 75 percent of those with some college would do so, and a full 82 percent of those who were college graduates would respect free speech rights in this case. (Respective percentages for communists are 56, 71 and 84.)

is difficult to imagine a liberal being able to build a long-lasting, statewide following among a majority of Wyoming voters. Progressive moderates are bound to appear, but, as in the case of Roncalio, they will need the aid of an appealing personality to survive, and will almost certainly have to keep their hands on the pulse of conservative sentiments in their state.

One of the major conservative themes in Wyoming history is a resentment of the federal government and federal bureaucracy. To take a recent example, Republican candidates for the seat held by retiring U.S. Senator Cliff Hansen were unanimous on at least one theme during their 1978 race—the federal government should "Butt out!" This is not new to Wyoming politics. Actually, political figures have been expressing this aspect of Wyoming thinking since statehood. Consider these examples:

I have been frustrated, annoyed, infuriated, exasperated, bewildered, appalled, alarmed and disgusted in my dealings with the federal government (Governor Ed Herschler before a committee of the U.S. House of Representatives, 1978).

The greatest evil of our time is centralization of power (Senator Joseph O'Mahoney during remarks before the National Association of Manufacturers, 1943).

. . . The Taylor Grazing Act will give the Secretary of the Interior practically dictatorship over our livestock industry of the West and can be compared to the dictatorship of Russia (Congressman Vincent Carter, 1934).

As an illustration of the 'paralyzing hand of bureaucractic sloth' the records of the State Engineer's office will show that the sturdy settlers, without capital or credit further than the God-given capital of brawn and energy, have reclaimed more acres of arid land than the millions of capital and army of employees in the service of the Government, in the same length of time, and more than that, each settler contributes his share, in the way of taxes, toward the support of our institutions (Report of State Engineer, A. J. Parshall, 1914).

Posing with the complete 1978 Code of Federal Regulations, Wyoming's Senator Cliff Hansen (retired) expresses his concern with the growth of federal regulations, demonstrating his conservative political philosophy. Courtesy of the office of Senator Cliff Hansen.

Unfortunately, the present water reclamation policy . . . seems to accomplish all reforms through federal agencies . . . whose meddlesome activity frequently acts as a hindrance to our development, and hence irritates our people (Governor B. B. Brooks' 1909 message to the Wyoming legislature).

In large measure, there is historical hypocrisy in this attitude. Actually, Wyoming has always been, and continues to be, heavily dependent upon the federal government in numerous ways. In the early years, Wyoming depended upon the U.S. Army for protection of people and commerce. Shortly thereafter, the federal government began a century long series of water reclamation (i.e. irrigation) projects without which Wyoming agriculture would not (and could not continue to) have prospered. Likewise, the government in Washington has provided many of the state's highways, and has done much to aid Wyoming's education, social services, capital construction, and health care, to name but a few examples.

Put simply, the federal government has been a welcome and essential element of the Wyoming economy. The federal government made its contribution to building the state's own economy and in helping to establish that group of businessmen, the cattlemen, who were to have such long-lasting cultural and political influence in the state. . . . Despite the fact that we have received more money from the federal government than we have paid in taxes, Wyoming just as consistently has decried so-called 'government meddling and interference.' Much of the reason behind that contradiction has to be because the romantic attitude of rugged, individualistic free-enterprising westerners had become part of Wyoming culture.[10]

Although this dependence upon the federal government has long been a key aspect of state dealings, it has not diminished the resentment that is felt regarding the federal government. Whether through public opinion polls (which showed, in 1978, that Wyoming people are somewhat distrustful of the federal government, and that 76 percent believe the "feds" waste a lot of their tax dollars), campaign rhetoric, or historical insight, Wyoming has long been resentful of the national government. As Professor Larson points out:

. . . federal activities in other areas (such as taxation, agriculture, education, civil rights, welfare, medical care, and apportionment of state legislatures) caused new flare-ups and warranted the conclusion that throughout its history, Wyoming had suffered more tension in its federal relations than any other state outside the South.[11]

Republican Dominance. As has repeatedly been shown in the previous pages, the Republican party dominates Wyoming politics. This is not to overstate the case; Democrats can and do win elections. But, to repeat one of the major points of Chapter 2, by nearly every standard—whether the number of registered voters, campaign funds and the ability to raise money, success at finding attractive candidates, winning elections, or maintaining control of the executive branch through administrative appointments—the Republican party is at a significant advantage.

Of course, considering Wyoming's other cultural tenets (conservatism, individualism, anti-Washington), the Republican advantage is even more understandable. The Republican party is, after all, associated with conservatism throughout America. The point here, which is admittedly a matter of perception and is debatable, is that the Republican party has been the dominant party in Wyoming for so long, has provided so many insightful leaders, and has had such close ties with influential allies in local government and businesses, that it has moved beyond its designation as merely another political party. Rather, it is so closely ingrained with, and attuned to, the state's political culture that it has become an integral aspect of the culture.

Ethnic Homogeneity (Similarity). As is obvious from a look at the map, Wyoming has no industrialized cities. Although Cheyenne, Casper, Rock Springs and others are cities by definition and by Wyoming standards, they are hardly cities in the cosmopolitan sense. Accordingly, the big city issues of race and poverty are not apparent in this state. There clearly are poor people in Wyoming, just as there are black, Chicano, Indian, Oriental, Italian, Polish, Arab, Irish, Jewish, and every ethnic combination among the state's citizenry. However, because there are no large concentrations of racial or ethnic minorities in the state—even in Rock Springs where an ethnic flavor is noticeable (particularly in its early architecture)—Wyoming's culture maintains a remarkable homogeneity, or uniformity, throughout.

This has important impacts upon the political culture. A recent paper focuses on Wyoming's homogeneity. The paper concludes that people in Wyoming (particularly youngsters attending overwhelmingly white schools):

. . . might well have little conception of the politics of race and the problems of trying to accommodate racial . . . differences into a broad consensus. . . . Similarly, Wyomingites generally do not look sympathetically at the politics of the poor. One significant reason for that outlook is that nationally those people who live in poverty are disproportionately black and members of other racial minorities. Because Wyoming has few of these groups, most Wyomingites have little understanding of their problems. Poverty is its own culture; 'To be impoverished is to . . . grow up in a culture that is radically different from the one that dominates society.' Such differences are not evident in the Wyoming culture.[12]

Even the presence of various Indian cultures probably does little to alter the state's overall cultural tone. The Indian population is a relatively small portion of the state's population. As such, Indian cultures form a correspondingly small part of the larger culture. It is such a small aspect, in fact, that Indian leaders have long gone to special lengths to preserve their tribal heritage, trying to guard against its being overwhelmed by the dominant white culture (See Sidebar 7–2).

The Minerals Boom: Energy Onslaught or Progressive Development?

As we are frequently reminded, the Oil Producing Exporting Countries, or OPEC as they are commonly known, conducted a highly successful oil embargo against the United States in 1973. The embargo began a series of events which have probably had as great an impact

on American living as any other series of events since World War II. The embargo began an energy crisis that continues today in the form of "energy consciousness" during the "energy era." As the size of cars has come down, and the price of fuel has shot up, the cry for energy independence has grown ever louder. With each call for self-sufficiency comes an even greater need for western resources, in general, and Wyoming resources, in particular. Thus, Wyoming in the 1970's, as with neighboring states, was like a teenager who grew six inches over the summer—things that had an orderly fit only recently no longer do; he is more conscious of himself, his world, and the vulnerability of the moment; and he will never be the same again. To the teenager, the whole world is aflutter, and he is uncertain whether he understands it all. So it is with the boy and so it is with Wyoming.

The changes that are taking place are redefining the culture of Wyoming. It remains to be seen whether the changes in the culture will encompass progressive infusions of new blood, resulting in overall improvements through economic prosperity, an expanded tax base, and enhanced energy self-sufficiency, or whether Russian roulette is being played with the Wyoming lifestyle. Indeed, the answer will be the legacy of the 1980's.

The Consequences of Rapid Growth: Dawn or Doom of a Western Culture. One of the major consequences of the energy boom in Wyoming and the high plains states is the incredible influx of new people—construction and energy workers, their families, and support personnel and their families (additional businessmen, policemen, teachers, etc.) This growth has hit the new "boom towns" the hardest.

Sidebar 7–2
Children and Wyoming Government: What They Know and How They Feel

by Maggi Murdock
(Professor of Political Science, Casper College)

Political socialization is the process by which members of a group learn about the political system of that group. In some form or manner every political system socializes or teaches its members in order to transfer the values and norms of the political system to the members of that system. The political system transfers information through a variety of agents (family, school, voluntary groups, peers, religious organizations, media and events) in order to socialize its members. While the obvious goal of political socialization in terms of the political system is to produce members that are supportive of the system so that the system might be maintained or continue, some agents such as events or the media or peer groups may transfer information about the political system that is less than supportive and, in fact, may be contrary to the goal of maintaining the political system, for the American government does not control all agents of socialization.

The amount and type of support that members of a political system have is of interest to political decision-makers and other members of a political system as well. It is for this reason that polls such as the Harris and Gallup polls are of such interest and utility in the American political system. Political scientists, however, have gone beyond an investigation of the attitudes of adult participants in the political system and examine as also important the political attitudes expressed by children to determine what attitudes they are being taught and they are learning.

In a study of the political attitudes of children in Wyoming undertaken in 1976, a group of children from the schools on the Wind River Reservation were asked what they knew about the tribal, state and national political systems. The children in this study were in grades three to eight and, while some of the children were white, the majority of the children were Native American. This study was different from most studies of children's political attitudes simply because the children resided in Wyoming: few studies such as this are done in a rural setting. Most studies of child socialization also focus on white children alone. The findings from this study point out the attitudes held by some Wyoming children:

- —In general, the children in this study were not radically different in their political attitudes than those children examined in other areas of the United States, but they did exhibit some differences in attitude.
- —While all of the children in the study expressed much support for the Federal government, the Native American children in the study expressed an even greater support than did the white children.
- —The children in this study knew less about the Wyoming state government, and expressed less support for the Wyoming state government, than they expressed for the federal and tribal governments.
- —Not unexpectedly, the white children in this study expressed less support for tribal government than Native American children and Native American children were more supportive of the tribe of which they were a member.
- —Like children studied in other areas of the United States, the children in this study appeared to not only support government, but also the people who ran each of these levels of government: the President, the Governor and the Tribal Chairmen.

These findings show something of the political attitudes of rural children in the United States, and certainly illustrate how a group of Wyoming school children feel about different levels of government. Studies such as this have limited usefulness unless they are applied practically: what kinds of information must be transferred to better acquaint Wyoming children with Wyoming government and make them more supportive of the Wyoming government? Such inquiries reveal the method of political socialization and how it can be applied to Wyoming government.

In its broad context, the energy boom of the 1970's and 1980's is the most recent in a series of boom and bust cycles which make up much of the history of the Rocky Mountain and Northern Great Plains regions.[13] From the building of the first transcontinental railroad in the late 1860's and early 1870's, to the drought and agricultural bust of the 1880's, to the periodic gold and silver rushes of the late nineteenth century, to the depressions of the 1890's (including the bankruptcy of the Union Pacific Railroad) and late 1920's and 1930's, to the uranium boom of the 1950's, to the recent development of the ski industry, and to the possible bust in tourism during the 1980's, the cycle has repeated itself.[14] Whether or not one views the present development in this historical context, it is apparent that the recent trend is as dramatic and significant as previous periods of growth have been in the region. In fact, energy related growth is the dominant feature of many western communities at present. A 1977 study estimated that 188 Rocky Mountain communities were affected by the current energy boom, three quarters of which had initial populations of under 2,000 residents.[15] It is not unusual for impacted communities to grow at annual rates of 20 to 25 percent, and some have doubled in size in just two years.[16] Examples are numerous: Craig, Colorado, one of 33 Colorado boom towns, had a 288 percent population growth between 1970 and 1977,[17] approaching 10,000 residents by 1978; during the 1970's the population of Rock Springs, Wyoming more than doubled its 12,000 base (some estimates say it tripled or more);[18] Wheatland, Wyoming, formerly a farming community of 2,350 residents in 1960 and 2,498 in 1970, grew to 3,705 in 1977 and an estimated 8,000 in 1979.[19]

The effects of the growth are, of course, both positive and negative. On the plus side, energy development stimulates local and regional economies. Jobs are created, wages rise, and many local businesses prosper.[20] In the broader view, development is often seen as a beneficial, or at least necessary, way of addressing two major national problems—the energy shortage and a weakened economy. In this regard, the intermountain West is a veritable storehouse of energy resources. The region contains billions of tons of coal. For example, Wyoming contains 40 percent of the known coal reserves. In addition, the intermountain states hold 95 percent of the known uranium reserves in the United States, vast oil, natural gas, and oil shale deposits (more oil is thought to be trapped in Colorado shale than is in the Middle East), and numerous other minerals and potential energy sources (e.g. geothermal).[21]

The negative position, to put it in the words of one observer, is that "many huge corporations and many decision-makers see the region as an area to be, in other words, 'sacrificed for the good of the rest of the country.' "[22] As one impacted community resident put it, "It looks like someone in Washington looked at a map of Wyoming and decided that it should be a National Sacrifice Area."[23] In the view of these people, the rush to respond to the energy shortage has been undertaken with too little planning and foresight. As a result, western communities are undergoing extraordinary social, psychological, cultural, and economic strains which threaten area lifestyles. In a recent paper on "Grassroots Organizing in Boom Towns," community specialist Earle Warner assesses the magnitude of impact problems, observing:

This social disruption in a boom town affects everyone, including the new arrivals (people often working in resource development) who find themselves in 'fractured' environments hostile to them—environments in which the newcomers find it difficult to put down roots. There is a widespread sense of hopelessness, a feeling of being trampled in the stampede to strip the land of its resources. Long-time residents and new arrivals, alike, feel the effects of the growth. They see the unbridled wealth which has come to some but which has brought new or greater poverty to many; wages and prices skyrocket; housing, regardless of quality is virtually impossible to find, and when found, is so expensive that few can afford it; and streets once placid and safe, are now filled with four-wheel-drive pickups, moving like urban rush-hour traffic.

The impact is not always as visible as street traffic or food prices. The traditional customs and social values, all too often lost now in urban settings, form the basis of the western way of life. Handshakes seal bargains; assistance is offered to automobiles disabled at the side of the road; and people readily greet and talk with strangers. There is neighborly caring, informal communication, toughness, and endurance and honesty. These customs and values have been part of daily living in a region with few people spread over immense geographic areas, and with few governmental or other external resources.

The explosive growth brought on by natural resource development tears apart the social and cultural support systems in which people's lives have been rooted. Communities, once they are glutted by growth and fractured by the boom of development, become unhealthy environments for long-time residents and newcomers alike. Craig, Colorado, and the Rock Springs area of Wyoming are two examples of communities experiencing significant problems from rapid growth. The Craig area's population went from 4,500 in 1973 to an estimated 10,000 in 1978. The social problems brought on by the growth are illustrated in the crime statistics. From 1973 to 1976, there was a sharp increase in the incidence of reported substance (alcohol, drug) abuse (more than 600%), family disturbances (more than 350%), and child behavior problems (delinquency, truancy) (1000%) and crimes against persons (900%). The mental health caseload in Craig tripled between 1976 and early 1978.

The population of the Rock Springs, Wyoming area grew from 11,674 in 1970 to between 40,000 and 48,000 in 1978. . . . The mental health caseload in Rock Springs increased 900% in five years, most of the patients being long-term residents. The crime complaints increased 60% in one year, 1972–1973.

The statistics are mere surface symptoms of the sickness rampant in many boom towns, a sickness brought on by uncontrolled growth and encouraged by decisions in which few local residents have any voice. The social and cultural community values are being overwhelmed. Long-standing informal social support networks have been broken. The sense of community, of belonging, is gone. The nature and quality of life have been destroyed. Craig and Rock Springs are premonitions of the future for as many as 200 communities in the Intermountain West and Plains region . . .[24]

For all that can be said, then, on both sides of the development question, this much is certain—the latest in the region's boom-bust cycles will undoubtedly have lasting impacts upon lifestyles and social interaction in the intermountain West. Much has happened in the 1970's; much is bound to happen in the 1980's; and much remains to be seen.

State Response. Faced with dramatic projections of further growth (some of which have not been borne out), Wyoming's legislature in the early and mid 1970's passed a series of measures to lessen the severity of the anticipated boom. The discussion that follows summarizes two major aspects of state planning—the consolidation of several environmental protection agencies into a unified Department of Environmental Quality, and creation of the Industrial Siting Council and Administration. Although the material in these pages may at first glance appear boring, the discussion gives specific examples of how a state government can address major issues of potential crisis proportion. Considering the importance of the development issue for the futures of both the nation and state, it is worthwhile to glance at these major aspects of state planning. The point of the material in this section, then, is twofold. The material shows something of state planning in response to rapid growth, but also provides case studies on the workings of the executive branch of Wyoming government.

In that sense, the section compliments Chapter 5. The discussion concentrates on state government because while federal programs and money are available, the primary responsibility for dealing with energy impact rests with the states and municipalities.

Much to the delight of Wyoming environmentalists, the Wyoming legislature, in 1973, combined several existing environmental programs into a new Department of Environmental Quality and generally widened its authority. The DEQ, as it is ordinarily called, is primarily responsible for "the prevention, reduction and elimination of air, land and water pollution and to assure proper reclamation for lands adversely affected by mining."[25] The DEQ also administers, or carries out, a variety of environmental programs offered by the federal government. As is typical of numerous federal programs, the national government makes money available to the states for specific purposes (more general programs are also available) and if specific requirements are met, such as having an appropriate agency at the state level to execute and enforce the federal program.[26] In this sense, federal and state governments *share* numerous responsibilities such as environmental protection; the federal government provides the money and establishes goals and procedures while the states interpret, implement and enforce them.[27]

In contrast with the DEQ, which protects the state's air, water, and land against potential polluters, the Industrial Siting Council (popularly called the Siting Council) protects Wyoming's social and economic environments against the "threat of serious injury."[28] While one attempts to keep Wyoming clean (DEQ), the other attempts to preserve the quality of life in the region's various communities (Siting Council).

Although there are procedural differences between the two agencies, the DEQ and Siting Council are quite similar in terms of administrative structure. Both are formally run by seven-member councils appointed by the governor. These councils, as is the case with much of state administration, are part-time citizens who periodically come together from throughout the state to set agency policies and make final administrative decisions. Each council appoints a full-time administrator who runs the agency's daily affairs and is accountable to the supervisory council. For the most part, council members serve as conscientious citizens; they receive no salary. Council members usually view their service as a responsibility that comes with living in a democracy.

Likewise, the DEQ and Siting Council are both regulatory agencies. This is the key to understanding the two agencies and, more importantly, to appreciating the kinds of things that Wyoming is doing in the face of the current boom. This means that anyone planning to construct a new facility which may be harmful to the environment must obtain a permit from DEQ before construction of the facility is even begun. Representatives of the facility must show, for example, that the facility will operate within state air emission standards. If this is demonstrated, a permit to construct will be issued. However, before the facility begins operation (even if the facility had previously been in operation, but has subsequently undergone major modifications) it must again be shown that state standards have been met. If so, a permit to operate will be issued. DEQ then monitors the operation to verify compliance. Violators are subject to penalties which may be imposed by state courts. Denial of the necessary permits may be appealed to the DEQ council and eventually to district courts.[29] But even assuming that petitioners on behalf of the facility in this example have shown that they are within the standards, they are a long way from opening for business. Remember, this example dealt only with air emission standards. Similar permits are required of other subdivisions within the DEQ, regarding emissions into the water, land quality, and solid waste management. Indeed, once these permits are obtained, the facility is still not ready to open, because it must also meet the standards of numerous other units of local, state, and national government. Licensing is clearly a long, complicated process. But remember, the stakes are high.

Just as the Department of Environmental Quality regulates the environment, the Industrial Siting Administration has regulated social and economic impacts (and to a lesser extent environmental ones as well) since its creation by the legislature in 1975. Essentially, this means that the petitioner must show that the new facility will not pose a threat of serious injury to the community in such social and economic terms as impacts on classroom space within the schools and the adequacy of sewer treatment facilities. This means that most new mines and all energy-generating or conversion facilities of major proportions[30] must prove that they will help offset new demands on community resources that will be caused by their presence. For example, if a large new power plant is going to double a town's population, thereby causing sharp increases in the number of classrooms, streets, fire-fighting and police equipment, or sewer treatment facilities that are necessary in the community, the petitioner will be required to go to considerable lengths to offset the new demands. Accordingly, the industry will be required to perform an extensive study on the likely consequences of its operation— and to show Siting Council officials that it will not "pose a threat of serious injury" to the

area—before the necessary permits will be issued.

As outlined in these pages, then, Wyoming has devised several major programs to provide for orderly growth, thereby preserving the region's way of life in the face of increasing (and increasingly necessary) pressure for resources. As energy companies are quick to point out, such programs do slow the process of achieving energy independence (Siting Council requirements may take up to 18 months of study, for example) and are not inexpensive. Environmentalists counter that when the impacts upon an area are potentially devastating, a deliberate pace is an asset and thorough studies are essential. Regardless of one's perspective on development and the proper role of government, this is clearly an area in which Wyoming's stake is extraordinary. As much as any issue in the foreseeable future, the handling of energy development is truly shaping the state's future.[31]

Water—A Political and Legal Issue

Few issues are as related to both Wyoming's past and future as is water. Whereas residents of eastern states have water in such abundance that its use is somewhat taken for granted, the opposite has always been the case in Wyoming. During this era of energy boom, it is fruitful to reflect upon the relevance of this resource as it bears upon the development of energy resources. Indeed, the water issue not only tells us something about both geographical limitations of the region and the challenging priority options in the face of the energy boom, but something of Wyoming's role in the federal balance, as well.

Historical Perspective. To say that Wyoming is a dry state, is to downplay the obvious. In fact, "semiarid is . . . an appropriate designation for all except the higher altitudes, since the average annual precipitation is about 14.31 inches."[32] Not only is there little rainfall to begin with, but other factors decrease the water that is there—low relative humidity, strong winds, and prolonged sunshine cause high evaporation levels. Evaporation rates are so high that "water stored in reservoirs is depleted by evaporation at the rate of four feet in one year."[33] Wyoming wind and evaporation have given rise to such tales as the claim "that snow does not melt, but blows back and forth until it wears out." Others say that "not much snow falls, but a lot blows through."[34]

Although these stories are humorous, they attest to the fact that relatively little water is to be found in the state. Even Wyoming's rivers, like the Snake and the Green Rivers, are but tributaries born in the mountains. By the time they "mature," so to speak, they have left for Idaho, Colorado, or east, toward the Missouri River.

The dry climate has had a tremendous impact on the shape of Wyoming. As much as anything, the lack of water explains the region's failure to develop even a single large commercial center (admittedly, there are other reasons as well, but the absence of large, navigable rivers makes economical shipping less feasible) and "more than anything else, seems to have placed a lid on population growth."[35] Likewise, the semiarid climate defined the nature of Wyoming's economy. Early settlers guessed correctly that this would be country best suited for ranching, mining, and some dry farming (particularly in the eastern part of the state where annual rainfall is slightly higher).

The climate also set the tone for much of the early construction in Wyoming. From early territorial attempts to divert streams from nearby mountains to Cheyenne to moves in the 1980's to enlarge the Buffalo Bill Res-

ervoir near Cody, water has attracted the attention of Wyoming builders. These endeavors, called reclamation projects, also brought an increased presence of the federal government to Wyoming. It was one thing, in other words, to have the desire to harness water for agriculture, but another thing to make it possible financially. One incentive program, for example, was the Carey Act of 1894, sponsored by Senator Joseph M. Carey. Designed to provide federal and state aid to western reclamation projects, the law provided for federal donations of up to one million acres of arid land (federally-owned land located in dry states) to each state that used its influence and resources to reclaim and settle the arid land. The intent of the act was to irrigate land in small tracts, creating modest family farms. The act was highly controversial, however, because of claims that some family operators were "fronts" for large financial (particularly ranching) interests.

Utilizing provisions from the Carey Act, irrigation projects were undertaken in the Big Horn Basin on the Greybull River and on the South Fork of the Stinking Water (later renamed the Shoshone).[36] Other reclamation projects abounded throughout the state, opening much of Wyoming to farming—in the Wheatland area (early 1890's), a Mormon colony north of the Greybull River near present day Burlington (middle 1890's), Sidon Canal near present day Byron, Cowley, and Lovell (early 1900's), the central Wyoming region surrounding Riverton (early 1900's), to name but a few examples. In particular, many early reclamation projects prospered (not all immediately, of course) due to the foresight and ingenuity of various political figures, such as State Engineer Elwood Mead and Senator Francis E. Warren.

The scarcity of water is also relevant to today's energy boom, because nearly all aspects of the boom—from extraction operations to population increases—affect, and are affected by, the availability and quality of water. At the outset of the most recent energy boom, many Wyoming-watchers anticipated an accompanying industrial boom of energy conversion facilities. In particular, gasification and liquefaction plants were envisioned as a means of transforming coal and oil shale into more manageable energy forms. Others saw the time when the state would be dotted with massive energy plants, converting raw energy sources into electricity to be used in the nation's more populous regions.

But these ambitious plans have not materialized, at least not in the proportions foreseen. As before, "a geographical limitation arose as a nemesis: lack of water."[37] Not only does little water originate in Wyoming, but three-quarters of that which begins in the state is obligated to downstream states. Because downstream appropriators had put "upstream" water to beneficial use prior to its use by Wyoming interests, various court cases and compacts between states legally preserve downstream user rights. This means, then, that before industries can begin large projects in Wyoming, they must first obtain rights to the necessary water. Pumping water in from the east is expensive and seldom feasible. As a result, industries often purchase the necessary water rights from farmers and ranchers. Even so, the natural and legal water rights hurdles have decreased the anticipated industrial onslaught. In 1975, when the federal government invited bids for the development of oil from shale on government land in Colorado, Utah, and Wyoming, for example, no bids were submitted on the Wyoming tracts. The question was not whether the oil was locked in the shale. It unquestionably was there, "but with present technology, too much water would be required to process it."[38] The

lack of water, plus air pollution levels and waste problems, forced the project to the back burner.

Water Law and Management. It is somewhat ironic that Wyoming should suffer from water problems, because Wyoming was the first state to adopt a thorough system of water management. As mentioned in Chapter 1, Article 8 of Wyoming's constitution says, "the water of all natural streams, springs, lakes or other collections of still water, within the boundaries of the State, are hereby declared to be the property of the State." Article 8 goes on to outline state management of its water by a Board of Control, state engineer, and superintendents of four water divisions. The importance of these provisions is twofold: first, it declares that water in the state belongs to the state; second, it provides a mechanism to administer that resource.

Article 8 goes a step further, declaring that "priority of appropriation for beneficial uses shall give the better right." The theory of "prior appropriation," as it is called, means that the first "person" to put water to beneficial use has the best right to that water. Most western states have followed Wyoming's lead in adopting this system rather than that based upon "riparian rights," the system born of Old English common law that allows all who own land along a stream the full and undiminished right to the water. Under the "prior appropriation" system, the key is *when* the user (or his ancestors) began using the water, rather than where his use is located. This means that while downstream residents are at the mercy of their upstream neighbors in a riparian system, downstream rights are protected in the prior appropriation system according to who used the water first.

The "prior appropriation" doctrine, and therefore Wyoming water law,[39] has several major features. First, "exclusive right is given to the first appropriator; and, in accordance with the doctrine of priority, the rights of later appropriators are conditional upon the rights that have preceded."[40] This means that would-be water users in Wyoming, called "appropriators," must first file an application with the state engineer and receive a permit (see Sidebar 7–3 for an illustration of this process). Water rights, then, are established in the order of these permits; the earlier the filing with the state engineer, the higher the appropriator's priority to use the water.

Sidebar 7–3
Summary of Procedure to Obtain
Rights to Surface Water in Wyoming

Wyoming's first surface water laws were enacted in 1875. More comprehensive laws were adopted along with the State Constitution in 1890. In brief, these laws state:

1. Any person, association, or corporation wanting to use surface water must first apply to the State Engineer for a permit. Application forms are available from the State Engineer's Office.
2. An engineer or surveyor, qualified to practice under Wyoming law, must make a survey and prepare the maps and plans necessary for application. Generally this engineer or land surveyor also has the necessary application forms.
3. The application form, maps and plans, and a $2 filing fee are submitted to the State Engineer as a package. The priority date is established by the date of receipt in the State Engineer's Office.
4. Upon approval of the application the State Engineer issues a permit for developing the proposed water project.
5. Construction, completion and beneficial use of the project must be made within the time specified on the approved permit.
6. The permittee must notify the State Engineer on appropriate forms of the dates construction began, when construction was completed, and when water was put to beneficial use. The appropriate forms are provided with the approved permit.
7. If the permittee cannot begin, complete, and/or put the water to use in the time

prescribed, he may ask the State Engineer to extend any or all of the time limits. He must cite good cause for needing an extension and request it before the original time limits expire. If a time extension is granted, the date of priority remains the same.
8. After the beneficial use of water has been made or a reservoir constructed and the notices as outlined in item 6 submitted, a final proof of appropriation or construction is submitted to the Board Control. This proof is advertised in the local newspaper and an inspection of the project made. If everything is found in order and no protests are filed, a Certificate of Appropriation or of Construction is issued by the Board and recorded in the county clerk's office in which the project is located. This is evidence of an adjudicated water right.
9. Limits of water for irrigation:
   a. Water rights with priorities dated March 1, 1945 and after are entitled to one cubic foot per second flow for each 70 acres of land irrigated.
   b. Water rights with priority dates on and before March 1, 1945 are entitled to one cubic foot per second flow per 70 acres and up to an additional one cubic foot per second flow per 70 acres during periods of surplus flow as determined by the local water commissioner.

Source: Brief Summary of Wyoming Water Law, available through the office of the state engineer.

Second, the prior appropriation doctrine "makes all rights conditional upon beneficial use—as the doctrine of priority was adopted for the protection of first settlers in times of scarcity, so the doctrine of beneficial use became a protection of late settlers against the wasteful use by those with earlier rights."[41] This means that a water right is valid only so long as it is actually put to "beneficial use" as determined by the state engineer and Board of Control. An appropriator may not, therefore, protect a right to water without using that right. Also, the state engineer and Board of Control are allowed considerable subjectivity in determining what are and are not beneficial uses. The legislature has been relatively silent on the point.[42]

Water rights which are not used may be ruled abandoned. Abandonment may be declared when a water right for surface or ground water has not been used for five successive years. Though statutory procedures must be followed, abandonment may be initiated by either the state engineer or the affected party. When a water right is declared abandoned, the user forfeits all water rights, easements, ditch rights, and the like, and the water again becomes subject to appropriation.

The third major feature of the prior appropriation doctrine is that unlike riparian systems, persons living away from the water source may be entitled to a water right. In other words, water appropriated through a valid water right may be transported anywhere for use.[43] In that sense, a prior appropriation water right is a legal property right. Accordingly, it may be bought, sold, or inherited like any other property right.

Next, this water law system preserves the property right of appropriators with older rights (meaning higher priorities) regardless of the available water supply. This means that during dry years higher priority appropriators get the full allocation until the available water is used. Rather than all appropriators taking less than their rights during dry periods, thereby sharing the shortage (so that lower priorities will at least get something), low priority appropriators simply get no water once the higher appropriators have used up the available supply.[44]

Finally, the legislature has determined that there shall be four "preferred uses" for Wyoming water. They are:

1. Water for drinking purposes for both man and beast.
2. Water for municipal purposes.
3. Water for use of steam engines and general railway use, water for culinary, laundry, bathing, refrigerating (including the manufacturing of ice), for steam and hot water heating plants, and for steam power plants.
4. Industrial purposes.[45]

These preferred uses do not interfere with priority allocations. In other words, that there are preferred uses does not mean that an appropriation application for drinking water gets a higher priority than an application for industrial use. As always, whichever permit is issued and used first has the priority right. Rather, "preferred use" means that in times of severe water shortage, other water rights may be acquired for, or forfeited to, the preferred uses through the laws of public condemnation. During a prolonged drought, for example, a city (having a preferred use) might go to court seeking an order (condemnation) taking away a local farmer's (a nonpreferred use) water right. If granted, the city would pay the farmer for his forfeited water right.[46]

With these features as the heart of Wyoming water law, the state engineer administers the water system through four water divisions.

Water Division No. 1 is made up of the North and South Platte River drainages, the Little Snake and the Niobrara River drainages. Water Division No. 2 contains all drainages north of the Niobrara and North Platte River drainages and east of the Big Horn Mountains. Water Division No. 3 is composed of the Big Horn and Clark's Fork River drainages; Water Division No. 4 includes the Bear, Green and Snake River drainages.[47]

A water division superintendent, who is subordinate to the state engineer, administers the waters of each water division. This means, for example, that the superintendents oversee the water appropriator's actual uses, making certain that there are careful measures of how much water is actually taken. These four superintendents and the state engineer make up the state Board of Control. The board meets periodically to adjudicate or finalize water rights and to consider other matters pertaining to water rights such as a change in the point of diversion, or a change or correction of water rights. Decisions made by the state engineer may be appealed to the Board of Control. Its decisions may be, in turn, appealed to district courts.[48]

State Rights or Federal Prerogatives? Finally, it is worth pointing out that the stage is set for continued state-federal strife on the issue of water rights. In 1977, President Carter submitted an environmental message to Congress suggesting, in part, a review of federal water policy. The review, a subsequent explanation said:

to be comprehensive . . . should not be limited to what has been traditionally viewed as strictly federal areas concerning water resources. This is because federal water resource policy and programs are influenced by other governmental institutions, primarily those of the states.

The message continued:

The review will respect the fact that the acquisition, use and disposition of rights to use water have his-

torically been a matter of individual state law. But this respect is tempered by the recognition that as demands on the Nation's limited water resources increase, it may be necessary to develop a national perspective both as to water quantity and quality and to ensure that federal policies promote the recognition of realistic goals through changes in existing institutions at all levels of government.[49]

In a series of papers on federal options, which appeared in the "Federal Register," one alternative for increased federal control over water explained:

The federal government could purchase rights to water and reallocate them to the most socially desirable or economically productive use. Purchases could be through voluntary sales or through eminent domain procedures.[50]

These statements, though merely a series of speculative alternatives and possibilities, sent shock waves through the West. In Wyoming, for instance, water was not (and is not) considered a negotiable issue. Snow and rain fall from the Wyoming sky to Wyoming soil to be transported in Wyoming streams or collected in Wyoming lakes. Thus, westerners contend, it is Wyoming water. And the most authoritative document of the sovereign State of Wyoming, the constitution, declares that Wyoming water is the property of the state. When the Congress admitted Wyoming to the Union, the reasoning goes, it accepted the provisions of her constitution, thereby ratifying state ownership of water.

There are, however, several problems with this reasoning. Notice, the problems are legal ones, not ethical matters of right and wrong. Combined, the arguments on both sides of the water question offer a classic case study of states' rights vis-à-vis federal rights.

The state's position in the water debate begins with the reasoning outlined above—water within the boundaries of Wyoming belongs to the State of Wyoming. As such, the state view continues, Washington has no jurisdiction over it. States' rights defenders argue that their position is strengthened in the U.S. Constitution, as well.

The Tenth Amendment states that "the powers not delegated to the United States by the Constitution, nor prohibited by it to the States, are reserved to the States respectively, or to the people." This means, then, that the powers that are not given to the federal government by the U.S. Constitution are withheld for the states. Although federal powers are discussed at various points in the Constitution, the primary listing is in Article I, Section 8. This list of enumerated powers gives the federal government sovereign powers—to coin money, establish an army and navy, and others. However, neither Article I, Section 8, nor other constitutional passages, makes mention of federal regulation of water. Therefore, the state view continues, management of water is reserved to the states—the federal government has little or no say about water management, especially, defenders of the state view say, since the U.S. implicitly admitted that it is the province of Wyoming to manage its state-owned water (when Congress admitted Wyoming to the Union). Accordingly, President Carter was exercising unwarranted and unconstitutional authority when he began a study of a federal water policy.

The view held by the federal government is, of course, quite different. As is the case with federal jurisdiction over civil rights, the federal perspective holds that national jurisdiction is more a matter of historical and legal interpretation and evolution than it is a matter of literal reading. This view explains, for example, that although Article I, Section 8 of the U.S. Constitution does not specifically give the national government jurisdiction over water, it grants both the authority to regulate interstate commerce and to do whatever is "necessary and proper" in exercising its commerce jurisdiction.[51]

The U.S. Supreme Court has repeatedly ruled that the commerce clause extends to the "navigable waters of the United States," including waters which are potentially navigable by "reasonable improvements." This, the federal side contends, is quite logical—the skies, streams and some lakes know nothing of state boundaries, and crops that grow as a result of rain and irrigation may yield sugar beets. These beets are ultimately turned into sugar products, which are sold throughout the nation. Thus, this perspective concludes, water clearly is engaged in, or bearing upon, interstate commerce. As such, it is subject to federal management and control.[52]

State partisans respond, "Fine, let the feds help manage Wyoming's navigable water. But who is going to make the Laramie, Shoshone, and Greybull Rivers navigable? Are barges lined up ready to head down Wyoming's two-foot deep streams toward the Gulf of Mexico?" If not, defenders of states' rights contend, the commerce clause is being abused. The result is seen as the same—the national government may have the authority to set broad national water themes over a minor part of Wyoming's water, but it has neither the right nor the authority to interfere with the management and control of Wyoming's most precious, state-owned (and hardly navigable) resource.

Federal partisans respond that much water in Wyoming is navigable, and that even more is potentially navigable. Likewise, they argue that the water that is not navigable has a significant bearing on agriculture, which is itself an aspect of interstate commerce. But the most effective argument is that the federal government is obligated to provide for the public good. For the national good, states' rights may have to fall. Besides, this precedent can be implied in the 1908 Winters Doctrine which established the concept of federal reserved water rights.

The point here is not to say which side, if either, is right. The question of "right" is far beyond the scope of these pages. Rather, the point here is to show, however briefly, a few aspects of federal-state rivalries. Although the water issues reviewed here are as yet unsettled, the rivalry seems to be a permanent feature of American politics, in general, and Wyoming politics, in particular. And no student of Wyoming politics should mistakenly think that this is an unimportant issue and an unimportant rivalry. As of this writing, the federal government appears increasingly willing (perhaps anxious) to preempt state water rights. If so, the rivalry may become even more pronounced and tense.

Financing State Government

Practically everything that state government does costs the state—which means taxpayers—some amount of money. This includes everything from the University of Wyoming's football team, to the lighting at the capitol; from the check-in stations that hunters report to, to the ports of entry that truckers report to. This, of course, is relatively obvious. But while the public tends to think their taxes are too high (see Sidebar 7–4), many taxpayers feel uncomfortable about this whole issue. It is strange that this aura of mystery hangs over state fiscal (monetary) matters, considering that the state budget (actually budgets) is little more than a statement of state priorities.

Sidebar 7–4
The Tax Burden in Wyoming

by Alan Evan Schenker
(Professor of Political Science, University of Wyoming)

Does the financial burden of supporting state and local government fall heavily upon Wyomingites? By one measure the reply is a strong YES, but by another measure it is an equally strong NO. Explaining this paradox can point up an unusual feature of Wyoming public finance.

In 1975, Wyoming had the *ninth highest state-local tax effort* in the nation: 13.4% of personal income.

According to a 1974 study, the state-local tax burden for a Wyoming family of four with a $10,000 income ranked 46th among the 50 states, at 5.8% of personal income.

How can we reconcile Wyoming being ninth from the top by one approach and fifth from the bottom by another? How can we reconcile the difference between 13.4 and 5.8 percent of personal income?

The answer is that Wyoming has a revenue system that is *both* very light for its own residents *and* heavy for other taxpayers, especially individuals and businesses that are outside the state.

This important phenomenon is called tax "exportation." For example: in 1977, Wyoming's state and local governments collected $150 million in taxes on mineral production. Most of these taxes were in effect paid by out-of-state buyers of minerals, for Wyomingites consume little of their own production. Similarly, Wyoming collected $74 million in state and local sales taxes, the equivalent of $730 for a family of four. But the U.S. Internal Revenue Service pays only $220 a year in sales tax. Much of the remainder is "exported."

It appears that Wyoming has been quite successful at achieving the goal implicit in that old adage, "A good tax is one that is paid by someone else."

Accordingly, this section is an introduction to a few of the basic aspects of financing Wyoming government. In other ways, the section is also a reminder of the fiscal challenges which face both the state and nation in the future.

Somewhat surprisingly, it is quite difficult to say exactly how much money the State of Wyoming either takes in or spends, because Wyoming does not have a unified budget (one document which details all state revenue and expenditures). Instead, state funds are accounted for through 13 funds which overlap in the sense that money is sometimes transferred from one fund to another or from state to local governments. This means, for example, that an agency might issue $10 million to another agency (acting within its legal authority, of course), which might then actually spend it. On paper it would look as though $20 million had been spent (or disbursed), $10 million by each agency. Actually, only half that amount would be involved. It is therefore quite misleading to combine the disbursements from the 13 funds and to assume that they are a total of state expenditures—there are simply too many intervening factors. As a result, various accounts of state finances often quote different figures in their search for the exact revenue and expenditure figures. This account will cover a few of the major themes of spending in Wyoming while attempting to avoid this pitfall.

Accounting for State Funds. As mentioned above, state revenues in Wyoming are accounted for through 13 distinct, yet overlapping, funds. As Table 7.1 shows, the funds, which are the means through which the Wyoming auditor keeps track of state expenditures, are of considerably different sizes and importance. Although the table seems to indicate that the Trust and Agency Fund, with revenues in excess of $430 million, is the major

fund for state spending, this is not the case. Most money in this fund "belongs to someone else," so to speak, and is being held temporarily by the state. Money in the state retirement system and workmens' compensation program are held in this fund until passed along to recipients; School Foundation, sales tax, and cigarette tax revenues are raised at the local levels, held temporarily by the state in the Trust and Agency Fund, and returned to the local recipients; the state's portion of mineral royalty money (the state's share of money from the extraction of minerals from federally owned land located in Wyoming) is held in the Trust and Agency Fund until the legislature appropriates them to state highways, schools, and impacted communities. Money from this fund is actually "passing through" state hands, in the very short run. Because the state is a trustee of these funds, it has very little control over how the money is spent. This means, for example, that a great deal of the money is given or loaned (through grants) by the federal government to various municipalities in Wyoming.

In terms of understanding the workings of the federal system, another important fund is the Federal Fund, which is the depository for much of the state's federal money. Except for federal contributions to such major policy areas as highways, game and fish, employment security, and the University of Wyoming, most state money from the federal government is held in this fund. Much of this money "passes through" this fund, on its way from the federal government to the localities. Federal contributions to the various health and social service programs that are administered at the local level (e.g., welfare, Medicare, nurses training) are typical. The money is essentially to be put to uses that are determined by the federal officials (administrators oper-

Table 7.1. Managing State Revenues—The State Funds

Fund Name	Purpose	Example of Use	Revenue for Fiscal Year 1979 (Combined Transfer and Receipts Income)	Major Sources of Revenue
General Fund	Accounts for all revenues and expenditures not provided for by law in any other fund. Is the largest accounting activity in Wyoming government and receives far greater tax revenues than any other fund.	Money from the fund finances the ordinary operations of state government, representing a wider range of activities than those of other funds.	$195,929,114	75% raised through the various state taxes: property tax; sales, use and excise tax; severance tax; franchise tax; motor carrier tax; other taxes.
Earmarked Fund	Accounts for state revenue which is specifically dedicated by law, whether earmarked or restricted to defray the cost of a particular governmental unit, activity, or function of state government, and to account for proceeds from bond issues.	Consists largely of accounts used by professional and commercial licensing boards, e.g., finances Employment Security Commission programs.	$ 49,059,999	39% raised through severance taxes; 19% raised through federal mineral royalties.
Federal Fund	Accounts for all revenue received from federal sources which are to be used in the activities and functions of state government which is not accounted for in the Trust and Agency Fund, or the Game and Fish Fund.	Finances Dept. of Health and Social Services programs, for example.	$ 68,481,194	100% raised through the federal government.
Trust and Agency Fund	Accounts for money which the state administers as a trustee for specific purposes, such as revenue held temporarily by the state government.	Payments to retired state employees, payments to equalize the money available to education throughout the state.	$432,589,886	Local taxes and individual retirement contributions

SOURCE: 1979 Annual Report of the state auditor. Assistance of the state auditor's office.

Table 7.1—*Continued*

Fund Name	Purpose	Example of Use	Revenue for Fiscal Year 1979 (Combined Transfer and Receipts Income)	Major Sources of Revenue
Debt Service Fund	Accounts for money deposited in State Treasury for the payment of principal and interest, and for the accumulation of revenues for bonded or other indebtedness.	University Building Excess Royalty Account, to build and repair university buildings.	$ 11,155,337	Originally funded through General Fund; mineral royalties, leases and bonuses from federal lands.
Highway Fund	Accounts for funds expended to build or improve Wyoming highways.	Highway construction with the approval of the Highway Superintendent and the State Highway Commission.	$148,267,538	Gasoline tax, federal grants and aid.
Game and Fish Fund	Provides for the control and management of wild life.	Stocking of ponds, lakes and streams.	$ 10,694,430	80% from hunting and fishing licenses.
Permanent Land Fund	Accounts for the resources received and held as trustee of the land grants by the federal government to the state, plus the proceeds from the sale of public lands and mineral royalties.	Funds go to education, through Permanent Land Income Fund	$ 17,403,930	75% from oil and gas lease royalties
Permanent Land Income Fund	Accounts for proceeds from sale of public lands, mineral royalties, and various fees for use of state land (such as grazing and mineral prospecting leases).	Distributed to the public schools.	$ 13,303,917	Rentals from grazing, agriculture and mineral prospecting on public lands, plus interest derived from investment of the Permanent Land Fund.
Permanent Mineral Trust Fund	Provides a permanent holding of revenues derived from taxes on coal, petroleum, natural gas, oil shale, and other minerals.	Loans to various political subdivisions.	$ 43,253,969	100% from taxes on Wyoming minerals.

Table 7.1—*Continued*

Fund Name	Purpose	Example of Use	Revenue for Fiscal Year 1979 (Combined Transfer and Receipts Income)	Major Sources of Revenue
University of Wyoming Fund (actually accounts for small portion of U.W. budget)	Accounts for money deposited by U.W. trustees and accrued interest.	Reflects approximately 34% of U.W.'s annual budget, other than General Fund appropriations.	$ 13,279,512	Student fees and mineral royalties.
Intragovernmental Fund	Finances and accounts for services and commodities furnished by units of state government which are entirely or generally self-supporting, from charges to other government units.	Maintenance, repair and upkeep of state computer services, administered by the Dept. of Administration and Fiscal Control.	$ 11,552,598	Fees charged for the use of state computer services, and use of state airplane services.
Enterprise Fund	Finances and accounts for the acquisition of commodities, and for operation and maintenance of programs which are entirely self-supporting from charges to the general public or institutional clients.	Training School purchases to replenish inventories.	$ 29,340,874	Liquor Commission collections from liquor sales.

ating within jurisdictions determined by Congress). Although state officials have little or no influence over their national counterparts (other than whether to apply for or accept various funds), they handle much, though not all, of the federal money because municipalities are "creatures" of the state in which they are located.[53] Although the analogy isn't perfect, it's as though a stepfather is giving money to his stepson for a specific purpose that they agree upon, but the money is first handed to the child's mother, because, after all, she has the primary responsibility for the son. While she holds the money she is performing a service similar to the Federal Fund. In large measure, the analogy might be extended to make one wonder whether the mother wants to handle the money because she doesn't fully trust the son, or whether she is somewhat jealous of the stepfather's increasingly large role in family matters.

Actually, the major fund, in terms of the legislature's wide-ranging discretion to address problems, is the General Fund, which typically handles between 50 percent and 60 percent of the state's income.[54] As seen in Table 7.2, the fund finances state matters as

Table 7.2. State of Wyoming General Fund Expenditures by Functional Category July 1, 1978 through June 30, 1979

	Expenditure	%
General Government	$ 42,958,942	26.5
Education	56,246,596	34.7
Hospitals, Health and Social Services	33,705,575	20.8
Manpower	1,208,777	.7
Correction and Law Enforcement	6,527,780	4.0
Safety and Regulation	4,596,669	2.8
Resources and Recreation	12,037,620	7.4
Transportation	1,434,817	.9
Professional Licensing	61,431	.1
Judicial	1,754,004	1.1
Legislative	1,540,780	1.0
Total	$162,072,991	100.0

SOURCE: 1979 Annual Report of the state auditor.

diverse as manpower services such as workmens' compensation (transferred from the Federal Fund), judicial programs such as supreme court expenses, and safety and regulation affairs like Civil Defense. The major portion of General Fund expenditures (82 percent) is spent on three major functional areas: general government (26.5 percent), education (34.7 percent), and hospitals, health, and social services (20.8 percent). The general government category covers administrative costs such as the Department of Administration and Fiscal Control's purchases of most state equipment (office supplies) and record-keeping that goes along with the state treasurer's investments of state money. The largest chunk of General Fund expenditures for education go to the University of Wyoming, with the community colleges and Department of Education also receiving large portions. Hospital, health and social services money from the fund finance various health and social service programs such as mental health, drug abuse, and aid to the poor; other of these monies support the state hospital and training school.[55]

As Table 7.3 shows, the largest portion of General Fund revenues is generated by the various state taxes. The property tax, listed first in the table, is a relatively minor source of money for the state. Although the state could levy a four mill tax on property, it has not levied any property taxes since 1972 (1.5 mills were levied). Instead, the property tax "is left to local governments as their primary tax source."[56] In fact, the property tax revenues that the state receives are levied by the municipalities and channeled to the School Foundation Fund as state revenue.

The largest source of General Fund tax revenues are the sales and use taxes. Sales taxes are the "gross receipts from sales of tangible personal property and specified services including receipts by public utilities, certain interstate carriers, food services, lodging and entertainment facilities."[57] In other words, consumers who make everyday purchases in Wyoming pay an additional tax to complete the sales, with exceptions for items such as prescription drugs, certain medical supplies, and occasional sales by religious and charitable organizations. The use tax is essentially the same as the sales tax, but covers items that are purchased out-of-state, but used, stored, or consumed in Wyoming. This tax is really aimed at Wyoming residents who seek bargains in neighboring cities located in other states (like Cheyenne residents who shop in Denver). Though the law is difficult to enforce, the Denver shopper is legally obligated to pay the Wyoming tax when he returns with a new color television set. Originally set at two percent of the purchase price when the taxes took effect in 1937, the sales tax was raised in 1967 to three percent on sales of 25 cents or more (the use tax has had a corresponding increase); counties have an option of levying an addi-

Table 7.3 State of Wyoming General Fund Revenue Actual—Fiscal Year 1975 through 1979 Projected—Fiscal Year 1980 through 1982

	FY1975	FY1976	ACTUAL FY1977	FY1978	FY1979	FY1980	PROJECTED FY1981	FY1982
Taxes								
Property Taxes	$ 4,627	$ 110	$ 122	$ 30	$ 12	$ 650	$ 0	$ 0
Sales and Use Taxes	61,165,697	61,133,825	69,404,240	88,118,605	105,285,938	117,284,588	137,535,088	162,455,077
Mineral Severance Taxes	9,175,489	19,998,972	22,900,587	26,636,621	33,293,903	37,930,500	42,976,000	48,535,000
Inheritance Taxes	1,566,666	1,398,751	3,577,931	2,056,068	2,004,806	2,000,000	2,000,000	2,000,000
Franchise Taxes	3,203,581	3,735,759	4,473,129	5,511,878	6,520,733	5,047,000	5,517,000	5,747,000
Motor Carrier Taxes	1,201,768	1,391,091	1,385,604	1,854,481	1,894,142	2,102,800	2,271,000	2,453,000
Other Taxes	15,907	0	0	0	0	0	0	0
Total	$76,333,735	$87,658,508	$101,741,613	$124,177,683	$148,999,534	$164,365,538	$190,299,088	$221,190,077
Licenses, Permits & Regulatory	1,721,191	1,816,082	1,922,819	2,746,396	2,595,889	2,383,979	2,540,675	2,631,955
Fines, Forfeitures & Penalties	199,357	244,648	246,074	382,419	323,214	285,000	315,700	350,100
Use of Property and Money	4,358,466	6,681,003	8,170,260	8,107,742	11,088,197	10,625,856	10,703,834	10,816,851
Charges for Sales and Services	5,193,623	6,375,433	6,993,253	11,084,731	11,112,642	10,361,020	13,299,001	14,364,013
Revenue from Other (Non-Federal)	1,469,178	2,436,899	6,878,418	6,875,302	17,561,756	10,703,750	11,388,721	11,456,233
Federal Aids and Grants	4,669,974	6,786,811	5,473,482	5,015,352	4,161,137	4,191,225	315,425	315,425
Non-Revenue Receipts	2,215,970	37,406	161,322	634,206	86,745[1]	1,230	1,300	1,370
TOTAL	$96,161,494	$112,036,790	$131,587,241	$159,023,831	$195,929,114	$202,917,598	$228,863,744	$261,126,024

(1) Does not include Accounts Receivable for:
Land Office—Emergency School Loans $3,900,000

SOURCE: 1979 Annual Report of the state auditor.

tional one percent on the purchase price of taxable items.[58] The importance of these taxes is probably obvious to anyone who has been a Wyoming consumer. Indeed, the revenues they generate are considerable. In fiscal year 1979 alone, sales tax revenues totalled $136,903,105.27 and use tax revenues were $27,233,842.28.[59] Combined, sales and use taxes accounted for 70 percent of General Fund *tax* revenues, and 54 percent of *all* monies in that fund during fiscal year 1979 (see Table 7.3).

The newest major tax in Wyoming is the minerals severance tax. First imposed in 1969 on mining companies for the privilege of extracting Wyoming minerals,[60] the tax has grown in recent years, both in terms of revenues generated and as a controversial issue, just as the pace of mining has quickened. Since 1977, the severance tax rate has been "two percent of the value of all non-fossil minerals except trona and uranium, 5.5 percent of the value of trona and uranium, four percent of the value of oil and gas, and 8.5 percent of the value of coal (plus the excise tax on coal)."[61] As is generally true of Wyoming taxes, revenues generated by the minerals severance tax

are divided among several of the state funds according to priorities determined by the state legislature. Accordingly, severance tax revenues are channeled to the Minerals Trust Fund, Capitol Facilities Fund, Water Development Account and Highway Fund, in addition to the General Fund. Both in terms of total revenue and as a portion of the General Fund, severance taxes are increasingly important in Wyoming. From fiscal year 1975 to fiscal year 1979, for example, severance tax contributions (with accumulated interest included) to the Permanent Minerals Trust Fund and General Fund increased from approximately $9 million to over $115 million.[62] Severance revenues generated 22 percent of the General Fund raised through state taxes (Table 7.3). As the energy development of the 1970's and 1980's continues, the size of the severance tax is sure to be one of the state's major political issue (See Sidebar 7–5).

Although the General Fund is an extremely important factor in Wyoming spending, it is not, of course, the only fund from which state money is expended. As shown earlier, Wyoming raises a great deal of money, through a variety of taxes (see Table 7.4) and other

Sidebar 7–5
Severance Tax Controversy

by Gary Sturmer
(Professor of Political Science, Northwest Community College)

A severance tax is a state levy, assessed on the commercial process of removal of mineral resources from their natural container, whether earth or water. The tax may be levied n a flat rate, or a graduated scale. Wyoming presently levies a severance tax on coal, uranium, trona, petroleum, natural gas and other valuable minerals.

Arguments: Pro

Boom and bust cycles, periods of extensive economic activity followed by periods of de-

pressed economic condition, associated with industries involved in the development of nonrenewable resources often create major social problems for the development area. The influx of people (employees and families) imposes demands on existing services (schools, hospitals, sewer systems, etc.), often exceeding existing capabilities. The social impacts of pollution are well documented. The cost of environmental cleanup necessitated by development, must also be considered.

Wyoming targets revenues generated by the severance tax through various programs designed to alleviate some of the impact problems.

Proponents of Wyoming's severance tax argue that the costs of mining operations are transferred to the consuming area through the tax, not imposed on Wyoming. Mining firms increase the price of their commodity to recoup the taxes they pay. This means that consumers of electricity generated with Wyoming coal pay for the use of Wyoming resources.

Arguments: Con

The economic impacts of the mineral development are felt through increased employment of the industry and through the concommitant growth of the service sector. Together these provide a substantially increased tax base, that could be utilized by levying property taxes, use taxes, local sales taxes and possibly even an income tax to finance programs targeted for impact problems.

Opponents of the severance tax express concern about the vulnerability of Wyoming's present tax base. The concern is that Wyoming may exacerbate the impacts of the eventual bust period that will occur when the mineral resources are exhausted, by maintaining or increasing dependence on a single tax for revenues.

The severance tax may lead to a decrease in production of the mineral resources. The increased price resulting from the severance tax levy, makes it more difficult for Wyoming resources to compete, therefore reducing the amount produced. In a period when the United States is trying to establish energy independence, there is some question if such a situation should be tolerated.

Table 7.4. Major Wyoming Taxes

Tax/Fiscal Year 1978 Revenue	Levied Upon
Alcoholic Beverages Fiscal year 1978 (July 1, 1977 to June 30, 1978) $3,794,115	Malt, fermented and spirituous liquors by volume.
Cigarette Tax Fiscal 1978—$4,874,491	A specified tax per cigarette levied on all sales by wholesalers in the state. Either stamps or imprints from a metering machine are affixed to each package of cigarettes. If the tax is not paid by the wholesaler, the importer or consumer is required to pay a use tax.
Coal Excise Tax Fiscal 1978—$2,191,701	Levied against the gross value of all coal produced in a calendar year (see also severance tax).
Commercial Vehicle Registration Fiscal year 1978—$1,522,028 to State Highway Fund, $826,925 remitted to counties.	Commercial vehicles, rental utility trailer, fleets of commercial vehicles and rental vehicles operating between this state and another state.
Corporate Franchise Tax Fiscal 1978—$353,668	Assessed valuation of corporate assets, capital and property located and employed within Wyoming. Unassessed property is taxed on the market value. Applies to all corporations organized within or that have obtained the rights to transact business within Wyoming. Mines and claims are taxed on yearly production.
Gasoline Tax Fiscal year 1978—$28,544,393	The volume of gasoline sold, used, or distributed for sale or use within the state.
Inheritance Tax Fiscal year 1978—$2,084,426	All tangible and intangible personal property within the state or belonging to a Wyoming decedent. All real property is taxed by the state of situs. An additional tax is imposed to offset credits allowed for deductions from federal estate taxes when the tax by statute does not equal the federal credit for state death taxes.

SOURCE: *Wyoming Tax Summary*, Wyoming Taxpayers Association, April, 1979. Assistance of the state auditor's office.

Table 7.4—*Continued*

Tax/Fiscal Year 1978 Revenue	Levied Upon
Insurance Companies Calendar year 1977—$5,742,243	Based on total direct premium income including policy, membership and other fees, all other considerations for insurance and annuity contracts, whether designated as premiums or otherwise less return premiums and dividends, excluding re-insurance premiums received on companies authorized to do business in the state. Also levied against those insured by unauthorized companies on the basis of premiums paid.
Motor Carrier Tax Fiscal Year 1978—$20,455,794	Taxes on motor carriers vary according to weight, use and type of fuel. Certain classifications are required to obtain licenses and operating authority.
Motor Vehicle Registration Fiscal year 1978—$9,883,691	All motor vehicles either purchased within or for the use on the highways of the state; owned by non-residents and remaining in the state for longer than 120 days in a 12 month period or operated for profit; or belonging to a person who becomes a resident of the state.
Oil and Gas Conservation Charges Fiscal year 1978—$423,117	Based on the production value at the well location.
Pari-Mutuel Tax Fiscal year 1978—$10,914	Horse races and professional roping events sponsored by counties, cities, incorporated towns, county fair boards, organizations and corporations approved by the boards of county commissioners.
Property Tax Fiscal year 1978—$214,750,660	All property, real and personal, is subject to taxations unless specifically exempt. Wyoming has a defacto classification system of assessment. In general, corporate properties are assessed at 25% of market value; agricultural property on the basis of use and productivity; minerals at 100% of gross value; residential and locally assessed commercial properties vary according to local assessment practice.
Public Utilities Calendar 1978—$616,788	Percentage of intrastate gross operating revenue of public utilities.
Sales and Use Tax Fiscal year 1978—$133,020,512 (includes local option sales tax)	Gross receipts from sales of tangible personal property and specified services including receipts by public utilities, certain interstate carriers, food services, lodging and entertainment facilities. Alcoholic beverages are also subject. The use tax is levied upon property for storage, use or consumption in Wyoming.
Severance Tax Fiscal year 1978—$63,406,428	Based on the privilege of extracting specified minerals and valuable deposits according to the fair cash market value of the product after the mining or production process is completed. The Department of Revenue and Taxation may establish the value in the event a bona fide sale does not occur at the point where mining or production is completed.
Unemployment Compensation Fiscal year 1977—$15,360,020	Annual earnings of employees by calendar quarter.
Workmen's Compensation FY 1978 Industrial Accident Account $10,081,387 Reinsurance Fund $7,952,090	Wages paid by employers doing business in Wyoming to personnel engaged in certain capacities. Extra-hazardous occupations are enumerated. Compensation for injury during employment is considered a liability of the employment unit.

sources, with which to address state responsibilities through a variety of funds. While a relatively minor source of General Fund revenue comes from federal grants and aid, approximately 25 percent of the money spent by Wyoming cities, counties, and state government comes from the national government.[63] This is a good example of how important revenues are outside of the General Fund. Still, in terms of understanding the somewhat complicated area of state finances, the General Fund offers an excellent starting place.

NOTES

1. Paul B. Horton and Chester L. Hunt, *Sociology* (New York: McGraw-Hill, 1964), p. 58.
2. Ibid., p. 59.
3. Daniel J. Elazar, *American Federalism: A View From the States,* 2d ed. (New York: T. Y. Crowell, 1972), pp. 84–125.
4. A statement by Professor Louis Pelzer as quoted in T. A. Larson, *History of Wyoming* (Lincoln: University of Nebraska Press, 1965), p. 191.
5. For more on this point, see Roy A. Jordan and Tim R. Miller, "The Politics of a Cowboy Culture," *Annals of Wyoming,* 52 (Spring, 1980): 40–45. Also, see Roy A. Jordan and Tim R. Miller, "Wyoming Political Culture," *Learning Modules of Wyoming Politics,* funded through a grant from the National Science Foundation, Local Course Improvement Program, Grant No. (SER77-03819) (Laramie: Center for Government Research, 1980), pp. 283–308.
6. Elazar, pp. 84–125.
7. Robert S. Erickson and Norman R. Luttbeg, *American Public Opinion: Its Origins, Content, and Impact* (New York: John Wiley and Sons, 1973), p. 66.
8. For more on liberalism and conservatism, both in general and in Wyoming, see Rolland M. Raboin, "Ideologies: The Liberal-Conservative Dimension," *Learning Modules of Wyoming Politics,* funded through a grant from the National Science Foundation, Local Course Improvement Program, Grant No. (SER77-03819) (Laramie: Center for Government Research, 1977), pp. 35–68.
9. Larson, p. 540.
10. Jordan and Miller, "Wyoming Political Culture," pp. 292–293.
11. Larson, p. 539.
12. Jordan and Miller, "Wyoming Political Culture," p. 298. The "poverty" reference is from Michael Harrington, *The Other America: Poverty in the United States* (Baltimore: Penguin Books, 1962), pp. 23–24.
13. In particular, the states which are most affected are Colorado, Wyoming, Montana, Utah, New Mexico, Arizona, Nebraska, North Dakota and South Dakota.
14. See Don Griswold and Jean Griswold, *Colorado's Century of 'Cities'* (Denver: Smith-Brooks, 1958) and Larson, *History of Wyoming.*
15. Dudley E. Faver, "Population Comparison," *Regional Profile: Energy Impacted Communities, a Report of Region VIII* (Denver: Collection Office, 1977), p. 76.
16. See John S. Gilmore, "Boom Towns May Hinder Resource Development," *Science,* 191 (February 1976: 536 and Alvin M. Josephy, Jr., "Agony of the Northern Plains," *Audubon,* 75:68–101. Also, see the Special Colorado Census, 1976.
17. David Longbrake and James F. Geyler, "Commercial Development in Small, Isolated Energy Impacted Communities," *Social Science Journal,* 16 (April 1979):52.
18. Earle Warner, "Grassroots Organizing in Boom Towns," in *Boom Towns and Human Services,* ed. Judith A. Davenport and Joseph Davenport, III (Laramie: University of Wyoming Department of Social Work, 1979), p. 93.
19. Judith A. Davenport and Joseph Davenport, III, "A Town and Gown Approach to Boom Town Problems," in *Boom Towns and Human Services,* ed. Judith A. Davenport and Joseph Davenport, III (Laramie: University of Wyoming Department of Social Work, 1979), p. 131. Also, *The Socioeconomic Impact of the Proposed Laramie River Station* (Laramie: University of Wyoming Division of Business and Economic Research, 1975), p. 72.
20. There is, however, often a reverse trend which affects local businesses. Many local businesses, faced with rising costs and demands, cling to outmoded business practices and fail as a result of outmigration of local money and inabilities to cope with added pressures and frustrations. See Longbrake and Geyler, pp. 51–63.

21. Warner, p. 92. Also, see Table I, "Comparison of Rocky Mountain Reserves with U.S. Reserves, from *Rocky Mountain Energy Resource Development: Status, Potential, and Socio-Economic Issues,* a report to Congress by Elmer B. Staats, Comptroller General of the United States (Washington, D.C.: U.S. Government Printing Office, 1977), p. 5.

22. Warner, p. 92.

23. Arthur L. Waidman, "The Role of the Church," in *Boom Towns and Human Services,* ed. Judith A. Davenport and Joseph Davenport, III (Laramie: University of Wyoming Department of Social Work, 1979), p. 101.

24. Warner, pp. 93–94.

25. Wyoming Department of Environmental Quality pamphlet. For a more thorough understanding of DEQ responsibilities, see Wyoming Statutes, 1977, 35–502.1 to 35–502.56. In particular, 35–502.2 on "Policy and Purpose" reads:

    Whereas pollution of the air, water and land of this state will imperil public health and welfare, create public or private nuisances, be harmful to wildlife, fish and aquatic life, and impair domestic, agricultural, industrial, recreational and other beneficial uses, it is hereby declared to be the policy and purpose of this act to enable the state to prevent, reduce and eliminate pollution; to preserve, and enhance the air, water and reclaim the land of Wyoming; to plan the development, use, reclamation, preservation and enhancement of the air, land and water resources of the state; to preserve and exercise the primary responsibilities and rights of the state of Wyoming; to retain for the state the control over its air, land and water and to secure cooperation between agencies of the state, agencies of other states, interstate agencies, and the federal government in carrying out these objectives.

26. These "red tape" regulations are often the brunt of criticisms by state and local officials who charge that there are so many rules that the federal money isn't worth all the trouble. Other examples of such rules include affirmative action minority hiring and promotion policies, minority subcontracting guarantees, and various accounting and reporting procedures.

27. Other programs such as revenue sharing and block grants either reduce or essentially eliminate the "red tape" requirements.

28. The Industrial Siting Administration also has environmental responsibilities. However, social and economic matters are its focus. For a more thorough statement of the Industrial Siting Administration's responsibilities, see Wyoming Statutes, 1977, 35–12–101 to 35–12–121.

29. It is even conceivable that a denial could reach the federal courts, if a significant issue of federal law is involved.

30. Such permits are necessary from the Industrial Siting Administration only when construction costs are estimated to exceed $50 million, computed in terms of the dollar's value in 1975.

31. Tim R. Miller, an interview with Blaine Dinger, Director of the Industrial Siting Administration in Cheyenne, Wyoming, Summer, 1978.

32. Larson, p. 4.

33. T. A. Larson, *Wyoming: A Bicentennial History* (New York: W. W. Norton, 1977), p. 163.

34. Larson, *History of Wyoming,* p. 5.

35. Larson, *Bicentennial History,* p. 7.

36. This is not to suggest that the lofty goal of one million reclaimed acres was ever achieved. Frequently, investors lost money due to cost overruns, etc. In all, several thousand acres were reclaimed through Carey Act provisions.

37. Larson, *Bicentennial History,* p. 163.

38. Ibid., p. 164.

39. For relevant statutes, see *Wyoming Water and Irrigation Laws,* comp. George Christopulos (State Engineer), 1975.

40. Ray Edward Johnston, "The Administration of Wyoming's Water Resources," (Masters thesis, University of Wyoming, 1960), p. 10.

41. Ibid.

42. Tim R. Miller, an interview with George Christopulos, State Engineer, conducted in Cheyenne, Wyoming, Summer, 1978.

43. Johnston, p. 10 and Larson, *Bicentennial History,* p. 164.

44. Larson, *Bicentennial History,* p. 164.

45. Donald J. Brosz, George L. Christopulos and Robert D. Burman, *Brief Summary of Wyoming Water Law,* (State of Wyoming, 1970), p. 3. This pamphlet is available through the state engineer's office.

46. Wyoming Statutes, Section 41–3.

47. Brosz, Christopulos, and Burman, p. 3.

48. Ibid.; also, Miller, interview with Christopulos.

49. Lynn Bama, "Who's Got the Water?" *Wyoming News* (February 1978), p. 16.

50. Ibid.

51. Edward S. Corwin and Jack W. Peltason, *Understanding the Constitution,* 7th ed. (Hinsdale, Ill: Dryden Press, 1976), pp. 65–66.

52. United States vs. Appalachian Electric Power Co., 311 U.S. 377, (1940).

53. The fact that municipalities are "creatures" of the state in which they reside has been articulated by John F. Dillon and is called "Dillon's Rule." It reads:

> It is a general and undisputed proposition of law that a municipal corporation possesses and can exercise the following powers and no others; First, those granted in express words; second, those necessarily or fairly implied in or incident to the powers expressly granted; third, those essential to the accomplishment of the declared objects and purposes of the corporations—not simply convenient, but indispensible. Any fair, reasonable, substantial doubt concerning the existence of power is resolved by the courts against the corporation, and the power is denied.

> Quoted from John F. Dillon, *Commentaries on the Law of Municipal Corporations,* 5th ed. (Boston: Little, Brown, 1911), Vol. I, Sec. 237. For a more detailed discussion of the law of municipal corporations by a political scientist, see Charles M. Kneier, *City Government in the United States,* 3d ed. (New York: Harper, 1957).

54. See, for example, League of Women Voters, *More Than You Want to Know About Wyoming Taxes,* publication #41 (1976), p. 12.

55. The exact figures for fiscal year 1979 are as follows: General government expenditures from the General Fund totaled $42,958,942—the State Treasurer's office expended $13,086,295 while DAFC spent $9,382,848. General Fund expenditures to education totaled $56,246,596—the University of Wyoming spent $34,398,100 of the total, the community colleges expended $13,567,813, and the Department of Education spent $5,615,274 of the total given to education. Total expenditures from the General Fund to the hospitals, health and social service category equalled $33,705,575—$17,824,477 by the Department of Health and Social Services, $6,406,608 by the State Hospital, and $6,455,535 by the Training School.

56. Kenyon Griffin, "The Politics of Taxation in Wyoming," *Learning Modules of Wyoming Politics,* funded through a grant from the National Science Foundation, Local Course Improvement Program, Grant No. (SER77–03819) (Laramie: Center for Government Research, 1977), p. 151.

57. The 1973 legislature amended the statutes to subject other services to the sales tax, including: hotel and motel room rentals, admissions to movies and places of amusement, intrastate telephone and telegraph services, laundry and dry cleaning, etc. Also, see Wyoming Statutes, 1977, (Sales) Secs. 39–6–401 to 39–6–417 and (Use) Secs. 39–6–501 to 39–6–603.

58. The following counties had exercised the county option through 1979: Campbell, Carbon, Converse, Crook, Hot Springs, Laramie, Natrona, Niobrara, Platte, Sheridan, Sweetwater, Teton, Uinta, Weston.

59. "Annual Report of the Department of Revenue and Taxation," *State of Wyoming 1979 Annual Report,* Volume II, p. 33.

60. The following minerals are subject to the tax: gold, silver or other precious metals, soda, saline, coal, trona, uranium, betonite, petroleum or other crude material, oil or gas, or other valuable deposits.

61. *Wyoming Tax Summary,* (Cheyenne, Wyoming: Wyoming Taxpayers Association, April 1979). Also, see Wyoming Statutes, 1977, Secs. 39–6–301 to 39–6–307.

62. "Annual Report of the State Auditor," *State of Wyoming 1979 Annual Report,* Volume I, p. 105.

63. U.S. Bureau of the Census, Department of Commerce, *Statistical Abstract of the United States,* 100th ed., pp. 294–295.